The making of
neoclassical economics

TITLES OF RELATED INTEREST

The making of neoclassical economics

John F. Henry
Department of Economics
California State University,
Sacramento

Boston
UNWIN HYMAN
London   Sydney   Wellington

Unwin Hyman Inc.,
8 Winchester Place, Winchester, Mass. 01890, USA

Published by the Academic Division of
Unwin Hyman Ltd
15/17 Broadwick Street, London W1V 1FP, UK

Allen & Unwin (Australia) Ltd,
8 Napier Street, North Sydney, NSW 2060, Australia

Allen & Unwin (New Zealand) Ltd in association with the
Port Nicholson Press Ltd,
Compusales Building, 75 Ghuznee Street, Wellington 1, New Zealand

First published in 1990

Library of Congress Cataloging in Publication Data

Henry, John.
 The making of neoclassical economics/John   Henry.
  p. cm.
 Includes bibliographical references.
 ISBN 0-04-445664-6
 1. Neoclassical school of economics. I. Title.
HB98.2.H46 1990
330.15'7—dc20   89-70717
             CIP

British Library Cataloguing in Publication Data

Henry, John F.
 The making of neoclassical economics.
 1. Economics. Theories of Cambridge School
 I. Title
330.15'5

ISBN 0-04-445664-6

Typeset in 10/12 point Palatino
and printed in Great Britain by Billing and Sons, London and Worcester

Contents

Foreword

Mainstream economics in the twentieth century has been primarily neoclassical economics. That this predominance has come to pass is something that has to be explained – and not merely on that school's own terms. Actually, the situation is far more complex. Neoclassicism predominates but is itself heterogeneous; moreover, there are diverse schools of heterodox economic thought. Contrary to the evident tendency of some economists to equate economics with neoclassical economics, economics is thoroughly heterogeneous. And this heterogeneity also has to be explained.

The origins of twentieth-century economics, in all its diversity but with the predominance of neoclassicism, reside principally in the period 1870–1900 or 1914. It was then that economics exhibited a major crisis of identity, in which every fundamental aspect of the discipline was contested, from its very name ('political economy' or 'economics') to the status of the English founding fathers, its central analytical problem, its scope and methodology and, *inter alia*, the content and place of the theory of value. The fact that one hundred years later these same issues remain controversial signifies that the complex question of identity is a continuing problem not resolved once and for all time.

The study of the origins, and indeed the nature, of twentieth-century economics is complicated by the fact that economics has come to serve three functions: to provide knowledge of the economy, of economic 'reality'; to serve as social control in the continuing legitimation and (re)construction of the economy; and, simultaneously and interactively, to serve as psychic balm, to set minds at rest that all is fundamentally well in matters economic. Such study is further complicated by the fact that economists have been motivated to pursue several distinct and partially reinforcing but also partially conflicting goals: the status and prestige of objective scientist; the role of technical expert in matters of economic policy in the continuing (re)construction of the economy; and the advocacy role of high priest in the legitimation of the market, if not also (however selectively) in the status quo structure of power, the delegitimation of government *per se* and the selective legitimation and delegitimation of various government policies. Any explanation of the genesis and predominance of neoclassical economics must willy nilly come to grips with these considerations.

The foregoing means that any interpretation of the making of neoclassical economics must draw upon insights not only from the traditional sociology of knowledge and standard history of economic thought, but also from the fields of intellectual history, the sociology of economics, the professionalization of intellectual disciplines, and such recondite areas as deconstruction, hermeneutics and the analysis of discourse in general.

It is important to note that the definition of 'neoclassical economics' is not perfectly self-evident. It has meant different things to different writers, some practicing neoclassical economics as they understood it, and others studying the history of neoclassical economics. These different meanings include (1) the subjective marginal utility theory of the 1870s and beyond; (2) the economics of Alfred Marshall; (3) the work of twentieth-century writers working in the tradition, or mould, established by Marshall and some others, most notably Leon Walras; (4) some combination of the foregoing; and, *inter alia*, (5) the Samuelsonian neoclassical synthesis of microeconomic price and resource allocation theory and Keynesian macroeconomics. The argument of the present volume is applicable to all of these definitions.

Neoclassicism has also had a variety of technical meanings as to its central problem: the mechanics of utility, price determination, or operation of the price mechanism; the working of the free enterprise system; the operation of pure markets; the mechanics of the pure theory or logic of choice; constrained maximization decision-making; the allocation of resources; and so on. Not all these meanings are mutually exclusive; indeed, many of them are mutually reinforcing. My own general view is that neoclassical economics comprises work in the tradition of Marshall, Walras and others on how the price mechanism of the market allocates resources in a context of the constrained maximizing choice from within individual opportunity sets. The argument of the present volume, however, is applicable to a variety of formulations of the central problem of neoclassical economics.

The foregoing discussion necessarily has had to allude to the concept of 'marginalism.' This concept, too, has had diverse meanings, and this also is part of the history of the practice as well as of the interpretation of neoclassicism. Marginalism has meant (1) the subjective marginal utility theory of value, (2) the economy as a process of adjustment at the margin, (3) the practice of constrained maximization by economic actors (for example, equating marginal cost and marginal revenue), and, *inter alia*, (4) price and resource allocation.

A related question concerns the so-called 'marginal revolution': whether such a revolution actually took place, and of what it consisted; and whether the so-called revolution took place in the 1870s, as is so often understood, or a short time later, (say) with the pre-eminence of Marshallian economics, or somewhat later, with the more firm establishment of an Austrian school, or (as George Stigler argues) much later, perhaps the 1960s, with the adoption of the now more-or-less conventional practice of using utility functions to formulate research problems. It will be perhaps obvious that each of these possibilities may presume something different as to the content of marginalism.

The question of the marginal revolution of the 1870s raises the larger question of whether or not there was a major paradigmatic shift between classical and neoclassical economics. In some respects there appears to be significant differences between the two, involving, for example, the change from the labor theory of value to a demand and supply price theory, and the change from macroeconomic growth and distribution theory to microeconomic static resource allocation theory. But in other respects, there appears to be significant continuity, for example in the focus on markets, in the rationalization of middle-class values and so on, perhaps even in the theory of market price as distinct from the metaphysics of value theory.

The period 1870–1900 or 1914, and the rise to predominance of neoclassicism therein, has become one of the, if not *the*, new leading areas of study in the field of the history of economic thought. Contemporary scholars such as James F. Becker, A. W. Coats, John Creedy, Mary Furner, Alon Kadish, Gerard Koot and John Malony have examined such divers topics as the role of expertise, the growth of professionalization concomitant with orthodoxy, the English historical school, the status of economics in the 1870s, the sociology of the discipline, the Oxford economists, the conflict between advocacy and objectivity, and such eminent figures as Alfred Marshall and Francis Ysidro Edgeworth. Among the other cognate topics that have recently come under historical and analytical scrutiny are the analysis of economics as a mode of discourse, by writers such as Michel Foucault, S. Todd Lowry and Keith Tribe, and the ongoing contest between internalist and externalist (absolutist and relativist) explanations of disciplinary change.

John F. Henry's study is a contribution of no small substance to this quest to understand the origins, driving force and rise to predominance of neoclassicism in economics. He perceives neoclassicism to be an emanation from the reigning capitalist system – not merely its explanation, and not merely a mode of its self-nationalization but its product. As Professor Henry puts it, his question is '*why* theory develops and why theories of a certain type develop when they do. To attempt any answer to this question requires an examination into the relation between society and theory.' Professor Henry does not consider his to be the final word in the attempt to understand the emergence of twentieth-century neoclassical economic theory. It is, of course, not the final word; but any effort at a complete, or at least more encompassing, explanation will have to deal with his explanation and, indeed, to have a place for it. Henry's argument, or some transformation of it, will be part of an eventual more complex and more encompassing explanation. No one is likely to agree with all the elements of his interpretation, but everyone will have to reckon with what he has to say. To have provided such a contribution, and I believe Professor Henry to have done so, is no slight accomplishment.

Modern economics, especially contemporary neoclassical economics, is distinguished by its emphasis on technique and by its particular paradigm of how pure markets operate in conjunction with economic agents practicing constrained maximization. Most contemporary economists know these techniques and the associated body of theory very well. What they do not appreciate are the origins and cultural premises of the predominant neoclassical paradigm and how their techniques give effect to those origins and premises, often with unknowing selectivity. In a certain sense, the techniques and the theories stand on their own independent bottoms. But in another respect, they are both conduits for certain premises and are functional as social control in the service, however selectively, of the regnant economic order and the status-quo structure of power and ideology. This is the case whether or not one likes that order or that power structure or that ideology. The same would be true, *mutatis mutandis*, if another school of thought were to have become predominant in economics.

It will be especially valuable to the reader if he or she systematically critiques the author's argument during the reading of this book. What are the author's questions, and what are his answers? What materials and lines of reasoning are brought to bear in support of the argument? What alternative questions and what alternative answers might be posed? What would a 'more complete' explanation of the making and the rise to predominance of neoclassicism take from Professor Henry's argument? On what grounds can one accept or dismiss his claims and his interpretations? If the reader will consider these questions seriously, Professor Henry's project in this study will be vindicated. For the subject is a serious one, and Professor Henry treats it seriously.

Finally, the reader should be cautioned that Professor Henry treats certain delicate or sensitive subjects, subjects that are part of the mind-set of most of us, in a very straightforward and often critical manner. Economists have long been noted for their candor. Adam Smith wrote that 'Civil government, so far as it is instituted for the security of property, is in reality instituted for the defense of the rich against the poor, or of those who have some property against those who have none at all'; and he lectured that the 'very end [of government] is to secure wealth and to defend the rich from the poor.' Vilfredo Pareto firmly believed that economics, no less than religion, was part of the total system of 'force and fraud' by which society was governed. And Frank Knight opined that, if religion were the opiate of the masses, it was also the sedative of the (upper) classes. All of which is to suggest that Professor Henry's account of the making of neoclassical economics is conducted at a very deep, and therefore sensitive, level indeed.

Warren J. Samuels

I dedicate this work to Tom Asimakopulos, Harold Wright, and Jack Weldon – three who made a difference.

In every cry of every man,
In every infant's cry of fear,
In every voice, in every ban,
The mind-forged manacles I hear.

William Blake

To him who does not know the world is on fire, I have nothing to say.

Berthold Brecht

Things are in the saddle and ride mankind.

Ralph Waldo Emerson

After all, if a man's salary is good enough, surely he can believe in anything.

Stephen Leacock

Preface

What follows is not to be read as a normal excursion into the history of economic theory. There is no attempt to examine all the major and many minor theorists, nor is there an investigation into the details of the work of these figures. Moreover, I am not interested in undertaking a systematic analysis of, or doing battle with others who are engaged in, this particular area of economic inquiry. Rather, this study tries to develop a general theory of the development of general theory itself.

The normal position taken by historians of science is to focus on the contributions of one or another figure, showing how these contributions were based on previous thought and led to subsequent analysis. As well, we usually find some degree of comparative analysis. More important, the standard adopted for the critical evaluation contained therein is that which is currently fashionable – in the case of economic thought, the neoclassical point of view. What I attempt here is an explanation of *why* the standard itself unfolded; why the neoclassical perspective, resting on a utility theory of value, became increasingly prominent, then dominant, in the nineteenth century. The argument rests on the underlying economic changes undergone by capitalist society during the period and the nature of capitalism as a minority ruling-class society.

By way of general argument, let us consider several points. First, we observe that the dominant ideas held by society undergo change. One aspect of this change is that of modification within a given ideological structure: an established theory is accepted as true, but specific parts of this theory are adjusted to accommodate changed circumstances or the development of new data. More significant than this, however, is that periodically we find a change in the general theory itself: Newtonian physics is replaced by atomic physics. It is this latter type of change that creates the greater upheaval in whatever field of inquiry is being studied, and which requires the more significant explanation as to why such change occurs.

What is termed 'neoclassical economics' was not always the prevailing view of the discipline. To reach its current position, it had to wrest ideological domination from the older, classical general theory. Why did this occur? What were the mechanisms by which this victory was won? While the argument contained herein may be found faulty, it is nevertheless true that such a change did occur, and that this change does require explanation.

Second, it is observed that established institutional structures are more or less taken for granted, are not subjected to critical scrutiny. We accept a price system, money, privately owned production facilities. To be sure, there is always some call for reform of given institutions, but only within the institutional framework itself. This is equivalent to the modifying type of change to which ideological structures are constantly subjected. Suggestions that the institutions themselves are the cause of problems and should be scrapped altogether are, under normal circumstances, held to be outside the pale and not worthy of serious consideration.

So it is with ideological formations. As long as ideas are contained within the dominant theoretical perspective, they may be entertained. Those challenging that structure are dismissed out of hand, regardless of merit. That is, just as institutional arrangements are accepted because they exist, so are ideas. And, clearly, there is a relationship between institutional arrangements and ideological formation, given that ideas about society must be concerned with the institutions of society. Thus, for example, in capitalist society, the vast majority of the population accepts the basic institutions of such a social organization – private property, exchange, etc. – and, consequently, accepts the general theory that supports those institutions. Calls for money *reform* will be heard (and such calls can indeed be scientifically silly – witness Major Douglas), while the suggestion that an economic system centering on exchange be eliminated will be met with, at best, silence.

What we find, then, is that society's position on normalcy or decency will be determined largely by the social institutions and ideas that are dominant. These ideas form the basic judgment as to what is rational. Yet these same ideas, as they establish the criteria of criticism, are themselves held to be sacrosanct, beyond criticism.

Last, given the monopoly of the prevailing ideological formation, theories fundamentally opposed to the dominant set of ideas are held in contempt. As the basis of judgment is determined by the ruling ideas, those notions that are in opposition to the ruling set are deemed invalid solely on the criteria established by the socially acceptable, normal view of things. Thus, say, communism is 'wrong' simply because capitalism is 'right.' All ideas are *not* treated equally.

The task set forth here, then, is to examine the historical evolution of the neoclassical standard, attempting to demonstrate its relation to institutional changes within capitalist society itself. What will be shown is that the theory reflects the dominant relationships within capitalist society and has been developed and modified to accommodate changes within this form of social organization. Hence, neoclassicism does not stand above or apart from society, but is, as with all social ideas, conditioned by that society. This calls into question the claim of scientific neutrality, held to be a hallmark of neoclassical economics.

Studies of this sort appear during periods of crisis: crisis in the underlying economic organization of society, which then generates crisis in the theoretical apparatus of that society. If an economy is reasonably well functioning, little attention is paid to the prevailing ideology which arises to defend that economy and which, increasingly, appears to have a life of its own, to exist within a social vacuum. During periods of social travail, however, questions are raised which the dominant ideology cannot answer – indeed, usually cannot even address. Then, the various fields of inquiry go through a paroxysm. We witnessed this in the 1930s and again in the 1960s. Currently, there appears to be renewed stability, an appearance encouraged, no doubt, by the renewed vigor of the neo-Walrasian theorists and the various fractures within the Keynesian and Marxist camps.

I think, though, that this apparent stability is just that – apparent. Everywhere we see economic dislocation, growing unease among astute politicians, major capitalists and even some economists. One of the effects of this unease is the renewal of the debates in economic philosophy and the appearance of a journal specifically dedicated to these debates.

Thus, while the surface phenomena appear relatively calm, the fundamental cracks in both society and theory which were laid bare in the 1960s continue to widen; theory becomes increasingly separated from practice and, thus, incapable of addressing those cracks. And, with the imminent crisis in the social order, economic theory will once again enter a period of turmoil. Tumultuous times raise questions concerning the very essence of the theories being questioned. Rather than accept doctrine as a matter of faith, the whole of the argument is brought under scrutiny and held up for critical evaluation. The present work may be considered one small contribution in the historically rather long critical evaluation to which neoclassical theory has been subjected.

In what follows, readers will see little that is new. To a large extent, I have followed the path already laid by critics such as Marx, Veblen and Dobb. For those who have not read the original accounts of the great neoclassicists, there may be some surprises. And for those who are not aware of the criticisms already set forth, some insights into the approach of Marx may be gained. But all the evidence has been already established. And, in the recitation of this evidence, there is nothing new.

What I have attempted is to take existing information and apply it in a particular way. My question was *why* theory develops, and why theories of a particular type develop when they do. To attempt any answer to this question, we must examine the relation between society and theory. Given that theory consists of a set of ideas, those ideas must come from somewhere. In the final analysis, society itself throws up and controls the dissemination of those ideas. Hence one must identify the relationship between social formation and change, and theory.

Readers will observe that this study places the development of general neoclassical perspective into a framework
established by the specific 'periods' of capitalist evolution.
Attempts at periodization are never neat: one period flows
into another; there are questions of lags, uneven development and so forth. Thus, it is true that the flow of ideas
does not match exactly the flow of history. So be it: that is
the way the world works. Rather than appearing as a tidy,
compartmentalized structure, the world economy, scientific
development – whatever – is somewhat messy. Problems
exist, and one cannot force the world to behave as one
would like merely because it would be more comfortable
were that the case.

Yet, in broad outlines, we do observe change. And change
occurs sequentially. As this is true, then, again in broad
outlines, the sequence of change can be segmented into
wholes that can be differentiated by degree and type.

It is readily seen (though not always admitted) that the
industrial structure of modern capitalism is not the same
as that of 1700. Small-scale producing units have given
way to large organizations as the dominant form of structure. And, while it may be possible to place this transition into periods of only a rough-and-ready nature, yet the
transition has occurred, and it has occurred as a periodic
movement.

Thus, while there may be valid quarrels with the dating of
various epochs and the specific time relationship of theory
to institutional change, I think that the assertion that a
relationship does exist is not arguable. Further, and more
important, evidence is brought forward to defend this position.

In the course of this examination, many points will be
made, some of which are outside the purview of most
economists. There is a strong temptation to prove every
point made, as this would provide the strongest case for the
argument. And, as the argument is in a decidedly minority
position, this would provide a more comfortable position for
the author. Yet, such a task would require a work probably
ten to twenty times longer than that which is offered. And
in the process, the main argument would probably get lost.

Thus, what is presented is a rather abbreviated, straightforward account. Where I think the information is well known, I let it stand on its own; where it appears that the average reader is unaware of the argument and historical fact behind the position, reference is made to authority to which the reader can then turn.

There are two last items by way of general introduction. First, I do not view this study as the final work in the attempt to understand the development of economic theory. Rather, it should be viewed as one contribution to that understanding. It is hoped that this examination will provoke criticism, further study, and – in the long run – a more complete analysis of the relationship between society and theory.

Second, I ask readers to read some rather long quotations from the authorities selected to represent the general position set forth. Some forbearance is requested in this task, but it does provide some rewards. More important, these quotations provide some of the evidence for the argument contained herein; in order both to capture the flavor of these positions and to provide some assurance that I am not quoting out of context – an intellectual crime that makes its appearance more often than one would like to admit – some extended quotations are necessary.

And a technical note: unless otherwise specified, all emphasized words or statements in the quoted remarks are in the original.

Finally, I would like to extend my sincere thanks to those who helped make this a better work than it otherwise would have been. Excellent and necessary criticism was received from Joseph Furey, Alessandro Roncaglia, Warren Samuels, Noel Thompson, Larry Randall Wray and Nancy Wulwick. As well, I would like to include in this list J. C. Weldon, one of the most clear-headed of our profession, who died before he could attend to my request for comments. He is missed.

For technical assistance, the following are to be commended: Michelle Beardo, Sharon Becker, Pat Buffington, Laurie Chow, Chris Goebel, Marilyn Hill, Carol Lucido and Gary McFarland. Charlene Heinen markedly improved the presentation with a strong dose of her editorial skills. Lastly, I owe thanks to Carolyn White, economics editor at Unwin Hyman, for her assistance in bringing this project to fruition, and to John A. D. Fraser, Anais Scott and Sue Hughes for their efforts in the production of this work.

J. F. H.

CHAPTER ONE

On the origin and dissemination of ideas

In any study that attempts to examine the ideological structure of a science, it is most important to specify the locus of ideas and the mechanism through which ideas become dominant. One position on such matters is to place the individual ideologist at the center of the process. Thus, histories of ideas focus on 'great thinkers' who are separate from society and social forces, whose ideas result solely from a superior intelligence or, in the religious version, divine inspiration. The argument contained herein takes exactly the opposite point of view: that ideas are social products, and that individual thinkers themselves are products of society.

Moreover – and this should be an important element in the history of any science – if an idea is to be successful, it must have a social mechanism of dissemination. Any idea, no matter how potentially significant, cannot become operable unless it has an impact on that which it is about. And to have an impact, the idea must be transmitted throughout society, or at least throughout a significant part thereof. An idea that does not go beyond the brain of the ideologist is stillborn; it either dies with its creator or must wait rebirth by another at a more propitious time.

Since the social origins and the dissemination of ideas are the central focus of this work, the conflicting approaches will be examined succinctly at this point, and a general schemata will be generated within which the substance of this work will then be argued.

1

On the social origin of ideas

Ideas are obviously the product of human activity. Since significant ideas can be traced to individual thinkers (though not without antecedents), it seems natural to credit such individuals with advancing knowledge independent of any social forces that surround them. In other words, there are 'great thinkers' who arise spontaneously and independently and produce the ideas that are then transformed into social action. Such an explanation may be termed the 'Great Man' version of the origins of ideas.

If this argument is correct, if ideas are independent of time, place and social forces, then ideological formations are social accidents, awaiting the birth and development of specific individuals who carry within them, in some sense, significant ideas. It follows, then, that change in society (or nature) is caused by the advent of ideas: ideas are primary; social forces are of secondary importance.

This idealist position is comforting to those seeking an explanation of historical movement that is independent of social laws. If ideas and ideologists are independently created, if history is a compendium of accidents, then there is no sense to human past and, further, no predictability to human future. Theories based on the possibility of the discovery of any historical regularity or necessity can then be identified as invalid, and the conclusions drawn from them can be dismissed as political rhetoric or wishful thinking.

In contradistinction to this idealist view is posed the materialist argument: that ideas (and, therefore, ideologists) are the product of social forces, and that they mirror or reflect social reality, attempting either an explanation or an obfuscation of that reality.

People are necessarily the product of society and, thus, of social organization. Society produces the environment in which individuals are born, educated and acculturized. There is no record of an individual raised apart from society who managed to develop into a thinker (Malson, 1972).

The ability to form ideas, to acquire knowledge from others through oral and written communication, to expand upon that knowledge, and to develop new knowledge are

2

all socially determined. People apart from society are not human except in the purely biological sense. They have no power of human communication or cognition. They thus have no ability to develop ideas that would advance an understanding of society or nature. Such people would be equivalent to a lower order of primate and would be responsible for as much thought or invention as the ape.

The above is a trivial, though necessary, point. It is trivial because it is patently true. It is necessary because it is so easily ignored by the accidentalists, who tend to see ideological formation as the work of unexplained geniuses somehow separated from society. Hence we are treated to the myth of the isolated, ivory-towered thinker. However, as noted by one of the most astute nineteenth-century thinkers, Lewis Henry Morgan,

> It fortunately so happens that the events of human prog-
> ress embody themselves, independently of particular men,
> in a material record, which is crystallized in institutions,
> usages and customs, and preserved in inventions and
> discoveries. Historians, from a sort of necessity, give to
> individuals great prominence in the production of events;
> thus placing persons, who are transient, in the place of
> principles, which are enduring. The work of society in its
> totality, by means of which all progress occurs, is ascribed
> far too much to individual men, and far too little to the
> public intelligence. It will be recognized generally that the
> substance of human history is bound up in the growth of
> ideas, which are wrought out by the people and expressed
> in their institutions, usages, inventions and discoveries.
> (Morgan, 1877, p. 302)

But society provides more than the nurturing ground for individuals. It also establishes reasonably well-defined constraints on people's mental constructions (their ideas). Ideas supporting the notion of slavery (or attacking that notion) develop and find reception only in the context of the establishment of a slave society. Primitive societies could not envision international security markets. Author-ities investigating the actual formation of ideas (rather than merely assuming their existence and creation) have demonstrated a distinct relationship between the form of social organization, its level of economic development, and the ideas produced within the context of the society (Bernal, 1971; Childe, 1964; Farrington, 1953; Lilley, 1965; Thomson, 1965, 1974).

This position does not mean that the individual thinker is of no account. It does, however, place the individual in a secondary positon. In this context, great thinkers are those who are most attuned to social developments, who have a level of training sufficient to analyze such developments, and who have enough prescience to place such developments into an ideological structure that itself aids in molding those developments.

It follows, then that individuals can influence the fate of society by virtue of definite traits of their nature. Their influence is sometimes very considerable but the possibility of its being exercised and its extent are determined by society's organization and the alignment of its forces. An individual's character is a 'factor' in social development only where, when, and to the extent that social relations permit it to be.

It has long been noted that great talents appear always and everywhere, whenever and wherever there exist social conditions favourable for their development. That means that any talent that *actually manifests itself*, i.e., any talent that becomes a *social force, is a product of social relations*. But if that is so, one can understand why people of talent can . . . alter only the individual features of events, not their overall trend; *they themselves exist only thanks to that trend; but for the latter, they would have never crossed the threshold between the potential and the actual.* (Plekhanov, [1898] 1976b, pp. 304, 310)

The social dissemination of ideas

For ideas to be viable, to have significance, they obviously must be transmitted as well as developed. And it is the social process of dissemination that creates the greatest force in the power of ideas.

It is conceivable that the same general idea or system of ideas will occur to different individuals at about the same time or in different periods. However, only at certain times does the idea bear with it a concomitant ability to realize itself in some sort of social acceptance. Consider the development of the ideas surrounding the Copernican system.

On the Revolution of the Celestial Orbs was published in 1543 (the year of Copernicus' death) and was judiciously dedicated to the Pope. But acceptance of the argument had to wait several centuries. Part of the reason for this delay was the normal process of science; a theory is propounded, then tested, evaluated and modified, and then accepted or rejected by those with sufficient expertise to judge it. Thus, the work of Tycho, Kepler, Galileo and others formed a compelling body of evidence that validated, in the main, the Copernican idea.

But scientific validation was not the only reason why acceptance of the theory was delayed. A more important issue was that the Copernican theory ran counter to prevailing ideas surrounding the nature of the universe and, thus, of man. The officials of the Roman Church had taught that the earth was the center of the universe and the Church was the center of the earth. The Pope, as the head of the Church, was directly responsible to and received authority from God. Hence the political power and economic welfare of the Church rested upon Divine authority. By removing the earth as the center of the universe, Copernicus also caused the rest of the argument – resting not on scientific truth but on mere assertion – to collapse.

Once the implications of the theory were understood by church officials, a great struggle ensued, the Church attempting to prevent the idea from being disseminated, and the Copernicans attempting to gain ideological dominance. For the Copernicans, however, the main instruments of communication were closed because the Church *was* the principle ideological force of the period and controlled the main organs of communication. In reserve, should all else fail, the Church had a powerful persuader – the Inquisition.

The contest was not directly over truth, for representatives of both sides recognized where truth lay.[1] Rather, one side was attempting to suppress truth, the other to allow truth to 'will out.' The former, behaving in characteristic fashion, cajoled, bribed, lied, threatened, tortured and murdered; the latter persisted. Obviously, the Copernicans eventually won, but not entirely by dint of their own efforts. To win, they had to have the ability to communicate their ideas and find a vehicle to allow those ideas to become socially acceptable. The vehicle that permitted both communication and acceptability was social revolution.

The basic, and so most often ignored, aspect of the Church is that it was and is a propertied institution. Given the origins and history of Christianity, the Church was a feudal institution that was dependent, therefore, on the maintenance of feudalism for its economic well-being (Dunham, 1964; Robertson, 1962). During the period in question, feudal Europe was wracked by peasant revolt and by social revolution led by the class eventually called capitalist. The attempt to maintain the feudal structure fell largely to the chief feudal ideologists – church officials. Hence the authority of the Church was most significant: to the extent that people accepted the position of the church fathers on corporeal matters, they would turn aside from their attacks on the feudal order; to the extent that church authority was undermined by seditious ideas, the population would carry on its struggle.[2]

The Copernican theory, because it undermined the authority of prevailing (pro-feudal) ideas, undermined the authority of the dominant feudal ideological institution. And, to the extent that it undermined that authority, it subverted the whole feudal system.[3]

Therefore, the forces that promoted social change and progress also promoted the ideas of Copernicus, while those that desired social stability – that is, retrogression – used their influence to retard dissemination of those ideas. And, because the latter forces actually maintained their dominance in most of Europe until the nineteenth century, they succeeded in preventing full dissemination of a correct, scientific theory.[4]

This illustration raises a fundamental point. No society, regardless of the form of its organization, has ever permitted freedom of ideas. All societies have imposed limitations on the extent to which ideas could be free. True, it is impossible to impose absolute restrictions upon what any individual may think. But this is unimportant. What is significant is that any society can and does impose restrictions on the flow of ideas by exercising social control over the instruments of communication. And the flow of information necessarily influences the ideas of any individual.

Consider two representative societies. Slave society is the form of social organization with the least amount of freedom. The majority of the population's actions are so proscribed that there can be little room for disagreement with such an assertion. In fact, the word 'slave' itself is used to describe a condition of unfreedom.

In slave society, ideas are controlled by the slave-holding class. Because it has an economic interest in promoting ideas conducive to the development and maintenance of slavery, and the same economic interest in prohibiting the anti-slavery impulse, it will promote and prohibit ideas at the same time. It can accomplish these ends because it controls the instruments through which ideas are disseminated. The newspapers, churches, educational institutions – any vehicle through which ideas can be transmitted – are controlled by the dominant class. If those instruments do not accept the control of slavers, they are closed.

> The ideas of the ruling class are in every epoch the ruling ideas: i.e. the class which is the ruling *material* force of society is at the same time its ruling *intellectual* force. (Marx and Engels, [1896] 1976, p. 67)

Slave-owners do not, of course, control *all* instruments of communication. For example, they cannot totally control what transpires at an illicit meeting in the slaves' quarters. They can, however, influence the outcome of the discussion by placing agents in such meetings to put forward the slave-owners' position (in modified form, to be sure) and later to report what took place.

The other representative society used to illustrate the argument is the freest possible egalitarian society, in which every member has exactly the same general rights and responsibilities in the decision-making process. Here, one segment of society does not rule over another, but all members have equal voices in framing authority. While there are no extant societies that typify this form of social organization, primitive tribal society can be held up as an historical model (Briffault, 1927; Childe, 1964; Morgan, 1877; Thomson, 1965).

In an egalitarian society, any idea may be brought forward for discussion. But not every idea will be allowed free and equal reign. One general set of ideas will be expressly forbidden – that of deceit intended to advantage some at the expense of others. Any individual or group of individuals who puts forward ideas designed to advantage only some of society is necessarily putting forward ideas that are to the detriment of others. This violates the principal of equality, and, assuming that the idea is recognized as detrimental, its holders will be quashed. Thus, even the most egalitarian society does not hold all ideas in equal favor.

In sum, then, it is argued that ideas are themselves social products; that if ideas are to be popularly disseminated, they must have some appeal to those bodies controlling the mechanisms of transmission. Since the means of communication are economic units and are controlled by those who have economic interests in mind, then the ideas they advance must be favorably disposed toward those economic interests. And subversive ideas – those not favorably disposed toward prevailing authority – must seek other than the dominant channels of communication for their dissemination; so they will be in the minority.

Science and fraud

Ideas must necessarily be one of two general types: they must be correct, or incorrect. Correct ideas are those that accurately reflect or correspond to the world of nature or of society, thus assisting in the creation of knowledge of those

8

worlds. These ideas can be tested in practice by subjecting them to conventional scientific tests of proof.

Correct ideas are not absolutely correct for all historical time. Such a position is theoretically absurd. Absolute correctness connotes absolute knowledge. In other words, that which is studied is known in all its characteristics and in its relationship with all other characteristics in the universe. The implication, then, is that the world has ceased changing, that motion itself has ended. For to know everything means that nothing about nature or society can change; there can be no new information. Since this cannot be the case, all correct knowledge is relative, or imperfect. It awaits further elaboration, refinement, modification and revision.

Correct knowledge may or may not be widely disseminated, depending on the relationship of that knowledge to the dominant social class. If that knowledge is conducive to the dominant class's interests, it will be transmitted; if not, it will be suppressed. It should be clear that the acceptance or rejection of an idea depends on the perception of the dominant class. Clearly, there is no reason to believe that a notion injurious to the long-run interests of that class will be immediately seen as such; so with ideas supportive of that class. Moreover, given sufficient time for ideas to demonstrate themselves in social practice, sufficient evidence will be eventually generated to allow a considered judgment to be made. In other words, I am not assuming omniscience on the part of the holders of power; just that in the long run they are capable of recognizing their interests.

Consider the status (and limits) of correct ideas in a slave society. An efficiency study is undertaken to arrive at the caloric intake an adult male slave must have if he is to survive to the age of fifty and work at maximum capacity for his adult life. Given the relationship between nutrition, longevity and efficiency, the correct amount will be arrived at. And, because the slave-holder has an economic interest in such information, it will be disseminated. On the other hand, a more substantial investigation would reveal that the economic relationship between the slave and the slave-holding classes is one of exploitation; the slave-owners control the surplus produced by the slaves, so it can be shown that slave society exists for the benefit of a minority of the population. This is contrary to the slave-holders' usual position that slavery is mutually beneficial, if not an outright burden for the slave-holders. The results of the latter investigation, the more significant of the two, will not be disseminated through official channels of communication; rather, it will be suppressed and its holders dealt with according to the customs of the period.

Incorrect ideas have two sub-sets: error and fraud. Error is of little consequence for historical inquiry. It is commonplace and is based upon misinformation, ignorance, accident and the like. To the extent that one has, or believes one has, no vested interest in error, it will be corrected as soon as it is pointed out. However, as error does confuse or obsfucate an issue, vested interests may well promote the continuation of simply erroneous information. In this case, though, error then enters the category of fraud.

Fraud is an entirely different matter. Fraud is also erroneous, but this class of error has social import. Because it has social import, a mere 'correction' will not eliminate it. In fact, those attempting the correction might find themselves in serious trouble.

We can define fraud as socially organized, conscious deceit. This definition contains two very important aspects. First, since fraud is socially organized, there must be a social foundation to its existence; fraud must serve a social function. Second, since fraud is consciously determined, those developing such ideas must know truth (or at least what benefits the dominant class). If fraud were mere accident, then, based on probability, intended fraud would sometimes be correct. But then, it could not be fraudulent. So fraud is established as a counter to or concealment of truth.

The significance of fraud cannot be overstated. A brief analysis of this social phenomenon reveals an important function that fraud serves in particular kinds of societies.

The social function of fraud

Since fraud is organized deception, the fundamental question is, Why should fraud exist – what social function does it perform? Since fraud is organized, it must be organized by those with the means to disseminate fraud among the population. That is, it must be organized by those who have control of the instruments of communication. It is conceivable that the segment of the population that does not control these instruments has an interest in developing fraud, but it does not have a mechanism at its disposal to communicate its ideas.

The segment that does develop and disseminate fraud must have a reason to do so. Since fraud distorts or conceals reality, it is only that portion of the population that advantages itself by such distortion and concealment that would be motivated to advance fraud as a social mechanism.

Students of ideology who have investigated this question have precisely identified the origins of fraud. Every serious examination has revealed a class basis to the phenomenon in which an exploiting class (one that exists on the basis of another class's production) develops and disseminates fraud to distort and conceal this exploitative basis to that class's existence (Childe, 1964; Farrington, 1966; Briffault, 1930; Dunham, 1964). In fact, major theoreticians of fraud have themselves revealed this class basis. Consider the following argument of Plato, speaking as a member of the old landed nobility and laying down 'correct' governing principles for a non-democratic minority ruling class (Thomson, 1977, pp. 318–28):

> But further we must surely prize truth most highly. For if we were right in what we were just saying and falsehood is in very deed useless to gods, but to men useful as a remedy or form of medicine, it is obvious, and laymen would have nothing to do with it . . .
>
> The rulers then of the city may, if anybody, fitly lie on account of enemies or citizens for the benefit of the state; no others may have anything to do with it . . .

11

If then the ruler catches anybody else in the city lying, any of the craftsmen, 'whether a prophet or healer of sickness or joiner of timbers,' he will chastise him for introducing a practice as subversive and destructive of a state as it is of a ship . . . (Plato, [*c*. 370AD] 1963, p. 634)

And the essence of this lie is as follows:

a sort of Phoenician tale, something that has happened ere now in many parts of the world, as the poets aver and have induced men to believe, but that has not happened and perhaps would not be likely to happen in our day and demanding no little persuasion to make it believable . . .

I hardly know how to find the audacity or the words to speak and undertake to persuade first the rulers themselves and the soldiers and then the rest of the city that in good sooth all our training and education of them were things that they imagined and that happened to them as it were in a dream, but that in reality at that time they were down within the earth being molded and fostered themselves while their weapons and the rest of their equipment were being fashioned. And when they were quite finished the earth as being their mother delivered them, and now as if their land were their mother and their nurse they ought to take thought for her and defend her against any attack and regard the other citizens as their brothers and children of the selfsame earth . . .

While all of you in the city are brothers, we will say in our tale, yet God in fashioning those of you who are fitted to hold rule mingled gold in their generation, for which reason they are the most precious – but in the helpers silver, and iron and brass in the farmers and other craftsmen. (Plato, [*c*. 370AD] 1963, p. 659)

Pareto, a fairly frank and considered examiner of the mechanism of class rule, reduces the techniques of this rule to force and 'cunning' (fraud):

To ask whether or not force ought to be used in a society, whether the use of force is or is not beneficial, is to ask a question that has no meaning; for force is used by those who wish to preserve certain uniformities and by those who wish to overstep them; and the violence of the ones stands in contrast and in conflict with the violence of the others. In truth, if a partisan of a governing class disavows the use of force, he means that he disavows the use of force by insurgents trying to escape from the norms of the given uniformity. On the other hand, if he says he approves of the use of force, what he really means is that he approves of the use of force by the public authority to constrain insurgents to conformity . . . (Pareto, [1916] 1935, p. 1512)

And, when faced with an organized show of force from the underlying population, the ruling class, given its calculations of the benefits relative to the (social) costs of intensifying its force, may well turn to fraud as the mechanism of rule:

To prevent or resist violence, the governing class resorts to 'diplomacy,' fraud, corruption – governmental authority passes, in a word, from the lions to the foxes. The governing class bows its head under the threat of violence, but it surrenders only in appearances, trying to turn the flank of the obstacle it cannot demolish in frontal attack. In the long run, that sort of procedure comes to exercise a far-reaching influence on the selection of the governing class, which is now recruited only from the foxes, while the lions are blackballed. The individual who best knows the arts of sapping the strength of the foes of 'graft', and of winning back by fraud and deceit what seemed to have been surrendered under pressure of force, is now leader of leaders. The man who has bursts of rebellion, and does not know how to crook his spine at the proper times and places, is the worst of leaders, and his presence is tolerated among them only if other distinguished endowments offset that defect. (Pareto, [1916] 1935, p. 1515[5])

Any inquiry into the origins of a specific fraud reveals the same general case; an exploiting body develops argumentation to prevent the underlying population from discovering the truth of its existence or, if that truth is exceedingly difficult to conceal, to rationalize that existence and inculcate the attitude that it is naturally ordered – one can do nothing to alter it. Where the need for fraud was of a particular type, that specific deception was produced. Consider the origins of racism, that pernicious fraud based upon supposed natural inferiority as determined by racial characteristics.

With the advent of the Spanish colonization of the Americas, the aboriginal population was forced into a situation of extreme servitude. The effects of this feudal system of exploitation of the Indians were acute: disease, malnutrition and suicide. The feudal colonizers required a rationalization to cover over their labor system and its effects on the producing class. Given the circumstances (an exploiting class of one race, the exploited of another), the argument eventually unfolded that the Indians were so inferior that they could be considered sub-human. Given this racial inferiority, the colonial efforts were to the advantage of the exploited, because the superior race could then promote the interests of the Indians, who were incapable of promoting their own interests. Further, since the colonial officials have the best interests of the aboriginal population in mind, they were free to use extreme methods of coercion in achieving this end (Cox, 1948, pp. 322–45; Hanke, 1959).

This illustration points up three fundamental specifics of fraud: the fraud follows social practice; it is conscious in its origins; and there must be at least one element in the fraud that appears rational. Let us consider each of these elements.

Fraud follows social practice in the following sense. There is no point to deception unless there is a need for it. Because the purpose of fraud is to create illusions concerning the real world, there must first occur real world developments about which illusions are necessary. For example, there is no point in arguing the innate inferiority of slaves until a slave system has begun to unfold. It should be noted, however, that any particular fraud can outlive its social origins and be adapted

14

to another practice altogether. Thus, innate slave inferiority can be transferred to serf inferiority, with modification required given the differences between serf and slave.

The second point is that of fraud's conscious origins. Consider the following argument:

> The falsification of thought in the interests of power is to an enormous extent sincere and well-intentioned. But we are probably too prone . . . to minimize the part played by intentional and deliberate fraud. Wherever access is afforded to detailed evidence, deliberate deception is found. From the tricks of the witch-doctor and the Pompeiian priest's speaking-trumpet down to the 'political intelligence' and the education of public opinion of our newspapers, there is a vast amount of fraud which cannot be wholly euphemised away by charitable interpretations . . .
>
> It is however not easy, in general, and it is unessential, to draw a sharp demarcation between conscious and subconscious intellectual dishonesty. Opinions have an ingenious tendency to flow in the channel of vested interest. The priestly class is favourably disposed towards mythology, the landowning class towards feudal principles, and stock-jobbers are particularly acute to perceive the dangers of communism. The adaptation of rational intelligence to the interests of power has little difficulty in justifying itself as a virtue and a duty. The necessity of sound principles, the principles upon which the existing order rests, is manifest. Subversive facts are a danger to society, and the social order must be protected even against itself. To abet dangerous tendencies of thought, to dwell unduly upon facts which, to the unsound judgment of many, might prove misleading, would be clearly culpable. It would be a betrayal of their welfare, for which the holders of power, who enjoy the privilege of sounder culture, must account themselves responsible. And if a slight modification in the complexion, in the presentation and nomenclature of facts conduces to a more wholesome attitude of the mind, so much the better. Do not our most reputed philosophers offer us, as the modest

15

conclusion of their meditations, the cogent argument that, since we have to live under existing conditions, we should believe anything that will help us to do so? (Briffault, 1930, pp. 34–5)

It is important to understand what is meant by this form of consciousness (understanding). Fraud may be developed by individuals who have a perfectly clear understanding of the society around them, are quite cognizant of the potential dangers to that society, and think through each particle of their argument in the process of developing a deception. If that is the case (and I believe it is, at least some of the time), it would be extremely difficult to prove. The mass of evidence necessary to prove the proposition would be overwhelming and generally not available.[6]

But this is not the meaning of consciousness from a class point of view. Any ruling class obviously wants to maintain its position. If that class is in power for any length of time, it must have some understanding of what is required to do so and the potential obstacles to remaining in its position of authority. Moreover, if a class is advantaged by a particular situation, then that situation must be 'good' in some sense. A 'bad' situation is one that produces unfavorable results. (Obviously, the same situation can produce both favorable and unfavorable results, depending on one's position in society.) If a class is conscious of what advantages it has, it will necessarily generate notions that tend to create and preserve that situation. For example, from a slave-owner's point of view, ideas advocating the equality of all people are foul. Therefore, ideas will be generated and transmitted that show the folly, ineptitude and outright evil of egalitarianism and egalitarians. For the slave-owners, egalitarianism is the destruction of civilization.

The last specific point of fraud concerns the rational kernel of irrational ideas. To be effective, fraud must be believed. To be believed, it must be believable. Thus, there are definite limits imposed on the nature of fraud and the type of fraud developed in any particular circumstance or within any general form of social organization.

Thus, when religion was used to inculcate belief in a divine right of monarchs, feudal magnates were perfectly satisfied to maintain such a belief in order to perpetuate feudalism. With capitalist revolution, however, 'divine right' had to be attacked in order to undermine the prestige and consequent authority of the feudal ruling class. When a controlled monarchy was restored following successful revolution, this particular fraud was no longer completely satisfactory; it had been discredited in the political contest that saw a new class victorious. Therefore, religion had to be restructured; but, given the rupture in the very foundation of religion, it proves to be less effective in the capitalist epoch.

Or consider the following hypothetical situation. Suppose an attempt were made to sanctify rule based on the size of the ruler's feet. Since foot size is randomly distributed among the population, it would soon be demonstrated that many of the ruled had the same right to authority based on their having the same foot size. Clearly, this would not be a suitable manifestation of the right to rule.

Fraud is useful only to those who have a purpose to deceive and a means to disseminate fraud among the population. The function of fraud is to conceal or pervert truth. But why? To conceal or pervert truth connotes that there is something worthy of concealment and perversion. From a social point of view, this means that something of significance must be hidden. A social injustice must be concealed, covered over, rationalized. The basic social injustice, and that to which all injustices can be linked, is exploitation. Thus, fraud will be found in all societies in which one class lives through the exploitation of another.

If the producing class is in power, there is no basis for fraud. This class cannot exist on the basis of exploitation (either there is no class to exploit, or the non-producing class is too small to be effectively exploited), so it has no interest in perverting or concealing objective reality. Instead, it has every interest in understanding that reality so as to improve its economic and social position.

Or, examining the same general argument from a negative position, if the producing class is not in power, then the purpose of fraud is to maintain its position of servitude to the dominant, exploiting class. Since fraud – deception – assists the ruling class, then the opposite – truth – can only assist the exploited class, the majority; effective democracy rests on truth.

But this is not our concern. We now turn to a brief overview of capitalist society – one form of exploiting social structure – to examine the relationship between this class, society, science and fraud.

Notes: Chapter 1

1 The theory was known since at least the third century BC, when the noted Greek astronomer, Aristarchus, put forward much the same argument as Copernicus.

2 It should be noted that the Protestant theological leaders of the period were equally opposed to the Copernican revolution, given that they, too, were interested in maintaining religious, though not necessarily Catholic, authority: see Dunham, 1964, pp. 312–13.

3 Here lay the crime of Galileo. By yielding to authority he knew to be wrong, hence illegitimate, he objectively placed himself on the side of that authority and against those fighting against it. Thus, he aided reaction and thwarted progress – and in so doing, assisted the maintenance of a murderous social order.

4 The Church eventually modified its position on this and other matters. Given the success of capitalist development, the only way feudal lords – both lay and clerical – could hold on to even a modicum of power was to come to terms with the new social power. To accomplish this, much of the older ideological formation had to be modified. It must be noted, though, that the revolutionary capitalists needed a religion to defend their interests. Only after the Catholic Church refused to cooperate did they turn to the development of their own brand of Christianity, Protestantism. The Roman Church 'reformed' when it was in danger of being frozen out altogether. The religious (economic) struggles in sixteenth-century Germany illustrate this proposition well: see Engels, [1850] 1966.

5 Actually, Pareto reverses the relative reliance on fraud and force. The usual mechanism of rule is that of fraud. A ruling class resorts to force only when required by the opposition of the underlying population.

6 There are enough examples to make the contention convincing. For example, to assist the conversion of the barbarian tribes of Europe to the Christian faith required the manufacturing of 'miracles' that can only be explained as examples of this form of deception. To convince Pepin, Pope Stephen produced a signed epistle from Peter, no less: see Manhattan, 1972, pp. 26–8.

CHAPTER TWO

Capitalism, science and fraud

Capitalism is one form of minority ruling class society. Since businessmen control the means of production, workers are coerced into selling their labor power in order to survive as a class. Obviously, if the producing class had control over economic resources, this particular social relationship could not exist. Further, in capitalist society production is undertaken for profit, which facilitates capital accumulation.

As with all other forms of social organization, capitalism requires a mechanism to organize the labor force. The less significant aspect of the necessity for this control is to assure that the proper quantity and quality of labor power is forthcoming to meet production. More important is the fact that the producing class must accept, in general, capitalism itself. Since the producing class is inevitably the majority, it must behave in such a manner as to allow any social organization to exist. That is, capitalism must have the loyalty, or at least the obedience, of workers.

There are two general ways in which any minority ruling class persuades the underlying population to perform its duties: physical coercion, or force; and mental coercion, or fraud. The former is the less preferred mechanism. Force is more costly and has a tendency to facilitate a correct understanding within the producing class of the nature of the social organization in question. That is, force is a more open form of class domination and, as such, is resorted to only when the ideological structure developed to persuade the lower class to accept the prevailing social system is eroded:

An antisocial organisation of power is not only under the necessity of maintaining itself unchanged, but of preserving equally unchanged the entire mental structure of ideas and values, principles and traditions, upon which it rests. Physical force is not so important a factor in the maintenance of power as is commonly supposed. It has its uses. The control of physical, and more especially of economic, means of compulsion is important. But, in general, reliance upon force, the multiplication of policemen, the display of machine-guns and tear-bombs, which we are becoming accustomed to associate with the maintenance of civilisation, are signs of weakness. They are indications of a desperate plight. All the policemen and bombing-planes in the world could not avail were not the minds of people successfully maintained in a condition of incapacity. It is not the unarmed condition of the oppressed which renders them powerless; it is their stupidity. (Briffault, 1935, pp. 54–5)

But capitalism, more than any other form of exploiting society, also requires science for its survival. There are two principle reasons for this. First, since capitalism developed out of previous, feudal, class society, it required a generally correct understanding of society in order to consolidate its position and attack the reigning ideas of the feudal ruling class. The best exposure of prevailing fraud is truth. Hence, to the extent that truth was useful to the emerging capitalists, truth (science) was promoted.

Second, one result of natural scientific inquiry is the promotion of technology. Given the economic impetus toward changing the level of productive forces, physics, biology and chemistry were advanced. This relationship is evident mainly during the competitive phase of capitalist development:

The bourgeoisie cannot exist without constantly revolutionizing the instruments of production, and thereby the relations of production, and with them the whole relations of society. Conservation of the old modes of production in unaltered form was, on the contrary, the first condition of existence for all earlier industrial classes. Constant revolutionizing of production, uninterrupted disturbance of all social conditions, everlasting uncertainty and agitation distinguish the bourgeois epoch from all earlier ones. (Marx and Engels, [1898] 1964, p. 7)

Therefore, within capitalist society one can observe a fundamental conflict. Both fraud and science are useful from a capitalist point of view. But, because fraud and science are in opposition, a tension exists in the ideological structure. Given the imperatives of class rule and capitalist control over the means of communication and over science itself (through funding, etc.), science will be advanced only to the extent that it does not conflict with the basic ideological support of capitalism. Depending upon the underlying characteristics of capitalist organization, either science or fraud will be dominant in any period; but, in all cases, they will exist concurrently.

The period of competitive capitalism

A useful starting point for this introductory examination is supplied by the work of the eminent British physicist and historian of science, J. D. Bernal. Bernal divides the capitalist epoch into five general periods, according to its relationship to the advancement of science (Bernal, 1971, Vol. 2, pp. 506–7, passim):

1 The fifteenth through the seventeenth centuries: the Heroic Stage;
2 1690–1760: the Transitional Stage;
3 1760–1830: the Industrial Revolution Stage;
4 1830–1870: the 'Heyday' Stage;
5 1870 to the present: the Imperialist Stage.

Obviously, the dating is somewhat arbitrary, since any classificatory system of this type does not fall into neat historical patterns. Different nation-states, for example, do not conform to the year limits above – developed for capitalism as a whole – but they still display the same general development. Nevertheless, various trends do unfold, and it can be observed that these trends are dependent on the underlying social characteristics of capitalism. Let us consider each stage in turn.

The heroic stage   This period incorporates the era surrounding the initial attempts at and early successes of capitalist revolution. Focusing on England, which can be viewed as a classical model in this regard, we observe growing opposition to the feudal order and its ideology in the late fifteenth and early sixteenth centuries, followed by the Civil War period of 1640 to the 'Glorious Revolution' of 1688 (Hill, 1949, 1979).

This time – frame differs from country to country, depending on the economic and political conditions of each. The Italian Renaissance, while challenging the monopoly of feudal ideology, failed in bringing about the political change that could have allowed full capitalist development. In France, the Heroic State was most pronounced in the eighteenth century and reached political fruition in the Revolution of 1789. From the standpoint of scientific achievement, the Heroic Stage covers the period from Copernicus to Newton.

During this historical time-frame, we observe a most dynamic political, economic and ideological struggle between the capitalists and their supporters and allies, and the feudal ruling class and its cohorts. Developing within the bowels of feudal society, capitalist production demanded new techniques with which nature could be harnessed and output and efficiency promoted. Thus, in mining, agriculture, transportation and armaments, new knowledge was called forth which would accurately reflect the changing emphasis of production and facilitate developments in these areas. It is no accident that the great scientists and scientific writers of the period – Galileo, Agricola, Biringuccio and, above all, Newton – were heavily influenced by the requirements of businessmen engaged in these areas of production (Hessen, 1931).

Equally important as the emphasis on production (and in the long run more important), but linked to it, was the necessity to develop a new world outlook, one that would reflect the interests of the rising capitalists and stand in contradistinction to that of the moribund feudal rulers.

If capitalists were to be successful in their program, they would have to bring forth a set of ideas that would rally the underlying population to their side and, as the opposite side of the same coin, dissuade them from obeisance to the feudal princes. This required an ideological system that was the opposite of the lords' and, furthermore, promised solutions to the problems faced by the lower orders. The ideological system that was promoted by the growth in scientific technique, and which, in turn, allowed further growth and development in those production techniques and fulfilled the political program of the new class, was materialism, the outlook of science:

> The revolutionary act by which natural science declared its independence . . . was the publication of the immortal work by which Copernicus, though timidly and, so to speak, only from his death-bed, threw down the gauntlet to ecclesiastical authority in the affairs of nature. The emancipation of natural science from theology dates from this, although the fighting out of particular mutual claims has dragged on down to our day and in many minds is still far from completion. Thenceforward, however, the development of the sciences proceeded with giant strides, and it might be said, gained in force in proportion to the square of the distance (in time) from its point of departure. (Engels, [1925] 1972, pp. 22–3)

This great revolutionary epoch restored, to a degree, the materialist world outlook of the ancient Greeks – Epicurus, Anaximander and their Roman spokesman, Lucretius – an outlook eventually defeated in Greece and replaced by the idealism of Aristotle, Plato and the various religious officials and their lackey (Farrington, 1953).[1]

But the materialism of the Heroic Stage did more than merely restore Greek science and philosophy: it advanced knowledge by quantitative and qualitative leaps that would have staggered the sages of the Aegean.

In England, the nurturing ground for the materialist philosophical position, this world outlook was put forward most clearly and cogently by Francis Bacon (1561–1626) and his pupil Thomas Hobbes (1588–1679). A long quote from Marx demonstrates the essential quality of this perspective and shows its development from Bacon through Locke:

The real progenitor of English materialism and all modern experimental science is Bacon. To him natural philosophy is the only true philosophy, and physics based upon the experience of the senses is the chiefest part of natural philosophy . . . All science is based on experience, and consists in subjecting the data furnished by the senses to a rational method of investigation. Induction, analysis, comparison, observation, experiment, are the principal forms of such a rational method. Among the qualities inherent in matter, motion is the first and foremost, not only in the form of mechanical and mathematical motion, but chiefly in the form of an impulse, a vital spirit, a tension . . .

In Bacon, its first creator, materialism still holds back within itself in a naive way the germs of a many-sided development. On the one hand, matter, surrounded by a sensuous, poetic glamour, seems to attract man's whole entity by winning smiles. On the other, the aphoristically formulated doctrine pullulates with inconsistencies imported from theology.

In its further evolution, materialism becomes one-sided. Hobbes is the man who systematises Baconian materialism. Knowledge based upon the senses loses its poetic blossom, it passes into the abstract experience of the geometrician. Physical motion is sacrificed to mechanical or mathematical motion; geometry is proclaimed as the queen of sciences. Materialism takes to misanthropy. If it is to overcome its opponent, misanthropic, fleshless spiritualism, and that on the latter's own ground, materialism has to chastise its own flesh and turn ascetic . . .

Hobbes had systematised Bacon without, however, furnishing a proof for Bacon's fundamental principle, the origin of all human knowledge and ideas from the world of sensation.

It was Locke who, in his *Essay on the Human Understanding*, supplied this proof. (Marx and Engels, [1844] 1975, pp. 150–2)

In sum, Bacon set forth the following doctrine:

(1) That science is the highway to knowledge.
(2) That scientific knowledge is based on observation. On the basis of observations, scientific theories are worked out, which must always be tested by fresh observations, which in turn suggest further theoretical developments – and so on.
(3) That scientific knowledge is objectively true, and that no other means of attaining objective truth exists.
(4) Bacon contrasted the method of science, not only to the unscientific amassing of 'undigested' facts, but to the method of 'dogmatism.' By this he meant the propounding of theories a-priori, that is, not based on observation, not tested by observation, but derived from principles which are supposed to be given in some way without reference to experience. (Cornforth, 1947, p. 23)

Bacon's general framework was systematized by Hobbes, who also rid Baconian thought of its semi-religious 'pullulations,' and developed a consistent atheistic materialism.

Concerning the thoughts of man, I will consider them first singly, and afterwards in train, or dependence upon one another. Singly, they are every one a representation or appearance, of some quality, or other accident of a body without us, which is commonly called an object . . .
The original of them all is that which we call sense, for there is no conception in a man's mind, which hath not at first, totally, or by parts, been begotten upon the organs of sense . . . (Hobbes, [1651] 1955, p. 7)

At the same time that Hobbes systematized materialism and philosophically threw God out the window, he nevertheless argued for the maintenance of religion in the form of a state-determined creed for the lower classes (Farrington, 1949, p. 169). This was determined in part by a theoretical inconsistency in the materialism of the period, but mainly by the political requirements of the revolutionary capitalists; it is an important consideration for what follows.

Consider, however, the significance of this revolution in thought, which lay on top of the revolution in economic and political organization. The materialists put forward the proposition that the world was knowable through observation utilizing humans' own sensory apparatus. If the world is knowable and can be discerned through human actions, then: (a) divine knowledge, divine interpretation and divine rule all appear as so much nonsense,[2] and (b) a very optimistic, progressive outlook is fostered – for if the world is capable of rational comprehension, the problems facing society are soluble (or, at least, appear so):

> But above all, if a man could succeed, not in striking out some particular invention, however useful, but in kindling a light in nature – a light which should in its very rising touch and illuminate all the border-regions that confine upon the circle of our present knowledge; and so spreading further and further should presently disclose and bring into sight all that is most hidden and secret in the world – that man (I thought) would be the benefactor indeed of the human race – the propagator of man's empire over the universe, the champion of liberty, the conqueror and subduer of necessities. (Bacon; quoted in Farrington, 1949, p. 54)

Hence, materialism, the product of scientific advance, which in turn promoted science, both undercut the feudal ideology of divine knowledge and drew support to the revolutionary class that championed science. It is no historical accident that this philosophy, with its corresponding attack on religion (if only implied and not thoroughgoing), was promoted in all capitalist revolutionary situations – France in the eighteenth century, Germany and Italy in the nineteenth, etc.

The transitional stage The period following successful capitalist revolution is the most difficult of all to understand. During this time, capitalists consolidated their economic and political power. This consolidation represents a reactionary phase, in which the new ruling class allied with its former enemies against the underlying population. In England, the period between the restoration of 1660 and the assumption to the throne of William and Mary after the 'bloodless revolution' of 1688 signalled the drawing to a close of the politically tumultuous 1600s.

Capitalists, since they are a minority segment of the population, cannot wage successful revolution with only their own forces: they require allies. These allies must necessarily be drawn from the lower classes – in the 1600s, these were principally small, petty producers such as farmers and craftsmen. To be successful, businessmen must advance their own interests as the interests of all the revolutionary classes; they must include in their program of action concessions to their revolutionary brethren. So in France, 'Liberty, Fraternity, Equality' was implied to apply to *all* anti-feudal elements.

In the struggle against the feudal elements, such a program was relatively easy to develop and maintain, because all the revolutionary classes had an objective interest in eliminating feudal constraints. The problem arose with the overthrow of the feudal lords, for then the major item on the agenda surrounded the establishment of the new order. The major political issue was no longer opposition to previously established rule, but who would seize the new authority.

If capitalists were to be successful in their bid for class power, they had to fend off former allies who desired a social order far different than that which the capitalists would impose. Thus, to secure victory for the class he represented, Cromwell had to dissolve the New Model Army, undermine the most radical elements such as the Diggers, and, when all else failed, march against the former backbone of the

27

Army, the Levellers, brutally exterminating them through open force of arms (Hill, 1949).

But physical suppression is only a short-term expedient. If the new class wished to consolidate its rule, it had to seek new allies in maintaining its control over the population. These allies were found, almost through a process of elimination, in the politically dispossessed feudal lords who not only had experience in class rule, but could be brought into a secondary position of domination rather than risk all.[3]

With the physical suppression of dissident elements and the drawing of the compact between capitalists and lords, the ideological thrust of the revolutionary (Heroic) period had to be modified lest it turn against the capitalists themselves. Thus we see ideas once advanced by the nascent capitalist ruling class come under attack by that same class once its control was established (Hill, 1980).

In keeping with the new alliance, feudal ideology, though in a modified form, was restored as an instrument of class rule. For example, the atheistic impulse of the previous period was channelled into relatively safe doctrines that, while still anti-Catholic or Anglican, became increasingly less anti-Christian (Dunham, 1964, pp. 329–56; Hill, 1964).

Let us return momentarily to the Heroic Stage. The materialism developed therein had two class elements: 'official' materialism, and 'subversive' materialism.

The official materialism of Bacon and Hobbes, while potentially unsettling, was not in itself problematic to the capitalists. Bacon had 'allowed' divine thought to exist side by side with rational thought, while Hobbes, though closer to an atheistic position, saw the advantage of an officially sponsored religion to maintain control over the lower-class elements. For the Hobbesians, materialism was to be the monopoly of the privileged classes and the scientists, while idealism (religion) was to be the dominant mode of thought of the underlying population.

Now the materialism of this period was not theoretically inconsistent with the maintenance of a divinely ordered universe. At this historical juncture, materialism, reflecting the scientific advances of the period in mechanics, was itself

28

a mechanical materialism. The universe (and society) was conceived of as a rational network in which all the pieces fitted and worked together in mechanistic harmony: thus the Newtonian 'clock,' in which there was movement but no change, only repetition. The problem with this view is how the 'clock' gets its start: who or what does the winding (Engels, [1888] 1941, pp. 20–32).

Mechanical materialism does not mandate a God to get things underway, but it does leave the door open to such a position. Hence we find the greatest materialists of the period invoking a divine order, not to explain how matter works, but to give structure to the realm of the material world. In fact, Newton offered a solution to the problems that materialism posed to religion in which he demonstrated that this universe was not inconsistent with a belief in God (Hessen, 1931, pp. 35–6).

So 'official' materialism was not hostile to religion in general. It *was* hostile, however, to the unthinking, purely scholastic form of feudal religion in which dogma dominated reason.

However, alongside this official materialism, there developed a 'subversive' materialism, as represented by the (officially ignored) Leveller, Richard Overton. His major work in the subject was 'Man is Mortal in All Respects' [1643], in which he reached a full, unreservedly atheistic, materialist philosophy of nature and society. During the early stage of the revolutionary movement, when the Levellers were the most important fighting element, Overton was viewed by capitalist officials as the 'chief representative of the terrible doctrine of materialism' (Hessen, 1931, p. 31).

What Overton and the Levellers advocated was a thoroughgoing revolutionary restructuring of society in which all hierarchical relations would be abolished (Morton, 1975). This was obviously not in the interests of capitalists, who, once the need for the Levellers was over, turned on them and physically eliminated the organization as a threat to their rule.

Exterminating the organization solved only part of the problem. A 'Leveller materialism,' should it permeate the population, was quite dangerous. So subversive materialism of the Levellers also had to be destroyed. Materialism had to be purged of its subversive elements.

The problem faced by the capitalists in the transition stage can be summed up as follows. Science and its materialist philosophy was perfectly correct in its place. But, for the good of the commonwealth and the establishment of order, it was necessary that this outlook be confined to those who knew best how to use it. The lower classes, given their incapacity to understand the dangers of this philosophy and, therefore, the political harm it could do to their own interests, had to be prevented from acquiring knowledge of that which could upset the harmony of the new-found order. In other words: Revolution, but not too much revolution; reason, but not too much reason; anti-clericism, but not too much.

This political problem was solved by two developments occurring after hostilities ceased: the skepticism of Locke (1632–1704) and the idealism of Berkeley (1685–1752). These two solutions were then combined by the so-called agnostic Hume (1711–1776). Let us deal initially with the argument proposed by Berkeley.

The essence of Berkeley's argument is evidenced by the proposition set forth in his *Treatise Concerning the Principles of Human Knowledge* [1710]:

> It is evident to any one who takes a survey of the objects of human knowledge, that they are either ideas actually imprinted on the senses; or else such as are perceived by attending to the passions and operations of the mind; or lastly, ideas formed by help of memory and imagination . . . By sight I have the ideas of light and colours . . .
>
> But, besides all that endless variety of ideas or objects of knowledge, there is likewise something which knows or perceives them . . . This perceiving, active being is what I call mind, spirit, soul, or myself . . . they exist, or, which is the same thing, whereby they are perceived; for the existence of an idea consists in being perceived.
>
> It is indeed an opinion strangely prevailing amongst men, that houses, mountains, rivers, and in a word all sensible objects, have an existence, natural or real, distinct from their being perceived by the understanding. But,

with how great an assurance and acquiescence soever this Principle may be entertained in the world, yet whoever shall find in his heart to call it in question may, if I mistake not, perceive it to involve a manifest contradiction. For, what are the forementioned objects but the things we perceive by sense? and what do we perceive besides our own ideas or sensations? and is it not plainly repugnant that any one of these, or any combination of them, should exist unperceived?

In the last place, you will say, What if we give up the cause of material Substance, and stand to it that Matter is an unknown Somewhat – neither substance nor accident, spirit nor idea . . . I answer, You may, if so it shall seem good, use the word matter in the same sense as other men use nothing, and so make those terms convertible in your style . . .

First, then, it will be objected that by the foregoing principles all that is real and substantial in nature is banished out of the world, and instead thereof a chimerical scheme of ideas takes place. All things that exist exist only in the mind; that is, they are purely notional. What therefore becomes of the sun, moon, and stars? What must we think of houses, rivers, mountains, trees, stones; nay, even of our own bodies? Are all these but so many chimeras and illusions on the fancy? – To all which, and whatever else of the same sort may be objected, I answer, that by the Principles premised we are not deprived of any one thing in nature. Whatever we see, feel, hear, or any wise conceive or understand, remains as secure as ever, and is as real as ever . . .

I do not argue against the existence of any one thing that we can apprehend, either by sense or reflection. That the things I see with my eyes or touch with my hands do exist, really exist, I make not the least question. The only thing whose existence we deny is that which philosophers call Matter or corporeal substance. And in doing of this there is no damage done to the rest of mankind, who, I dare say, will never miss it. The Atheist indeed will want the colour of an empty name to support his impiety; and the Philosophers may possibly find they have lost a great handle for trifling and disputation. [But that is all the harm that I can see done.] (Berkeley, [1710] 1929, pp. 124–6, 128–9, 168, 142)

Berkeley's general position is that of subjectivist idealism: because ideas are all we can know and ideas are the product of individuals, the only certainty that exists is that of one's own idea. The world, thus, is a product of the individual's notion of what that world is, a most important proposition in connection with the individualist view of society (see below, Chapter 4).

Berkeley does not hesitate to reveal the purpose of his theory:

> For, as we have shewn the doctrine of Matter of Corporeal Substance to have been the main pillar and support of Scepticism, so likewise upon the same foundation have been raised all the impious schemes of Atheism and Irreligion . . . How great a friend material substance has been to Atheists in all ages were needless to relate. All their monstrous systems have so visible and necessary a dependence on it, that when this cornerstone is once removed, the whole fabric cannot choose but fall to the ground . . .
>
> Matter being once expelled out of nature drags with it so many sceptical and impious notions, such an incredible number of disputes and puzzling questions, which have been thorns in the sides of divines as well as philosophers, and made so much fruitless work for mankind, that if the arguments we have produced against it are not found equal to demonstration . . . yet I am sure all friends to knowledge, peace, and religion have reason to wish they were. (Berkeley, [1710] 1929, pp. 176–8)

Further, Berkeley denies causality:

> To all which my answer is, first, that the connexion of ideas does not imply the relation of cause and effect, but only of a mark or sign with the thing signified. The fire which I see is not the cause of the pain I suffer upon

my approaching it, but the mark that forewarns me of it
. . .
   Hence, it is evident that those things which, under
the notion of a cause co-operating or concurring to the
production of effects, are altogether inexplicable and run
us into great absurdities, may be very naturally explained,
and have a proper and obvious use assigned to them,
when they are considered only as marks or signs for our
information . . . (Berkeley, [1710] 1929, pp. 160–1)

Since the only thing known is one's ideas, there can be
no necessary connection between those ideas as caused
by laws of nature or society. Ideas are purely random,
accidental, individualist. If there is order to the universe,
it is divinely determined. The best that can be done is
to draw purely formal relationships between ideas that
are subsumed under the rubric of 'signs' or symbols.
The physical and chemical activity of the sun does not
cause light; light is merely the sign for the relationship
between our idea of the sun and our idea of, say,
color.
   Berkeley, then, unequivocally raises idealism to primacy
and completely negates the materialist view of nature and
society. This facilitates the restoration of religion, but in
a different form from that of the feudal church. Under
feudalism, God was an objective entity existing apart from
man and human ideas and directing worldly affairs. Now,
God is subjective, depending solely on one's ideas, thus
becoming a more personal, less dogmatic, God than that of
the previous period.[4]
   Even Berkeley, however, did not launch a frontal attack
on science itself. His position on the relationship of science
and religion is summed up by Cornforth:

Scientific results are true, valid and useful – but we must
not overestimate their significance. They only deal with
the order of our sensations. For sensations come to us
in certain orders and in certain combinations, in which
invariable rules and laws can be discerned. And science
discovers and systematises these rules.

Science is therefore not a materialist theory of the world; it is only a set of rules and predictions of the order of human sensations.

Science is therefore circumscribed within its own limited sphere, and has no bearing at all on the nature of things. Therefore nothing that science can establish can possibly contradict the main tenets of religious faith.

Or to put the issue in another way –

We accept science. We welcome scientific discoveries. We take up 'a scientific attitude.' But we recognise that science is not about what it appears to be about. (Cornforth, 1947, p. 48)

The significance of Locke for this investigation is his skepticism, or equivocation. Having supplied the philosophical proof of the materialism of Bacon and Hobbes (as pointed out by Marx in the quote above on pp. 24–5), Locke then argued:

It is evident the mind knows not things immediately, but only by the intervention of the ideas it has of them. Our knowledge therefore is real only so far as there is a conformity between our ideas and the reality of things. But what shall be here the criterion?

Since the mind, in all its thoughts and reasonings, hath no other immediate object but its own ideas, which it alone does or can contemplate, it is evident that our knowledge is only conversant about them.

Knowledge then seems to me to be nothing but the perception of the connection of an agreement, or disagreement and repugnancy, of any of our ideas. In this alone it consists . . .

So that if any one will examine himself concerning his notion of pure substance in general, he will find he has no other idea of it at all, but only a supposition of he knows not what support of such qualities which are capable of producing simple ideas in us; which qualities are commonly called 'accidents' . . .

From all which it is evident, that the extent of our knowledge comes not only short of the reality of things, but even of the extent of our own ideas. Though our knowledge be limited to our ideas, and cannot exceed them either in extent or perfection . . . yet it would be well with us if our knowledge were but as large as our ideas, and there were not many doubts and inquiries concerning the ideas we have, whereof we are not, nor I believe ever shall be in this world, resolved. (Locke, [1690] 1912, pp. 300, 267, 194, 286)

For Locke, knowledge is based on experience as derived through our senses – a materialist proposition. Yet, because we can never come to a complete understanding of the 'substance' of the material world, we are limited to knowledge of our own ideas rather than the objective world itself – an idealist proposition.

Since Locke held that an objective world existed independent of our ideas, he was basically a materialist. But, given his insistence upon the unknowability of the 'substance' of matter, he left the door open to religious interpretations of the world. Since the immortality of the soul cannot possibly be discovered through scientific investigation, this 'substance' provided a limit to science. Hence, science and religion each had its proper place, and one need not encroach on the other or hold the other in antagonistic opposition.[5]

Locke, followed by Berkeley, wrote at the very end of the English capitalist revolutionary period, the time when the conciliation between capitalists and lords took place. Hume, writing two generations later, developed the skeptical aspect of Locke's materialism into a full-blown philosophy. For Locke, there were areas that could not be known. For Hume, *nothing* could be known.

Starting from an empirical foundation, Hume quickly generated a subjectivist idealist conclusion, in the process eliminating causality, the very heart of science:

A like reasoning will account for the idea of external existence. We may observe, that 'tis universally allow'd by philosophers, and is besides pretty obvious of itself, that nothing is ever really present with the mind but its perceptions or impressions and ideas, and that external objects become known to us only by those perceptions they occasion . . .

Now since nothing is ever present to the mind but perceptions, and since all ideas are deriv'd from something antecedently present to the mind; it follows, that 'tis impossible for us to so much as to conceive or form an idea of any thing specifically different from ideas and impressions . . .

When I examine with the utmost accuracy those objects which are commonly denominated causes and effects, I find, in considering a single instance, that the one object is precedent and contiguous to the other; and in inlarging my view to consider several instances, I find only that like objects are constantly plac'd in like relations of succession and contiguity . . .

Nay, even to these objects we cou'd never attribute any existence, but what was dependent on the senses; and must comprehend them entirely in that succession of perceptions, which constitutes our self or person. Nay farther, even with relation to that succession, we cou'd only admit of those perceptions, which are immediately present to our consciousness, nor cou'd those lively images, with which the memory presents us, be ever receiv'd as true pictures of past perceptions. The memory, senses, and understanding are, therefore, all of them founded on the imagination, or the vivacity of our ideas. (Hume, [1739] 1967, pp. 67, 170, 265)

It seems evident, that men are carried, by a natural instinct or prepossession, to repose faith in their senses; and that, without any reasoning, or even almost before the use of reason, we always suppose an external universe, which depends not on our perception, but would exist, though we and every sensible creature were absent or annihilated . . .

But this universal and primary opinion of all men is soon destroyed by the slightest philosophy, which teaches us that nothing can ever be present to the mind but an image or perception, and that the senses are only the inlets through which these images are conveyed, without being able to produce any immediate intercourse between the mind and the object. The table, which we see, seems to diminish, as we remove farther from it: But the real table, which exists independent of us, suffers no alteration: It was, therefore, nothing but its image, which was present to the mind . . .

By what argument can it be proved, that the perceptions of the mind must be caused by external objects, entirely different from them, though resembling them (if that be possible) and could not arise either from the energy of the mind itself, or from the suggestion of some invisible and unknown spirit, or from some other cause still more unknown to us . . .

This is a topic, therefore, in which the profounder and more philosophical sceptics will always triumph, when they endeavour to introduce an universal doubt into all subjects of human knowledge and enquiry. Do you follow the instincts and propensities of nature, may they say, in assenting to the veracity of sense? But these lead you to believe that the very perception or sensible image is the external object. Do you disclaim this principle, in order to embrace a more rational opinion, that the perceptions are only representations of something external? You here depart from your natural propensities and more obvious sentiments; and yet are not able to satisfy your reason, which can never find any convincing argument from experience to prove that the perceptions are connected with any external objects. (Hume, [1748] 1964, pp. 124–6)

As summarized by Cornforth, Hume's position was that:

a)   The known world consists of atomic sensible events.
b)   We can, for our convenience, study the order and combinations of such events experimentally, and formulate scientific laws giving the rules observed in such order and combination. But we cannot discover any necessary causal connection between events. Nor can we discover any permanent ground for the passing phenomena of sense – no objective external material world, nor any permanent self or soul that knows.

c) My knowledge is moreover limited to the present events in my own experience. My knowledge cannot penetrate to anything outside the limits of that experience, either in the present, the past or the future. (Cornforth, 1947, p. 57)

Hume's form of argumentation led to the following conclusion regarding science and religion:

The sciences, which treat of general facts, are politics, natural philosophy, physic, chymistry, etc. where the qualities, causes and effects of a whole species of objects are enquired into.

Divinity or Theology, as it proves the existence of a Deity, and the immortality of souls, is composed partly of reasonings concerning particular, partly concerning general, facts. It has a foundation in reason, so far as it is supported by experience. But its best and most solid foundation is faith and divine revelation. (Hume, [1748] 1964, p. 135)

So, contrary to the claims directed against him, 'the infidel Hume' (who personally was irreligious) was not destructive of religion. His philosophy was 'destructive of a certain sort of dogmatic theology, which seeks to base religion on metaphysical proofs of the existence of God and the immortality of the soul. But it was perfectly compatible with religious *faith* – religion not based on reasonings or proof or metaphysics of any kind, but simply on faith and inner experience' (Cornforth, 1947, p. 59).

In Marxist theory, Hume (along with Kant) is known as one of the great Agnostics (Engels, [1888] 1941, p. 22; Lenin, [1908] 1970, p. 24). That is, he placed science and religion, materialism and idealism, side by side, each with its proper sphere of activity and influence, and adopted a 'live and let live' position with regard to both (Cornforth, 1947, p. 59):

Hume simply showed that, if science is concerned solely with the order of events in one's own experience, then it cannot possibly conflict with religion. A scientist can be religious or not as he chooses – scientific knowledge simply throws no light at all on the truth or otherwise of religious faith. On the other hand, the religious man has no cause to fear or to quarrel with science. (Cornforth, 1947, p. 60)

In my opinion, Hume's agnosticism has been misunderstood. Hume represents the culmination of a period of intense conflict between science and religion. The fundamental problem raised by materialism (if applied consistently) was its atheistic conclusion. But religion, representing the principle form of idealism at that time, was the dominant fraud of the period. Capitalists, to be sure, desired struggle against (feudal) religion insofar as religion impeded their development; but they did not desire struggle against religion in general. The problem was to advance materialism insofar as this outlook benefited capitalist development, but at the same time to prevent this view from becoming dominant within the society as a whole. Hence materialism had to be adulterated with a liberal dose of idealism. The task was that of reconciling the irreconcilable, science and fraud, a task which, if completed, could only mean the domination of the latter. Essentially, Hume, under the colors of Locke, secularized the straightforward idealism of Berkeley, which was too reactionary for the time period in which it was developed.

Hume's so-called agnosticism and Locke's skepticism have been misunderstood by quite able scholars. Dunham, for example, argues that Locke's position (and by imputation that of Hume) is one of tolerance, and that toleration permits both science and religion equal sway:

I do not know how the English have managed to confine intellectual ferment within the intellectual world, but I fancy that a persistent tolerance has had much to do with it. On the whole, a man is much more content with what is if he is allowed to speak boldly about what ought to be.

This is in itself a social good, which confers yet other benefits: the community can, in its slow discursive way, ponder the notions and perhaps even effectuate some of them. At any rate, toleration was the great social discovery, by the Dutch and English, in the seventeenth century. In 1690, we find John Locke asserting it with an eloquence that the subsequent libertarian years have never surpassed . . . (Dunham, 1964, p. 347)

In a limited sense, this is correct. But toleration itself is a form of class rule:

> The outcome of that conflict between the irrepressible functions of intelligence which insisted on adapting itself to the facts of experience and the traditional fictions necessary to the maintenance of antisocial power has been a compromise so strange and incongruous that it has, in some respects, crippled the human mind more effectively than did the primitive imbecility of ancient uncontesting loyalties.
>
> So violent grew the conflict between opinions that sought the support of argument and experience and opinions founded on the authority of ancient tradition that it became a matter of social necessity to devise some formula of accommodation between irreconcilable opposites. The social urgency which led to the expedient took, in fact, the very concrete form of dissatisfaction arising from the practice of suppressing opinions unfavourable to established power by burning, massacring, or casting into prison those who held them . . . In the course of the last few centuries, those who pretended to found their opinions on valid grounds have become so moved with moral indignation that the authority of opinions founded on no grounds at all became seriously threatened.
>
> The moral indignation of the people who were in danger of being burned alive or imprisoned led them to put forward the bold demand that opinions founded on valid grounds should be 'tolerated.' Daring as it was, that demand was, owing to the dwindling authority of opinions founded on no grounds at all, eventually conceded. Valid and reasonable opinions became nominally tolerated; that is to say, the right to burn alive those

40

who held them was formally waived. It was agreed that reasonable and intelligent opinions should enjoy a degree of consideration nominally equal to that enjoyed by groundless, unreasonable, and lunatic opinions.

Thus did the noble principle of freedom of opinion become established as one of the foundations of the charter of democratic liberty. By an astounding legal fiction, sane and insane opinions, groundless and valid opinions were, it came to be held, equal in the eyes of impartial and judicial judgment.

The famous formula of compromise was, as is well known, by no means strictly observed, for opinions resting on valid grounds have never enjoyed, and can never in a traditional civilisation enjoy, the same status and the same degree of consideration as opinions founded on no grounds at all. But the formula has had the pleasant result of enabling groundless traditional opinions to appeal to the noble principle of democratic liberty when endangered by intelligence . . .

The net effect of that noble principle on human intelligence is to obliterate the criteria between valid and groundless opinions, between sane and insane thought. All opinions being equally entitled to respect and consideration, equally free to be inculcated and propagated, every invidious, prejudiced, and intolerant discrimination between opinions resting on valid grounds and opinions resting on none is to the judicially impartial and dispassionate mind inadmissible. (Briffault, 1935, pp. 133–6)

A proposition is either true or untrue. Toleration connotes that truth shall be permitted the same degree of freedom as untruth (fraud). From an objective point of view, this means that truth will be permitted as long as it does not conflict with the interests of the class controlling the instruments of communication. If that class is a minority ruling class, then fraud will necessarily be dominant. At best, we are left with the proposition, 'It's all a matter of opinion' – a notably untrue and illogical statement (Dunham, 1953, pp. 145–56).

Further, we can observe that this tolerance is allowed only to the extent that it can be confined within the constraints of prevailing authority. In England, for example, famed British tolerance become quite intolerant during the period surrounding the French Revolution, when habeas corpus was suspended, the Combination Acts were imposed, etc. 'Dangerous ideas' were afoot and had to be suppressed.

In this transitional period, then, capitalists reacted to the continued development of a materialist or scientific outlook. Materialism was contained, adulturated, but not destroyed. It is telling in this regard that the favored position on materialism during this stage of development was not that of Berkeley but that of Locke and Hume. Capitalist growth mandated that materialism, albeit in modified and limited form, remain at least on a par with idealism. The nature of capitalism in its competitive stage promoted such a compromise.

Given the nature of competition, with no capitalist or group of capitalists able to secure effective control over pricing, profit-maximizing operations mandated an emphasis on cost-reducing, output-increasing changes in the techniques of production. By promoting changes in technology, the more innovative capitalists could seize the advantage over their competitors, thus increasing profits, allowing greater investment and more control within the industry. The profit motive, then, was a most important factor in the promotion of the sciences that underlay those technological developments (Bernal, 1971, vol. 2; Lilly, 1965).

In addition, capitalists obviously desired knowledge of society and its workings and relationships in order to promote the social environment best suited to profit maximization. What has come to be called social science was initially promoted in order to better understand, and therefore control, social development – again, in the interests of profit maximization.

Hence science and scientific advance continued its development during the Transitional Stage. At the same time, the constraints of establishing and controlling the new capitalist order required that the population be submissive to the interests of capitalists as the new ruling class. This required the development of fraud designed specifically for the lower classes and of a sort amenable to the new social order.

The industrial revolution stage   The Industrial Revolution Stage represents the fruition of the growth of science in the earlier stages, coupled with the economic and political consolidation of capitalism as a form of social organization and with sufficient capital accumulation. This consolidation burst forth in a spate of technological advances that induced a transformation throughout the entire system of production.

> The period is a crucial one for the development of humanity. It was then and only then that the decisive turn was taken in man's mastery of Nature in the double substitution of multiple mechanisms for the human hand and of steam-power for the weaker forces of man and animal and the inconstant and localized forces of wind and water. The two basic transformations of the new sixteenth and seventeenth centuries which made those of the eighteenth possible were the birth of experimental quantitative science and of the capitalist methods of production. (Bernal, 1971, vol. 2, p. 519)

This stage represents a watershed in social organization in which production is transformed from (generally) small, individualistic forms to that of the large-scale, collectivized factory system with its concomitant growth of new industrial towns. It is important to recognize that the transition to factory production was not a mere quantitative change in the technique of manufacture, but represented a fundamental change in the whole of economic activity (Marx, [1869] 1906, pp. 405–556). The introduction of the factory system placed the locus of production in large, collectivized units and displaced the lower forms of production based on small-scale techniques. The old craft system was destroyed as a dominant form of economic activity:

> The modern bourgeois society that has sprouted from the ruins of feudal society has not done away with class antagonisms. It has but established new classes,

new conditions of oppression, new forms of struggle in place of the old ones.

Our epoch, the epoch of the bourgeoisie, possesses however, this distinctive feature; it has simplified the class antagonisms. Society as a whole is more and more splitting up into two great hostile camps, into two great classes directly facing each other: Bourgeoisie and Proletariat. (Marx and Engels, [1848] 1964, pp. 2–3).

With the destruction of the older forms of production and the growth of large-scale producing units, workers were cast from their historical working and living conditions and arrangements and thrust into a collectivized environment. This upheaval in the social relations of capitalism generated the early, organized forms of working-class opposition. It is at this point that we first observe the Luddite-type, semi-craft form of resistance, which, while not solely of a machine-breaking sort, nevertheless promoted a basically reactionary ideology – that of attempting to restore the previous social arrangements (Thompson, 1968). The second form of opposition was that of the nascent progressive element, represented by early proto-Chartism, which contained both a demand for amelioration of conditions and a (minority) revolutionary threat (Thompson, 1968; Hammond and Hammond, 1967).

We also observe the first attempts to formulate an ideology reflective of the changing class relations, that of socialism. Its earliest forms were necessarily utopian in orientation. By this is meant the attempt to implant upon all of society the result of reasoned speculation concerning what was considered a just form of social organization – not the attempt to realize an impossible goal:

Then came the three great Utopians: Saint Simon, to whom the middle class movement, side by side with the proletarian, still had a certain significance; Fourier; and Owen, who in the country where capitalist production was most developed, and under the influence of the antagonisms begotten of this, worked out his proposals for the removal of class distinction systematically and in direct relation to French materialism.

One thing is common to all three. Not one of them appears as a representative of the interests of that proletariat which historical development had in the meantime produced. Like the French philosophers, they do not claim to emancipate a particular class to begin with, but all humanity at once. Like them, they wish to bring in the kingdom of reason and eternal justice, but this kingdom, as they see it, is as far as heaven from earth from that of the French philosophers.

For, to our three social reformers, the bourgeois world, based upon the principles of these philosophers, is quite as irrational and unjust, and, therefore, finds its way to the dust hole quite as readily as feudalism and all the earlier stages of society. If pure reason and justice have not, hitherto, ruled the world, this has been the case only because men have not rightly understood them. What was wanted was the individual man of genius, who has not arisen and who understands the truth. (Engels, [1880] 1968, pp. 33–4)

What Saint-Simon, Fourier and Owen (among others) reacted to was the observed injustices of the period. Applying the mode of reasoning of the French rationalists, they subjected prevailing society to critical evaluation, found it wanting, and proposed remedies based upon this reasoned inquiry. Philosoophically, they were, in the final analysis, idealists – fervently believing that a considered idea would be accepted by reasonable people (in particular by members of the dominant class) and implemented through social reform.[6] They held that the working class would benefit through such a social reordering and, moreover, that all of society would find its situation improved – at least at the moral level.

During this period, we observe an extremely close, if tenuous, connection between science and business organizations:

It was in this period, far more so than later in the nineteenth century, that the manufacturers, the scientists, and the new professional engineers mixed together in their work and social life. They intermarried, entertained

45

lavishly, talked endlessly, experimented and associated in new projects. This was the age of the 'Lunar Society' of Birmingham and the Black Country which used to meet at members' houses on full-moon nights and counted among its members John Wilkinson (1728–1808), the ironmaster who lived and dreamed iron and was buried in an iron coffin; Wedgwood (1744–1817), the potter; Edgeworth, the genial Irishman full of wild and noble-minded projects for social improvement; the serio-comic radical Thomas Day of 'Sanford and Merton'; the poetic but practical Dr Erasmus Darwin (1731–1802) of Lichfield; Joseph Priestley (1733–1804); the melancholy, indefatigable Scotsman James Watt (1736–1819) with his younger compatriot, Murdock (1754–1839), the inventor of coal-gas lighting; and finally, the heart and centre of the whole movement, the wealthy, enterprising, jovial, and hospitable Matthew Boulton (1728–1809), the Birmingham button-maker who became, as the first manufacturer of steam engines, almost literally the prime mover of the Industrial Revolution. As he wrote to the Empress Catherine, 'I sell what the whole world wants – power.'

Closely linked with these by personal ties was the more serious group of the Scottish renaissance of the eighteenth century . . . Adam Smith (1723–90) with his *Wealth of Nations*, the intellectual father of laissez-faire capitalism; Dr Black (1728–99), the originator of the pneumatic revolution; Dr Hutton (1726–97), the founder of modern geological theory.

Others, like Dr Roebuck (1718–94), a medical man turned chemical manufacturer and founder of the Carron Works, the first deliberately planned ironworks, and Dr Small (1734–75), the tutor of Thomas Jefferson, belonged equally to England and Scotland.

Such a combination of science and manufacture was only to be found in the Britain of the late eighteenth century. Its existence marks a period of dynamic equilibrium of technics and science, a transition between a period in which science had more to learn from industry than to give to it and one where industry came to be based almost entirely on science. (Bernal, 1971, vol. 2, pp. 529–30)

This is not to say that the relationship between science in its more general, abstract sense was directly related to improvements at the plant level. Scientific advance allowed the accumulation of knowledge which could be applied to the machine process. At the same time, science could learn from the practical experience and problem-solving techniques of machinists, etc.

In any case, science was now viewed as increasingly utilitarian in that it could provide capitalists with technical results that meant higher profits. At the same time, science had to be controlled, institutionalized, lest it step beyond the bounds of socially ordered convention; its utilitarianism had to be confined to advancing the interests of the dominant class rather than society as a whole.

In this regard, the case of Joseph Priestley is instructive. He was trained as a Congregationalist minister but had a scientific bent, which eventually led him to the discovery of oxygen. For his work, Priestley had the support of various manufacturers and was maintained by one Lord Shelburne.

Priestley's rational outlook in science carried over to religion, and he developed a position on Christian thought that attacked the Trinity, predestination and the existence of the soul. Not disavowing religion, however, he argued that the function of the true Christian was toward the 'greater benevolence to man' – that the fruits of scientific achievement must not be limited to advancing the interests and well-being of a few, but should be applied to all.

Priestley had the misfortune to step outside the bounds of respectable dissent during the early stage of the French Revolution, a period when almost *any* non-conventional argument, particularly those dealing with religion, was viewed with suspicion. In 1791, the authorities incited a mob that burned down his house, destroying both his laboratory and library. Out of favor with his benefactors and the government and shunned by his colleagues, he migrated to the United States (Bernal, 1971, vol. 2, pp. 531–3).

Another aspect of the relationship between science and established authority during the period was the unresponsiveness of the great universities to scientific advance.

Progress took place in the dissenting academies and the Scottish universities, where religious control was either less strictured or non-existent. This continued a tradition established during the Heroic Age, when scientists were forced to promote their ideas outside the constraints of institutionalized centers of education. Thus, the Royal Society was founded in 1662 as a mechanism existing outside and in opposition to conventional academe. The one major exception to this general argument was the establishment of the so-called 'invisible college' at Oxford between 1646 and the Restoration of 1660, which developed in connection with, or as an adjunct to, the center of such progressive thought at Gresham College, London. Here, Boyle, Petty, Wren and Hooke led the attack on the philosphy of Aristotle (idealism), which was a foundation of feudal ideology (Bernal, 1971, vol. 2, p. 453). It is noted that both Oxford and Aristotle survived.[7]

The Industrial Revolution Stage occurred at the end of the competitive epoch of capitalism development. From the standpoint of the development of capitalist society, it represents the closest link in the connection between the dominant class and scientific advance. In the next two stages, science, as a system of rational inquiry and human advance, draws away from capitalism, a sharp break occurring during the last, imperialist, stage.

The 'heyday' stage   From 1830 to 1870, science under capitalism developed its greatest general theoretical advance. According to Engels, three major developments separated this period from those of previous scientific achievements:

> But, above all, there are three great discoveries which have enabled our knowledge of the interconnection of natural processes to advance by leaps and bounds: First, the discovery of the cell as the unit from whose multiplication and differentiation the whole plant and animal body develops – so that not only is the development and growth of all higher organism recognized to proceed according to a single general law, but also, in the capacity of the cell to change, the way is pointed out by

48

which organisms can change their species and thus go through a more than individual development. Second, the transformation of energy, which has demonstrated that all the so-called forces operative in the first instance in inorganic nature . . . are different forms of manifestation of universal motion, which pass into one another in definite proportions so that, in place of a certain quantity of the one which disappears, a certain quantity of another makes its appearance and thus the whole motion of nature is reduced to this incessant process of transformation from one form into another. Finally, the proof which Darwin first developed in connected form that the stock of organic products of nature surrounding us today, including mankind, is the result of a long process of evolution . . .

Thanks to these three great discoveries and the other immense advances in natural science, we have now arrived at the point where we can demonstrate as a whole the interconnection between the processes in nature not only in particular spheres but also in the interconnection of these particular spheres themselves, and so can present in an approximately systematic form a comprehensive view of the interconnection in nature by means of the facts provided by empirical natural science itself. (Engels, [1888] 1941, pp. 46–7)

These advances comprise the basis of a fundamental break with an advancement upon the science of the previous centuries:

The materialism of the last century was predominantly mechanical, because at that time, of all natural sciences, mechanics and indeed only the mechanics of solid bodies – celestial and terrestrial – in short, the mechanics of gravity, had come to any definite close. Chemistry at that time existed only in its infantile, phlogistic form.

Biology still lay in swaddling clothes . . . As the animal was to Descartes, so was man a machine to the materialists of the eighteenth century. This exclusive application of the standards of mechanics to processes of a chemical and

49

organic nature . . . constitutes a specific but at that time inevitable limitation of classical French materialism.

The second specific limitation of this materialism lay in its inability to comprehend the universe as a process – as matter developing in an historical process.

This was in accordance with the level of the natural science of that time, and with the metaphysical, i.e. anti-dialectical manner of philosophizing connected with it. Nature, it was known, was in constant motion. But according to the ideas of that time, this motion turned eternally in a circle and therefore never moved from the spot; it produced the same results over and over again. This conception was at that time inevitable . . .

This same unhistorical conception prevailed also in the domain of history. Here the struggle against the remnants of the Middle Ages blurred the view. The Middle Ages were regarded as a mere interruption of history by a thousand years of universal barbarism. The great progress made in the Middle Ages – extension of the area of European culture, the bringing into existence there of great nations, capable of survival, and, finally, the enormous technical progress of the fourteenth and fifteenth centuries – all this was not seen. Consequently a rational insight into the great historical inter-connections was made impossible, and history served at best as a collection of examples and illustrations for the use of philosophers. (Engels, [1888] 1941, pp. 26–8)

Science was abandoning its mechanical or static materialist framework and entering that of dialectics – the view of nature or society as being in a constant state of change.

The great basic thought that the world is not to be comprehended as a complex of ready-made things, but as a complex of processes, in which the things apparently stable no less than their mind-images in our heads, the concepts, go through an uninterrupted change of coming into being and passing away, in which, in spite of all seeming accidents and of all temporary retrogression,

a progessive development asserts itself in the end . . .
(Engels, [1888] 1941, p. 44)

The 'Heyday' Stage represents the period of transition from competitive capitalism to monopoly capitalism, or imperialism.[8] The technological advances induced by the application of science to machine production were raising the level of technology in various industries to a level inconsistent with the maintenance of competition. The cost of operation was now sufficiently high to restrict entry, and the level of output technology allowed meant that markets could be satisfied with fewer, much larger, producing facilities.

Moreover, it was during this period that manufacturing and financial capitalists finally secured political power, beginning in England with the Reform Act of 1832 and, in the United States, with the Civil War that saw Northern capitalists defeat and wrest political power from Southern slave-owners. At this time also, the working class began its mature period of development, as testified to by the Chartist movement.

The nature of competition itself induced these changes, changes that resulted in the undermining of competition. Given the structure of competitive capitalism, businessmen were under a social constraint to introduce new inventions quite rapidly into their productive processes. As individual businessmen cannot effectively dictate market price under competitive conditions, they are forced to accept that price as a constraint. To increase profits, then, requires reduction in costs. These cost-reducing, output-increasing innovations allowed greater profits for those capitalists who were among the first to introduce them. But the very act of innovation tended to reduce the level of competition. As long as market prices could not be dictated or controlled by those determining the level of production, the growth in output allowed by technological change generally caused market prices to fall. For those tardy in innovating, price eventually fell to a level lower than their unit cost of production. Obviously, this meant elimination from the market. However, the higher level of technique incorporated into the production process also meant a higher total fixed cost of production, which connotes higher entry costs; so the potential increase in the number of business firms was restricted. In addition, since technology usually incorporates advances in production itself, the introduction of higher levels of technology meant that fewer producers were required to satisfy the requirements of any given market. The result of the historical power has been the transformation of industry from a large number of small producers to that of a few, large producers (Veblen, 1904, chs 2, 3; 1967, pt 1).[9]

With the beginning of this transition, capitalism began to demonstrate its regressive nature. During the competitive epoch, capitalism provided a progressive social system insofar as it advanced technology, generated ever larger levels of output (which, potentially at least, could be used to increase the standard of life of the population), and continually stripped the social order of its pre-capitalist, feudal vestiges. Capitalism represented a dynamic, energetic, liberalizing order. But with the transition to monopoly, capitalism began to display a certain moribundity. Instead of welcoming the change it fostered, capitalism preferred quiescence or conservatism. And this was at the very time when science was beginning to promote a view of never-ending change.

At the same time, the growth in the working-class movement was promoting change, including changes of a revolutionary nature. The Chartists, for example, did not limit themselves to mere parliamentary reform: one wing, not surprisingly led by Irish nationals, advocated fundamental change in the whole social order. The working class played a large role in the (capitalist) revolutionary movements of 1848–9 on the Continent, and it developed some independent movement that promoted social change far greater and more fundamental than that envisioned by businessmen.[10]

What all this means is that capitalists and science began their parting of the ways. The continued growth in the materialist outlook, now taking on the added dimension of a dialectical component, was turning against capitalism as a social system. Rational, scientific inquiry was raising fundamental questions concerning the continued existence of capitalism, a society becoming increasingly less rational. If businessmen desired maintenance of the social order, they obviously had to promote an outlook that would reduce or prevent altogether a scientific understanding of it.

In the Heroic Stage, science dominated fraud. In the Transitional and Industrial Revolution Stages, something of a balance is struck between these two ideological systems; it was imperative that fraud be raised to a dominant position. Engels describes the change in England:

> The industrial revolution had created a class of large manufacturing capitalists, but also a class – and a far more numerous one – of manufacturing workpeople. This class gradually increased in numbers, in proportion as the industrial revolution seized upon one branch of manufacture after another, and in the same proportion it increased in power. This power it proved as early as 1824, by forcing a reluctant Parliament to repeal the act forbidding combinations of workmen. During the Reform agitation, the workingmen constituted the Radical wing of the Reform Party; the Act of 1832 having excluded them from the suffrage, they formulated their demands in the People's Charter, and constituted themselves, in opposition to the great bourgeois Anti-Corn Law party, into an independent party, the Chartists, the first workingmen's party of modern times.
>
> Then came the Continental revolutions of February and March 1848, in which the working people played such a prominent part, and, at least in Paris, put forward demands which were certainly inadmissible from the point of view of capitalist society. And then came the general reaction. First the defeat of the Chartists on the 10th April, 1848, then the crushing of the Paris workingmen's insurrection in June of the same year, then the disasters of 1849 in Italy, Hungary, South Germany, and at last the victory of Louis Bonaparte over Paris, 2nd December, 1851. For a time, at least, the bugbear of working-class pretentions was put down, but at what cost! If the British bourgeois had been convinced before of the necessity of maintaining the common people in a religious mood, how

much more must he feel that necessity after all these experiences? Regardless of the sneers of his Continental compeers, he continued to spend thousands and tens of thousands, year after year, upon the evangelisation of the lower orders . . . (Engels, [1880] 1968, pp. 23–4)

The Imperialist Stage With the advent of monopoly (more technically, oligopoly) as the general characteristic of capitalism, capitalism ceased to be the progressive social system it had been. With industries dominated by a few large businessmen, effective collusion could occur and profits be maximized through the cartelized control (restriction) of output in order to raise the selling price of commodities (Veblen, [1923] 1967).

Consider the effect that the monopolization of output has on science. As output is restricted, so necessarily is the technology that would allow unfettered increases in production. This does not mean that one observes no technological increase, just as it does not mean that production stagnates. However, the rate of increase in both areas tends to slow, falling below that which science, if allowed unhampered development, would allow (Lilley, 1965, pp. 180–91). This is particularly evident during periods of depression, a social phenomenon to which monopoly capital is notoriously prone.

Moreover, the scientific effort is increasingly directed into narrower channels – wherever production linked to technological change is most profitable. This direction is increasingly toward armaments, a development made necessary by the tendency toward war displayed by imperialism (Bernal, 1971, vol. 3, p. 707).

What one observes, then, is both a restriction and a narrowing of scientific energies, with increasing emphasis on technique rather than on general, theoretical inquiry. The height of this development occurred in the 1920s and 1930s, when various capitalist countries were forced into fascist-type organizations in order to survive the threat of a potentially revolutionary working class. Here science – if it can be called that – and particularly the social sciences, reached its most vulgar depths (Brady, [1937] 1971).

The fundamental problem of monopoly capital in its relationship with science is this. The promotion of science, which is still necessary under conditions of monopoly, leads to a dialectical, materialist outlook. The working class, which is increasingly concentrated by conditions of large-scale production and of a size and level of organization sufficient to overthrow capitalism (as witnessed by the Paris Commune of 1871), becomes a serious threat to the continued rule of the dominant class. Should this class adopt the outlook of science (become conscious of its existence as a class), and should it be effectively organized, the existence of capitalist society would be placed in jeopardy. Given that the working class is the majority, it could, should the above conditions be met, establish itself as the dominant class fairly easily. Hence it is imperative that capitalists, through their control of the instruments of communication (which are monopolized along with the means of production in general), attempt to persuade the working class to accept the continuation of capitalist society (that is, to keep it unconscious of its economic and political interests), even though the *appearance* of things would seem to indicate the need for fundamental change.

One could not ignore that great advances in science were taking place during the Imperialist Stage. The theory of evolution was increasingly understood and amplified; physics was undergoing a veritable revolution with the work of Rutherford, Einstein and Bohr; and chemistry was continually advancing knowledge of both the organic and inorganic world (Bernal, 1971, vol. 3). Moreover, many of these developments were directly useful in industry. What could be done, however, was to conceal the growth in understanding, by erecting a fraudulent philosophical system that effectively denied the existence of this reality altogether. Hence, the last 100 years have witnessed the appearance or revitalization of various philosophies – positivism, pragmatism, existentialism, etc. – that bear one essential characteristic in common: the denial of an objective, real world that exists independent of one's ideas and can become known through observation and experimentation. In other words, materialism had to be denied.

The problem is neatly summed up in the facts surrounding the German scientist Ernst Haeckel. At an 1863 Congress, the young Haeckel vigorously defended Darwin's theory of evolution and outlined its implications for the scientific study of the origins of man. Obviously, the conclusion he drew was totally atheistic. His fellow scientist, Virchow, considerably more sophisticated in his knowledge of social reality, agreed with Haeckel that scientists must establish facts; but he pointed out a limit to this inquiry. The scientist had no business in philosophizing upon those facts, that is, in developing scientific theories on the basis of those facts. Consciousness or the understanding of the essence of facts in their relation to each other was the domain of Church and State:

> That is, I think, the point where science makes its compromise with the Churches, recognizing that this is a province that each can survey as he will, either putting his own interpretation on it or accepting the traditional ideas; and it must be sacred to others. (Virchow, quoted in Farrington, 1966, p. 16)

Essentially:

> The scientist might gather facts but he must not draw conclusions, at least in the sphere of consciousness. He was to be free to trace the evolution of the physical structure of living things from the moneron to man, but not free to associate therewith any conclusions on the evolution of the psychic activities that depend on the physical structure . . . Darwinism was now opposed on the ground that the Social Democrats had taken to it. Science was to be restricted because the people were becoming interested in its conclusions. Not truth but political expediency was to be the controlling factor in the growth of science. (Farrington, 1966, pp. 16–17)

As for Haeckel, his youthful enthusiasm was met by official disdain, particularly after his publication of *The Riddle of the Universe*, a popular work that addressed the underlying population. When it was found that Haeckel was being read by factory workers, his work and personality were viciously attacked:

> it was discovered in his own country that his works were 'a fleck of shame on the escutcheon of Germany,' 'an attack on the foundations of religion and morality'; and in Glasgow that the impeccable author himself was 'a man of notoriously licentious life' . . . (Farrington, 1966, p. 18)

So the problem was that of encouraging the discovery of useful facts while controlling the interpretation of those facts. To this end, the modern idealists, led now not by church officials but by university professors, natural scientists included, rose *en masse*.

Consider the argument of Ernst Mach, a leading physicist of the last century:

> We see an object having a point S. If we touch S, that is, bring it into connexion with our body, we receive a prick. We can see S, without feeling the prick. But as soon as we feel the prick we find S.
>
> The visible point, therefore, is a permanent fact or nucleus, to which the prick is annexed, according to circumstances, as something accidental. From the frequency of such occurrences we ultimately accustom ourselves to regard all properties of bodies as 'effects' . . . which . . . we call sensations. By this operation, however, our imagined nuclei are deprived of their entire sensory contents, and converted into mere mental symbols. The assertion, then, is correct that the world consists only of our sensations.
>
> . . . Such a view can only suit with a half-hearted realism or a half-hearted philosophical criticism. Bodies do not produce sensations, but complexes of sensations . . . If, to the physicist, bodies appear the real, abiding existences, whilst sensations are regarded merely as their evanescent, transitory show, the physicist forgets, in the assumption of such a view, that all bodies are but thought-symbols for complexes of sensations (complexes of elements).

Here, too, the elements form the real, immediate, and ultimate foundation, which it is the task of physiological research to investigate. By the recognition of this fact, many points of psychology and physics assume more distinct and more economical forms, and many spurious problems are disposed of.

. . . When . . . research in physics and in psychology meets, the ideas held in the one domain prove to be untenable in the other . . . If we regard sensations, in the sense above defined, as the elements of the world, the problems referred to are practically disposed of, and the first and most important adaptation effected . . .

The philosophical point of view of the average man – if that term may be applied to the naive realism (read materialism) of the ordinary individual – has a claim to the highest consideration . . . The fact is, every thinker, every philosopher, the moment he is forced to abandon his narrow intellectual province by practical necessity, immediately returns to the universal point of view held by all men in common.

To discredit this point of view is not then the purpose of the foregoing 'introductory remarks.' The task which we have set ourselves is simply to show why and to what purpose for the greatest portion of life we hold it, and why and for what purpose we are provisorily obligated to abandon it. No point of view has absolute, permanent validity. Each has importance only for some given end.

We must regard it as an additional gain that the physicist is now no longer overawed by the traditional intellectual implements of physics. If ordinary 'matter' must be regarded merely as a highly natural, unconsciously constructed mental symbol for a complex of sensuous elements, much more must this be the case with the artificial hypothetical atoms and molecules of physics and chemistry . . . We are on our guard now, even in the province of physics, against overestimating the value of our symbols. Still less, therefore, should the monstrous idea ever enter our heads of employing atoms to explain psychical processes; seeing that atoms are but the symbols of certain peculiar complexes of sensuous elements which we meet with in the narrow domain of physics . . .

The obscurity of this intellectual situation has, I take it, arisen solely from the transference of a physical pre-possession to the domain of psychology. The physicist says: I find everywhere bodies and the motions of bodies only, no sensations; sensations, therefore, must be something entirely different from the physical objects I deal with. The psychologist accepts the second portion of this declaration. To him, it is true, sensation is given, but there corresponds to it a mysterious physical something which conformably to physical prepossession must be different from sensation. But what is it that is the really mysterious thing? Is it the Physis of the Psyche? Or is it perhaps both? It would almost appear so, as it is now the one and now the other that is intangible. Or does the whole argument rest on a vicious circle?

I believe that the latter is the case . . . It is the transitoriness of sense-perceptions that so easily leads us to regard them as mere appearances in contrast with permanent bodies. I have repeatedly pointed out that unconditioned permanent things do not exist in nature, that permanences of connexion only exist . . . (Mach, 1897, pp. 9, 10, 22, 23, 25, 152, 153, 195, 196)

With Mach, as with the other modern schools of philosophy (to which we shall return), we see a retreat to the idealism of Berkeley. As Lenin has argued, the modern positivists added nothing new to the basic argument put forward by the good bishop almost two centuries past; the only differences were those of terminology and emphasis (Lenin, [1908] 1970). Modern positivism may appear to be based in a materialist foundation given its claim to be an empirical philosophy. As the above quote from Mach should make clear, this is illusory: while 'things' may be accepted as real, they are not independent of our perception of them. (On this, see Cornforth, 1950.) The problem of the modern idealists was the same, merely more difficult than that of Berkeley. Nineteenth-century science was far richer, far more advanced – there was more to conceal, more to distort, more to prevent from reaching the underlying population. Hence, official philosophy had to become more difficult and muddled. Nevertheless, it was still the same problem of 'appeasing' science and idealism:

> And just as appeasement in any sphere always leads to the disruption of one's own camp in the interests of the enemy, so it is with the philosophy of science. It leads to the disruption of scientific thought by many obscurities and muddles, the importation into scientific thought of nonsensical and meaningless terms. It leads to the presentation, not of a picture of the objective world we live in, its laws of motion and our own place in it, but to a picture of what Sir James Jeans later called 'the mysterious universe.' Everything becomes doubtful and obscure; and strange shadowy entities – 'elements' and so forth – take the place of material and controllable facts and processes. (Cornforth, 1947, p. 74)

Two basic results sprang from this attack on science. The first was promotion, within science itself, of disorientation as to the function of scientists and the nature of scientific inquiry. The logical conclusion of this is the so-called 'Crisis in Physics,' which is equally applicable to the other natural sciences and continues into the present period:

> The physical theories of the twentieth century are no freer than those of early centuries from influences derived from idealistic trends from outside science. For all their symbolic and mathematical formulations they still embody much of the flight from reality that derives ultimately from religion, now more and more clearly concerned to provide a smoke screen for the operations of capitalism. The influence of the positivism of Ernst Mach on the theoretical formulation of modern physical theories was a predominating one. Most physicists have so absorbed this positivism in their education that they think of it as an intrinsic part of science, instead of being an ingenious way of explaining away an objective world in terms of subjective ideas.

60

Though positivism appeared in the first place in the field of physical science, its implications were far wider . . . it marked a general retreat or withdrawal of intellectuals from concrete to abstract problems and from a naturalistic to a formal approach. Underlying that movement was a reluctance to face facts; for facts, especially social facts, were becoming increasingly hard for bourgeois intellectuals to face. Positivism did indeed provide an admirable alibi for those who wished to be above the battle on the right side. As the Irishman said, 'I know you were impartial in this fight, but which side were you impartial on?' Only the most stupid reactionaries objected to it . . . (Bernal, 1971, vol. 3, p. 746; vol. 4, p. 1093)

The second result was destruction of the generally optimistic view of the early capitalist period, in which it was held that all problems were solvable once enough information was known and human action taken. Now this optimism was inundated by pessimism, a pessimism induced by official philosophy that argued, no matter how many facts were accumulated, that one still could not be sure of anything, including the very existence of a real world. Thus, no hope could be or should be held about reaching solutions.

So, with the advent of imperialism, the dominant ideology turns once more to idealism, albeit a more 'scientific' form than that of the older, more openly religious, type. From its materialist thrust developed during the Heroic Stage, capitalism, first gradually and then with a vengeance, retreated into the idealist world of its feudal counterparts. And the extent and speed of this retreat were determined by the growth and consolidation of capitalism itself, alongside of and within which emerged the working class – the antipodal force to the capitalists.

With this cursory outline in mind, we now turn to an examination of the origins and evolution of modern, neoclassical economic theory, focusing on its very foundation, the utility theory of value.

Notes: Chapter 2

1   As well, one cannot ignore the influence of the Arabic scholars, who, more than any other single social group, maintained a scientific attitude during the highly unscientific Middle Ages: see Briffault, 1930, pp. 133–53.

2   At the same time, it cannot be ignored that Bacon and Hobbes themselves saw a place for religious thought. Bacon placed religious ideas alongside those acquired by human knowledge, thus dichotomizing rational and irrational thought. Hobbes saw religion as useful for state control of the lower classes. It should be noted that Bacon overtly argued that religion should not interfere with science: in fact, a 'correct' religion would not be in opposition to science: see Farrington, 1949, p. 107.

3   It should be remembered that it took some time for the lords to accommodate themselves to their new position. The English had to go abroad to find a suitable – malleable – monarch following James II's rebellion of 1687–8.

4   At the same time, a theoretical inconsistency, applicable to all idealists mandates that, for Berkeley, God is the primary source of ideas: see Lenin, [1908] 1970, pp. 22–4.

5   As well, it should be noted that Locke abhorred the atheistic impulse of his period. 'The duty of mankind, as God's creatures, to obey their divine creator, was the central axiom of John Locke's thought': see Dunn, 1983, p. 119.

6   Official treatment of Robert Owen is enlightening. In the early stages of his development, Owen was received by Royalty and Parliament as a sage, a veritable Messiah of utopian deliverance. Once he abandoned his purely reformist position and began to develop a revolutionary outlook, his fortunes with the upper classes fell and he was no longer welcome in their company: see Morton, 1978.

7   Interestingly, the group centering around Greshman and Oxford, which laid the foundation for the Royal Society, included in their 'curriculum' economic concerns as well as those of science and philosophy: see Ornstein, 1963, p. 91.

8   Following Lenin, imperialism and monopoly capital are equated in meaning and substance: see Lenin, [1916] 1939.

9   It should be noted that the growth in the size of the market caused by the reduction in price *may* outpace the growth in the size of the optimal plant, thus allowing for an *increase* in the number of plants. Clearly, while this may be a possibility, it has not been the case for most industries in the long run.

10 In fact, this independent working-class movement was largely responsible for the revolutions of this period stopping short of complete elimination of the feudal classes. Businessmen, having unleashed the revolutionary movement, soon saw to their horror the working class pushing that revolution forward to include changes

in the interest of workers. Fearing the workers far more than their feudal enemies, capitalists called a halt to the revolutionary upsurge and attacked the working class rather than continuing their fight against the feudal lords: see Marx, [1852] 1970b.

CHAPTER THREE

The theory of value from the heroic age to the industrial revolution

From the period of capitalist revolution through the early Industrial Revolution Stage, the dominant trend with respect to value theory (general perspective on society) was toward the labor theory of value. From Petty through Smith, this particular general view was refined, modified and consolidated as the principal basis from which society was examined.

There were two primary reasons for this development. First, with a successful capitalist transformation of society, the older theories of value had to be overthrown and one amenable to a burgeoning capitalist society had to be put in their stead. This ideological struggle replicated the underlying contest between the feudal and capitalist elements for economic and political supremacy. Second, to consolidate their position, capitalists required knowledge of the workings of their society and a means by which their economic interests could be advanced.

In regard to the former argument, the dominant theory of value during the feudal period was that of 'just price,' the point of view of the independent, small producer that reflected the costs of production of the principal producing classes of society – craftsmen and peasants (Meek, 1975, pp. 12–14). This position was quite amenable to the interests of the feudal ruling class, because 'just' implied that which would perpetuate the existence and efficient operation of the then-current economic system.

This theory, however, was increasingly supplanted by one reflecting the continued deterioration of petty production under the later forms of feudal society and the rise of large, monopoly merchants who secured feudal mercantile privileges that permitted the extraction of monopoly prices for their commodities. This view also was amenable to the feudal ruling class because of the close relationship – indeed, alliance – between the lords and the large merchants.

> The Price of Wares is the present Value . . . The Market is the best Judge of Value; for by the Concourse of Buyers and Sellers, the Quantity of Wares, and the Occasion for them are Best known. Things are just worth so much, as they can be sold for . . .
>
> The Price of Wares is the present Value, And ariseth by Computing the occasions or use for them, with the Quantity to serve that Occasion . . .
>
> The Value of all Wares arise from their Use; Things of no Use, have no Value, as the English Phrase is, 'They are good for nothing . . . The Value of all Wares, arriveth from their Use; and the Dearness and Cheapness of them, from their Plenty and Scarcity. (Barbon, [1690] 1903, pp. 13–16, 39, 41)

> for no Goods have any Value, but from the uses they are apply'd to, and according to the Demand for them, in proportion to their Quantity.
>
> Every thing receives a value from its use, and the Value is raised, according to its Quality, Quantity and Demand. Tho Goods of different kinds are equal in value now, yet they will change their Value, from any unequal Change in their Quality, Quantity, or Demand. (Law, [1705] 1966, pp. 10, 83)

At this point in history, the utility theory of value represented the class interests of the merchants. This class generally did not engage directly in production but controlled the mechanisms of exchange; their profits appeared to be solely the difference between purchase cost and selling price. This surplus, then, was the result of a 'good bargain.' And, as merchants were interested in pursuing their economic interests, they obviously benefited from a high selling price. Feudal monopoly privileges secured this advantage.

Production was still predominantly in the hands of workers owning their own means of production, whose work therefore yielded no surplus-value to any capital. If they had to surrender a part of the product to their parties without compensation, it was in the form of tribute to the feudal lords. Merchant capital, therefore, could only make its profit, at least at the beginning, out of the foreign buyers of domestic products, or the domestic buyers of foreign products; only toward the end of this period – for Italy, that is, with the decline of Levantine trade – were foreign competition and the difficulty of marketing able to compel the handicraft producers of export commodities to sell the commodity under its value to the exporting merchant. And thus we find here that commodities are sold at their values, on the average, in the domestic retail trade of individual producers with one another, but, for the reasons given, not in international trade as a rule . . . (Engels, [1868–96] 1956, p. 114)

The mercantilists, then, focused their attention on the market, in particular the demand side of the relationship. Since they tended to charge 'what the traffic would bear,' their prices would be those their customers would allow; if they were higher, sales would be reduced and, in the extreme, would fall to zero. It was a short step from there to viewing price as the result of supply and demand conditions with the consumer the ultimate arbiter, based upon his view of the satisfaction the commodity afforded relative to its exchange value – a utility calculation.

But this was appearance only. The mercantilists were not fools: they fully understood that their profits were the result of advantages of time and place secured by monopoly trading privileges. As such, they were in violation of stated Christian (as well as other religious) principles that promoted a view of the 'correct' price as being based solely on production costs. Thus, their monopoly profits had to be ideologically concealed through the ruse that the merchants were merely satisfying the subjective desires of their customers, that segment of the community which determined the selling price of their wares. The merchants, then, had clean hands, and their profits were ostensibly the result of the vagaries of the market over which they seemingly had no control.

Such a fraudulent argument may serve the interests of a class that had no direct role in production and secured its economic advantage solely through political affiliation with the dominant class, but it did not facilitate the attempts of the new, capitalist ruling class in forming its society. To consolidate their position and therefore advance their interests, businessmen had to overthrow this view or at least reduce its significance, replacing it with one that would assist in accomplishing their social ends – accumulation.

The primitive labor theory of value

From the beginning, the most important element in this pursuit was organizing the labor supply. The erosion of feudal society created new conditions of existence for most of the population. The elimination of the older strictures on production freed a large mass that had to be effectively organized and controlled if it was to be employed profitably. This freed labor power was seen as the foundation of national welfare (the capitalists' welfare).

Indicative of this view was the change in the prevailing sentiment concerning the appropriate level of population. In England prior to 1640, it was argued that the country was overpopulated, as was proved by abundant poverty, vagabondage, etc. Following the revolution, the opposite view prevailed. Now England was *under*populated, its welfare dependent upon a growth in the laboring class through either natural reproduction or immigration (Appleby, 1978, pp. 129–57). This about-face was the result of a progressive social system replacing a decadent, moribund society: capitalists could use the population and its skills to a far greater extent than could the regressive feudal system.

We do not propose a recitation of the famous and not-so-famous economists/philosophers who participated in the development of the labor theory of value from Hobbes and Locke through Smith. However, some representative quotes are in order to allow a fuller understanding of the primary issue of the period.

Suppose a man could with his own hands plant a certain scope of Land with Corn, that is, could Digg, or Plough, Harrow, Weed, Reap, Carry home, Thresh, and Winnow so much as the Husbandry of this Land requires; and had withal Seed wherewith to sowe the same. I say, that when this man hath subducted his seed out of the proceed of his Harvest, and also, what himself hath both eaten and given to others in exchange for Clothers, and other Natural necessaries; that the remainder of Corn is the natural and true Rent of the Land for that year . . . (Petty, [1662] 1962, pp. 43–4)

For many Ages, those Parts of the World which are engaged in commerce, have fixed upon Gold and Silver as the chief and most proper Materials for this Medium . . . But as Silver itself is of no certain permanent Value, being worth more or less according to its Scarcity or Plenty, therefore it seems requisite to fix upon Something else, more proper to be made a Measure of Values, and this I take to be Labour.

By Labour may the Value of Silver be measured as well as other Things . . .

Thus the Riches of a Country are to be valued by the Quantity of Labour its Inhabitants are able to purchase . . . (Franklin, [1729] 1959, p. 149)

The true and real Value of the Necessaries of Life, is in Proportion to that Part which they contribute to the Maintenance of Mankind; and the Value of them when they are exchanged the one for the other, is regulated by the Quantity of Labour necessarily required, and commonly taken in producing them; and the Value or Price of them when they are bought and sold, and compared to a common Medium, will be govern'd by the Quantity of Labour employ'd, and the greater or less Plenty of the Medium or common Measure . . .

and he that gives him some other in exchange cannot make a better Estimate of what is a proper Equivalent, than by computing what cost him just as much Labour and Time; which in Effect is no more than exchanging one Man's Labour in one Thing for a Time certain, for another Man's Labour in another Thing for the like Time. (anonymous; cited in Meek, 1975, pp. 42–3)

These ideologists were not fully cognizant of the scientific requirements for a correct theory of value, nor did they arrive at a full, consistent theory during the early stages of this development. We can call their labor theory of value 'naive' or 'primitive,' for four reasons.

1 Various inconsistencies abounded in these early attempts to formulate a scientific theory of value. To illustrate, one need only refer to Petty's theory of value.

For Petty (as with Cantillon and others), both labor and land were productive of value, though labor was given the primary role. If Petty had been correct in his formulation, he necessarily would have had to include all the gifts of nature – sun, water, air, etc. – because all these are required in production of agricultural output. But he did not. The reason for his specifying land only is readily understood. At that time, agriculture was the principal productive activity of England. Land was a commodity and commanded a return for its use. Hence, it appeared that this natural resource contributed, in turn, to the value which, when distributed, was returned primarily to workers and owners of land. As the sun was not owned, no such return was forthcoming for its use, and thus it could not be said to contribute to value.

Petty's position was indicative of the investigator insufficiently removed from his subject; he allowed the property arrangements of the society around him to influence his evaluation of that society. However, given the level of capitalist production relations during Petty's time, this can be seen as a 'natural' error.

2 The labor theory of value during this time focused on aggregate production more than on providing an explanation of exchange values.

During its formative stage, the theory principally reflected the requirements surrounding the organization of the producing class – the primary consideration of the capitalist class. The subsidiary question, that of explaining the rate of exchange among commodities produced by labor, became more significant only after the initial problem had more or less been resolved.

However, the 'intuitive' primacy given to production was not incorrect. Before exchange can take place, production of goods for exchange must occur. Hence the emphasis on production by the early theorists was not inappropriate, but merely incomplete.

3   When attempts were made to formulate exchange values based on this primitive labor theory of value, the prevailing tendency was to equate value not with the hours of physical and/or mental labor expended in production, but with the costs of that labor (Meek, 1975, pp. 22–3). Hence, we observe a great deal of economic theorizing based on a labor-cost theory of value – which, of course, proves internally inconsistent.

However, it must be noted that a labor-cost perspective can be seen as connected with the rudimentary development of capitalist production. Given that costs of production are more obvious than hours of labor expended in the determination of prices, it should be no surprise that such an emphasis would be found at this level of intellectual development.

4   Another aspect of the primitive labor theory of value was to develop argumentation focusing, as did Locke, on specific labor producing specific use values: a carpenter's labor produces a house.

From this point of view of *general* theory, such a position is insufficiently abstract. It is necessary to investigate society and social exchange not from the concrete, specific forms that labor may take, but from the aggregate, social, general perspective. Hence one cannot directly compare the labor of the carpenter with that of the dentist, though both drill: the forms of labor (the skills incorporated in the labor expended) are altogether different. However, both carpentry and dentistry involve the expenditure of human effort, and this more abstract level of analysis allows for general comparison.[1]

All these deficiencies can be explained with reference to both the nature of scientific inquiry and the development of that which the early theorists were attempting to analyze. Obviously, scientific truth does not come all at once: it is

70

the result of a long process of investigation, speculation, discovery, testing, modification, refutation and rectification of ideas based upon the extent to which they conform to the objective reality of the phenomenon being investigated.

Also, it is impossible to fully comprehend a phenomenon that is in its early stages of development. A social system, for example, that is just beginning to unfold does not openly display all of its characteristics, and much of that which is observable is still in its rudimentary form of development. For example, in the England of Petty, the social relationships between capitalists and workers were not well developed. Small-scale, petty production, the primitiveness of the selling of labor power, the continued existence of feudal carryovers – all concealed or confused the fundamental characteristics of the new social order.

Thus, what we observe in the seventeenth and eighteenth centuries is a gradual though uneven growth in this particular perspective – growth containing many elements of error and inconsistency, but growth nevertheless. It is to be noted that this labor theory was held even by basically idealist philosophers such as Hume (Marx, [1905–10] 1969, pt 1, p. 374), which indicates the growing strength of this outlook among those actively involved in developing ideological formations during the period. The labor theory of value was gradually becoming the dominant theory, reflecting the dominance of the new social order with its progressive social program.[2]

Adam Smith and the mature period

With the publication of *The Wealth of Nations* in 1776, the labor theory of value reached its mature stage of development. Capitalism had now reached its Industrial Revolution Stage of development and displayed its essential characteristics quite openly. It remained for Smith, an intellectual with sufficient knowledge and prescience, to put forward the first *general* theory of the capitalist economic process. Using *The Wealth of Nations* as a case study, one can more fully understand the point of view of the labor theorists.

The labor theory of value, as with all general theories, contains within it a social program. Examining society from the vantage point of production, Smith set forward basic requirements for the most rapid accumulation of capital given the (competitive) capitalism of the period. At this time, the older feudal monopoly privileges remained and, to the extent that they siphoned economic surplus away from the capitalist class, were to be attacked and eliminated. Hence *The Wealth of Nations* argued from an anti-mercantilist, free trade position. Given that the British government still contained feudal elements which were allied with the monopoly traders, Smith limited government's role to the nominal duties of maintaining a system of defense, administering justice and developing various public works and institutions favorable to the long-run interests of the dominant class (Smith, [1776] 1937, p. 651).

The whole of *The Wealth of Nations* was directed toward recognition of the basic social requirements of capital accumulation for that period of capitalist development (Smith, [1776] 1937, Bk II). Given the social division of labor, the class relations of society and the identification of productive labor, the social program set forth by Smith was that of advancing the material interests of capitalists, who carried within their economic activity the potential for progress and, thus, for improvement of the welfare of the population (Rogin, 1956, pp. 57–65).

To facilitate understanding of the economic relations of society, and therefore to contribute to the establishment of a social program through which society could be advanced, Smith necessarily had to maintain an objective standard of analysis. Personal, subjective criteria, dependent solely on individual prejudice, had to be eliminated from consideration, and society had to be approached from a point of view that examined relationships as they actually existed. To carry out such an objective investigation, it was necessary first to examine the relations of production. Given that production in any society is primary, that exchange and consumption depend upon society's ability to function reasonably well in the realm of production, Smith, as with all labor theorists, had to develop a standard of measurement that would reduce production to some objective unit of account. A labor valuation allowed this.

Statistical matters aside, reducing production (or the results of production) to the amount of labor contained in or expended upon output provides a measurement that is capable of objective quantification. Armed with the same information and applying the same techniques of measurement, different investigators would arrive at the same estimate of production regardless of any subjective bents they might have. Thus, the social output could be reduced to a single common factor and changes in the division of the output could be accurately measured (Dobb, 1972, pp. 1–33). Given the attempt by Smith to discuss the actual workings of capitalism in order to propose policy that would assist in the accumulation process, such an objective standard was absolutely necessary. Wishful thinking would be no substitute for analysis if Smith's intent and the interests of capitalist progress were to be served.

With such a standard of valuation, then, Smith was driven to an examination of the social relations in production – the relations among people and classes in the production process itself. It is clear that Smith had a class analysis of society: capitalists, landlords and workers formed the basic social units of society in that period.

The labor theory of value coupled to a class analysis of society identified surplus as originating in the working class and being expropriated by the owners of the means of production through a (non-defined) exploitative mechanism:

> The profits of stock, it may perhaps be thought, are only a different name for the wages of a particular sort of labour, the labour of inspection and direction. They are, however, altogether different, are regulated by quite sufficient principles, and bear no proportion to the quantity, the hardship, or the ingenuity of this supposed labour of inspection and direction. They are regulated altogether by the value of the stock employed, and are greater or smaller in proportion to the extent of this stock . . .
>
> In the price of commodities, therefore, the profits of stock constitute a component part altogether different from the wages of labour, and regulated by quite different

principles. In this state of things, the whole produce of labour does not always belong to the labourer. He must in most cases share it with the owner of the stock which employs him. (Smith, [1776] 1937, pp. 48–9)

Since the class relations in production were based on the expropriation of social labor by capitalists and landlords, a conflict arose within society based on these relations and realized itself in the distribution of the product of social labor.

What are the common wages of labour, depends everywhere upon the contract usually made between those two parties, whose interests are by no means the same. The workmen desire to get as much, the masters to give as little as possible. The former are disposed to combine in order to raise, the latter in order to lower the wages of labour.

It is not, however, difficult to foresee which of the two parties must, upon all ordinary occasions, have the advantage in the dispute, and force the other into a compliance with their terms. The masters, being fewer in number, can combine much more easily; and the law, besides, authorises, or at least does not prohibit, their combinations, while it prohibits those of the workmen. We have no acts of parliament against combining to lower the price of work; but many against combining to raise it. In all such disputes the masters can hold out much longer . . .

We rarely hear, it has been said, of the combinations of masters, though frequently of those of workmen. But whoever imagines, upon this account, that masters rarely combine, is as ignorant of the world as of the subject. Masters are always and everywhere in a sort of tacit, but constant and uniform combination, not to raise the wages of labour above their actual rate . . . Masters too sometimes enter into particular combinations to sink the wages of labour even below this rate . . . Such combinations, however, are frequently resisted by a contrary defensive combination of the workmen; who sometimes too, without any provocation of this kind, combine of their own accord to raise the price of their labour. Their usual pretences are sometimes the high price of provisions, sometimes the great profit which their masters make by their work. But whether their combinations be offensive or defensive, they are always abundantly heard of. In order to bring the point to a speedy decision, they have always recourse to the loudest clamour, and sometimes to the most shocking violence and outrage. They are desperate, and act with the folly and extravagance of desperate men, who must either starve, or frighten their masters into an immediate compliance with their demands. The masters upon these occasions are just as clamorous upon the other side, and never cease to call aloud for the assistance of the civil magistrate, and the rigorous execution of those laws which have been enacted with so much severity against the combinations of servants, labourers, and journeymen. (Smith, [1776] 1937, pp. 66–7)

People of the same trade seldom meet together, even for merriment and diversion, but the conversation ends in a conspiracy against the public, or in some contrivance to raise prices. (Smith, [1776] 1937, p. 128)

The interest of the dealers, however, in any particular branch of trade or manufactures, is always in some respects different from, and even opposite to, that of the public. To widen the market and to narrow the competition, is always the interest of the dealers. To widen the market may frequently be agreeable enough to the interest of the public; but to narrow the competition must always be against it . . . The proposal of any new law or regulation of commerce which comes from this order ought always to be listened to with great precaution, and ought never to be adopted till after having been long and carefully examined, not only with the most scrupulous, but with the most suspicious attention. It comes from an order of men whose interest is never exactly the same with that of the public, who have generally an interest to deceive and even to oppress the public, and who accordingly have, upon many occasions, both deceived and oppressed it. (Smith, [1776] 1937, p. 250)

This view of the social order gave rise to a concept of the state not far different from that developed later and more thoroughly by Marx (Lenin, [1917] 1977).

Wherever there is great property, there is a great inequality. For one very rich man, there must be at least five hundred poor, and the affluence of the few supposes the indigence of the many. The affluence of the rich excites the indignation of the poor, who are often both driven by want, and prompted by envy, to invade his possessions. It is only under the shelter of the civil magistrate that the owner of the valuable property, which is acquired by the labour of many years, or perhaps of many successive generations, can sleep a single night in security. He is at all times surrounded by unknown enemies, whom, though he never provoked, he can never appease, and from whose injustice he can be protected only by the powerful arm of the civil magistrate continually held up to chastise it. The acquisition of valuable and extensive property, therefore, necessarily requires the establishment of civil government. Where there is no property, or at least none that exceeds the value of two or three days labour, civil government is not so necessary. (Smith, [1776] 1937, p. 670)

Civil government, so far as it is instituted for the security of property, is in reality instituted for the defence of the rich against the poor, or of those who have some property against those who have none at all. (Smith, [1776] 1937, p. 674)

There is, however, a fundamental difference between Smith and Marx on the question of the state. For Smith – indeed, for economic science in general up to that point – this class cleavage did not result in irreconcilable conflict between the classes with an end result of social revolution. In Smith's theory, the class conflict was reconcilable through the forces of the competitive market, the 'invisible hand' that was set forth (in good eighteenth-century tradition) as natural law. Even though classes existed and the state was developed to

76

ensure the interests of the upper class (particularly in the dispensation of justice), competition would ensure that the public good would be enhanced through the operations of individuals attempting to maximize their individual interests (Smith, [1776] 1936, p. 14):

> But the annual revenue of every society is always precisely equal to the exchangeable value of the whole annual produce of its industry, or rather is precisely the same thing with that exchangeable value. As every individual, therefore, endeavours as much as he can both to employ his capital in the support of domestic industry, and so to direct that industry that its produce may be of the greatest value, every individual necessarily labours to render the annual revenue of the society as great as he can. He generally, indeed, neither intends to promote the public interest, nor knows how much he is promoting it. By preferring the support of domestic to that of foreign industry, he intends only his own gain, and he is in this, as in many other cases, led by an invisible hand to promote an end which was no part of his intention . . . (Smith, [1776] 1937, p. 423)

Various commentators have seen this proposition as contradictory. If class conflict is primary and arises out of the very foundation of capitalist society, how is it possible to mollify that conflict within that same society (Hunt, 1979, p. 55)? There is obviously a point to this line of argument. However, I think that, in Smith's analysis of capitalism of that period, an argument can be made for consistency.

During the period, capitalism was extremely progressive. Given that it was the beginning of the Industrial Revolution Stage, the economic breach between the capitalist owners of the means of production and the propertyless working class had not yet fully developed. The prevailing mode of production was still that of the small workshop. Hence, as capitalists were progressive and accumulation resulted in greater social output, Smith felt that all classes would benefit economically from the larger national income, even though different classes had different objective interests.

In retrospect, obviously, one can observe that Smith was mistaken, but at that time this individualistic perception of social welfare appeared correct, given the dynamic, small-scale capitalist society confronting Smith.

Hence Smith's social program of *laissez-faire* was itself an attempt to influence social progress by eliminating monopoly restraints on the program and allowing the capitalist accumulation process full reign. Also, the assumptions of competition required that there be relatively small differences in individual wealth between members of different classes (or entry into markets would be restricted); and the competitive process would maintain this relatively equal distribution of income as long as government remained neutral.

This last point we want to make in reference to Smith's general theory is that of its determinism:

> It is not surprising that classical Political Economy should have stirred its age, and exerted an influence which was revolutionary both to traditional notions and to traditional practice. In the history of thought in the social sciences its arrival was epoch-making because it created the concept of economic society as a deterministic system: a system in the sense that it was ruled by laws of its own, on the basis of which calculation and forecast of events could be made. For the first time a determinism of law in the affairs of men was demonstrated to exist, comparable to the determination of law in nature. In thus stressing the essential unity of economic events, Political Economy at the same time stressed the interdependence between the various elements of which the system was composed. To introduce a change at any one point was to set in motion a chain of related changes over the rest of the system; and these movements could be defined as having a certain order of magnitude in relation to the size of the initial impulse. The form and magnitude of such related movements were given by the series of functional relations stated by the equations of which . . . the classical theory of value in effect consisted; so that its theory of value was an essential, and not merely an incidental, feature of classical Political Economy. (Dobb, 1972, p. 34)

This determinism was one aspect of the mechanical materialism being advanced throughout this period. In the feudal period, phenomena leading to change were the result of divine interference. Since this could not be fathomed by human knowledge, it appeared to be the result of fate – of accident. For the labor theorists, however, the world was a knowable entity: Human intelligence could discover the relationships and movement of society much as the natural scientists could develop discernible knowledge about the universe. In fact, there was a marked tendency during the period for social scientists to equate the social order with that of nature, resulting in a 'natural law' view of society (Routh, 1977, passim).

We shall return to this point later; now we merely note that this view represents yet another aspect of the progressive and scientific attitude of Smith and earlier classical economists. Their position was that a society existed that was not the product of divinity or of one's ideas but an objective world that contained its own laws. These laws could be understood by man, and with that understanding, imbecilic regulations would be abolished and progress for all humanity would be assured. This, then, generated a very optimistic view of the future of society.

True, natural law could not be dictated; but it could be understood. And, given the record of capitalism to that point, allowing natural law to operate fully *seemed* to guarantee a beneficent future.

The utility theory of value in the eighteenth century

Throughout the period in question, the dominant theory of value was based on the objective factor of labor. This does not mean that subjectivist theories, in particular that of utility, were altogether absent or even in decline. Actually, as Schumpeter argues, the latter perspective 'had the wind until the influence of *The Wealth of Nations* – and especially Ricardo's *Principles* – asserted itself. Even after 1776, that theory prevailed on the continent . . .' (Schumpeter, 1954, p. 302). If a catalogue of all economic writers of the period were drawn up, it may well turn out that a majority (perhaps an overwhelming portion) maintained a utility theory of value. How then can it be said that the labor theory of value was dominant?

The problem arises in examining things from a static rather than a dialectical point of view. One should not be surprised that the appeal of the older, mercantilist theory of value persisted during the period. First, most European countries remained feudal in their economic and political organization, and, since the mercantilist theory represented one aspect of later feudal development, the point of view of this class still carried great weight. Second, as argued in Chapter 2, the success of the capitalist revolution resulted in an alliance between the revolutionary capitalists and their former feudal enemies. Within this context, the capitalist ideology, based on materialism, was modified, and idealism, the position of the decadent feudal lords, was elevated to a position of rough equality with materialism, at least insofar as the education of the lower classes was concerned.

Science, however, continued its development, and, along with it, the materialist perspective was promoted. England represented the most progressive country at that time (though attention should be paid to Holland), and it was here that the greatest advances in both material production and intellectual achievement were realized. One aspect of this growth was the labor theory of value, part of the attempt to examine society from a scientific, objective point of view.

Thus, if one examines the growth of ideas and sees the significance of new developments for future growth and change, that is, if one examines ideas from the perspective of progress, then the labor theory of value represents the dominant position, not in terms of numerical weight, but in terms of social import. It was no historical accident that it was England that saw the greatest development in this approach, while the Continent – still basking in feudal backwardness – was the proud receptacle of the mercantile waste products. Hence the older, utility, theory remained ensconced in these countries, while in England it was increasingly held in disrepute, though it continued as an undercurrent. On the Continent, the greatest strides against the utility theory of value were taken by those intellectual segments of the population directing their efforts against feudalism, particularly the Physiocrats (Meek, 1963).

With regard to the utility theory of value, we shall refer to only two writers of the period, one of whom (the least important) was 'rediscovered' when the utility theory reached its nineteenth-century zenith. We shall dispense with Daniel Bernoulli rather quickly, focusing on the Italian abbott, Ferdinando Galiani, best known for his work in monetary theory and for his attack on the Physiocrats.

In Bernoulli's 1731 paper (published in 1738), submitted to solve what has become known as the 'St Petersburg Paradox', he developed a direct relationship between the marginal dollar of net assets, the marginal utility of that dollar, and the price that an individual is willing to pay in order to engage in a game of chance with a known probability of its outcome. In arguing the proof of his propositions, the Swiss mathematician also developed the concept of diminishing marginal utility (Schumpeter, 1954, pp. 302–4).

It is important to note that Bernoulli's problem did not deal with the attempt to explain either production or exchange value. Rather, in his model the various constraints were given (prices of lottery tickets, possibility of success, wealth levels of the individual) and the only question was that of the subjective desire of the individual to play at various combinations of the above. Hence, the only thing 'explained' was the individual's willingness to gamble, given various probabilities of success relative to wealth holdings. The whole approach, then, was directly opposite to that of the economists developing the labor theory of value.[3]

Galiani's work is of an entirely different matter. There is no question that in his *Della Moneta* of 1750, Galiani developed a very modern utility theory, in which value could not be understood except in relation to utility and scarcity, where utility referred not to the usefulness of the commodity in the ordinary sense but to that which provides pleasure or procures welfare. Moreover, his concept of relative scarcity can be seen as a primitive marginal utility concept (Schumpeter, 1954, pp. 300–2).[4]

At the same time, however, Galiani, after devising a fairly

modern theory of demand, shifted his focus and turned to labor as the only factor of production and source of value:

> It is only toil (*fatica*) which gives value to things. (cited in Marx, [1859] 1970a, p. 57)

> The real wealth . . . is man. (cited in Marx, [1905–10] 1971b, pt 3, p. 267)

In this later argument, then, he presages the value theory of Smith, Ricardo and Marx, going so far as to specify the foundation of value as what would become known as socially necessary labor.

For Schumpeter, as one would expect, 'this spoils his theory of value' (Schumpeter, 1954, p. 302). But it does illustrate the ambiguity of even predominately utility theorists during the period. Given the growth in capitalist production and the increasing disfavor in which the large merchants found themselves, the social climate demanded that at least some heed had to be taken of the objective theory of value. Even Galiani admitted more of social forces into his utility theory than modern theorists would allow, suggesting that utility itself was shaped by historical and institutional factors (Spiegel, 1971, p. 205).

What Galiani was attempting, then, was the salvaging of the older theory of value in the face of social movement away from the form of society which had generated that theory. In this regard he is somewhat akin to the Humesian attempt to reconcile materialism and idealism.

Conclusion

The labor theory of value was originated and reached its first sophisticated level of development during the Heroic and Transitional Stages of capitalist growth. No argument will be given to those who point out the errors and inconsistencies of the early theorists, including Smith himself. These existed, to be sure. Such a line of argumentation misses the point, however. What we do observe is a continued growth and refinement of the theory as capitalist society increasingly displays its underlying relationships. Hence, what the eighteenth century unveils is a growing attempt to understand society from a scientific perspective. In such a development there will be errors and inconsistencies, but these will be weeded out as long as scientific advance continues.

At the same time, the utility theory of value remained, but in a secondary position. This was the last period in which this was to be the case. With the completion of the Industrial Revolution Stage, and with developments contained within the French Revolution, the utility theory was to achieve, first, equality with, then domination over, the labor theory of value. Subsequent chapters examine the social process through which this development came about.

Notes: Chapter 3

1 One major exception to this general problem was the argument put forward by James Steuart, in which not only is labor put forward in its general, abstract form, but the labor of workers under capitalist relations is distinguished from labor in other forms of social arrangements – such as that of self-employed craftsmen: see Marx, [1859] 1970a, p. 58.

2 The progressive characteristics of capitalism in this stage of development was in its (half-hearted, to be sure) attack on feudal ideologies, which allowed the release of new intelligence, and the *potential* for material advance now that the restrictions on production necessitated by the maintenance of feudalism were shattered. That the reality did not live up to the potential during this period can be traced to proper profit-maximizing behavior coupled to an unorganized working class.

3 Of course, Bernoulli never considered his work as a contribution to the theory of value. Only later, with the enshrinement of the utility theory and the search for predecessors, was it put in this light.

4 Dmitriev goes even further, arguing that Galiani's contribution was so advanced that 'Very little that is new can be found in the writings of the Austrian school when we compare them with Galiani's theory . . .': see Dmitriev, [1898–1902] 1974, p. 189.

CHAPTER FOUR

The interregnum:
from Smith to Ricardo

In the period between *The Wealth of Nations* and Ricardo's *Principles*, there unfolded two developments of significance for economic theory: the French Revolution, and the industrial revolution in England. The first unleashed a burst of activity covering the entire political spectrum from communism through aristocratic reaction. The latter generated the first collectivized working class and its concomitant development of nascent trade unionism and resistance to such collectivization (the manufacturing and agricultural 'machine-breakers').

In both England and France, the two countries in which these developments found the greatest response to historical movement, the reaction to the threat of revolutionary (or, at least, incendiary) thought and action was immediate and ruthless. In England the Combination Acts were instituted, habeas corpus was suspended, and severe penalties were imposed for minor offenses. In France, after the Jacobin attempt to impose a dictatorship of the small businessmen, the Girondists (large capitalists) cleansed France of both the petty producer and working-class threat (the first Paris Commune) and imposed their rule by means of a military dictatorship with the assistance of sections of the nobility. In all this, *any* non-conventional ideological thrust was viewed with disfavor and its champions treated summarily. Witness the reception in England of Paine's *The Age of Reason*.

From the standpoint of social movement, the times were extremely dangerous (or were thought to be) for the continued rule of the capitalists. The revolution in France, though capitalist in orientation, had unleashed ideas that threatened any established form of social organization. In England, a class was forming that could seize upon such ideas and convert them into a social practice that would unseat those holding political and economic power. All this had its effect on political economy. In a most important sense, Adam Smith represents the culmination of a long gestation period. Rather than being the progenitor of the science of political economy, he personifies the end-product of a line of development stemming from the English revolutionary period. As discussed, in the previous century the labor theory of value was making continued progress and was becoming dominant over those ideological systems supportive of reaction. Following Smith, economic theory divided itself into two camps – that which continued the advance of the previous period, and would soon find itself in the minority, and that which represented the apologetic attempt to conceal the underlying relationships of society and thus assist in the continued rule of the business class. Böhm-Bawerk, himself no friend of the objective approach to economic theory, observed:

> The position taken by Adam Smith towards the question of interest may be termed one of complete neutrality. In [his] time the relation of theory and practice still made it possible to observe such neutrality, but his followers soon could no longer do so. Changed circumstances made it necessary for them to show their colors on the interest question . . . (Böhm-Bawerk, [1884] 1959, p. 49)

So, while the labor-theory-of-value approach continued in the post-Smithian era, it was embarking upon its defensive period, its only great theorist being Ricardo. Meanwhile, the utility theory of value and its ancillary components were making enormous strides, eventually to swamp the scientific approach.

This proposition can be demonstrated by reference to four major theorists of the period: Bentham, Say, Malthus and Lauderdale. The first three made contributions which, while not necessarily original, all played a significant role in the eventual unseating of the labor theory. Moreover, each theorist can be understood to have developed his argument in reaction to the political and economic developments surrounding him. Lauderdale is introduced here not as an original thinker or great theorist, but as one who saw fairly clearly the threat to the dominant classes contained in the labor theory of value, and who manufactured an argument conducive to their continued rule.

On utilitarianism

In retrospect, Jeremy Bentham's influence on future developments was clearly greater than that of the other three notables. Not only did he have an immediate impact on many major theorists and propagandizers (in particular, James Mill and Ricardo), but his theoretical system continues, in one form or another, to be propounded in the present period.

Bentham is best known for his systemization of utilitarianism. Obviously, since utilitarianism had a long developmental period, Bentham did not originate this particular point of view (Albee, [1901] 1957; Stephen, [1900] 1950).

The *philosophy* which preaches enjoyment is as old in Europe as the Cyrenaic school. Just as in antiquity it was the *Greeks* who were the protagonists of this philosophy, so in modern times it is the *French*, and indeed for the same reason, because their temperament and their society made them most capable of enjoyment. The philosophy of enjoyment was never anything but the clever language of certain social circles who had the privilege of enjoyment . . .

In modern times the philosophy of enjoyment arose with the decline of feudalism and with the transformation of the feudal landed nobility into the pleasure-loving and extravagant nobles of the court under the absolute monarchy. Among these nobles this philosophy still has largely the form of a direct, naive outlook on life which finds expression in memoirs, poems, novels, etc. It only becomes a real philosophy in the hands of a few writers of the revolutionary bourgeoisie, who, on the one hand, participated in the culture and mode of life of the court nobility and, on the other hand, shared the more general outlook or the bourgeoisie, based on the more general conditions of existence of this class. This philosophy was, therefore, accepted by both classes, although from totally different points of view. Whereas among the nobility this language was restricted exclusively to its estate and to the conditions of life of this estate, it was given a generalised character by the bourgeoisie and addressed to every individual without distinction. The conditions of life of these individuals were thus disregarded and the theory of enjoyment thereby transformed into an insipid and hypocritical moral doctrine. When, in the course of further development, the nobility was overthrown and the bourgeoisie brought into conflict with its opposite, the proletariat, the nobility became devoutly religious, and the bourgeoisie solemnly moral and strict in its theories, or else succumbed to the abovementioned hypocrisy, although the nobility in practice by no means renounced enjoyment, while among the bourgeoisie enjoyment even assumed an official, economic form – that of *luxury*. (Marx and Engles, [1896] 1976, pp. 441-2)

Moreover, Bentham's theoretical system is not the only form of utilitarianism possible, though it is telling that his efforts have been best received in the present period. Our first task is to separate the Benthamite brand of utilitarianism from utilitarianism in general, then specifically to detail the import of his system for the development of neoclassical economic theory.

Initially, if one is sufficiently broad in one's definition, one can argue that all social theories are necessarily utilitarian. All social theories are designed to perform some function – either to assist in the attempt to uncover laws of social organization and development, or to facilitate the concealment of those laws. That is, all social theories are designed to either advance the science of society or to promote fraudulent ideas concerning society. Thus, all such theories are developed with some use in mind and, in that sense, are utilitarian. This, though, is obviously too broad a view of what is commonly meant by 'utilitarian.'

Let us narrow our definition to be more compatible with the conventional view:

> The creed which accepts as the foundation of morals, Utility or the Greatest Happiness Principle, holds that actions are right in proportion as they tend to promote happiness, wrong as they tend to produce the reverse of happiness. By happiness is intended pleasure, and the absence of pain; by unhappiness, pain, and the privation of pleasure. To give a clear view of the moral standard set up by the theory, much more requires to be said; in particular, what things it includes in the ideas of pain and pleasure; and to what extent this is left an open question. But these supplementary explanations do not affect the theory of life on which this theory of morality is grounded – namely, that pleasure, and freedom from pain, are the only things desirable as ends; and that all desirable things (which are as numerous in the utilitarian as in any other scheme) are desirable either for the pleasure inherent in themselves, or as means to the promotion of pleasure and prevention of pain. (Mill, [1861] 1969, p. 210)

There are two general matters with which we must deal briefly in connection with this definition and the thrust of utilitarianism in general. The first is its generally avowed conservative bent. It is quite true that the utilitarian ethic in the hands of Bentham and his followers produces a decidedly conservative outlook. But this is not necessarily the case. One of the greatest utilitarians was Claude Helvetius, a consistent democrat who promoted the utilitarian creed against the interests of the French nobility in the pre-revolutionary period (Horowitz, 1954). In the hands of Helvetius, utilitarianism became one aspect of French critical rationalism that subjected all institutions to severe scrutiny. Since the French ruling class was not advancing the well-being of society, it was not useful, and hence should be eliminated.

At this point in the development of French ideology, the most progressive revolutionary class was that of the capitalists. Since it was the most advanced class and led the attack on the nobility, it could and did represent its interests as those of society as a whole. Thus, what was useful to this class was beneficial to all of society except for the dominant class and its allies. Helvetius's philosophy took the following position. His view of the utilitarian principle expressly argued from the point of view of society as a whole and not (at least not consciously) from that of a particular segment of society or from that of the individual. He did not hold the later utilitarian principle of 'the greatest good for the greatest number' but, rather, developed his argument in the context of the whole of society. His was the philosophy of *Man*, not of some men (Horowitz, 1954, pp. 71–89).

Philosophically, Helvetius was a materialist. His argument that man acquires knowledge of objects through the senses and ethical values, such as virtue, was soundly rooted in the nature of social organization itself (Plekhanov, 1976a, pp. 79–86).

In eighteenth-century France, then, the utilitarian principle was a progressive force precisely because the class it then represented was progressive. For Bentham's period, utilitarianism served as a conservative instrument because capitalists were by that time conservative:

The commercial and industrial classes in England, after being in the forefront of a protracted and victorious revolution, were forced to conclude a union with the older aristocracy. This alliance had as its chief purpose heading off popular resistance movements. From the Digger Movement to the Chartists movement, peasants and workers demanded democratic reforms that the middle classes were unwilling to grant. Due to this pressure the bourgeoisie was inclined even in philosophy to affect compromises with idealism and orthodox theology. The smug complacency of the English Enlightenment made its representatives glorifiers of an achievement rather than prophets of revolution. We have merely to observe the radically different uses the utilitarian self-interest doctrine was put to for definite ideological corroboration of this. In England, utility doctrines were paraded about as a natural ally of theology, while the superior intellects in France were attempting to prove the natural hostility of utilitarianism to theology. The 'cool' self-love of Joseph Butler was a far cry in theory and in practice from the 'passionate' self-love of Helvetius. Superficial formal similarities cannot disguise the intense hostility of their doctrines. Reconciliation was the leit-motif of English thought in the latter half of the eighteenth century. Like Bentham, most English theorists contented themselves with advising the French on how to 'remodel' their government along parliamentary lines. (Horowitz, 1954, p. 32)

The second issue of general import is the relationship between utilitarianism and the utility theory of value. Utilitarianism does *not* inevitably lead to a utility theory of value. Although there is disagreement on this point (Schumpeter, 1954, pp. 408–9), it has been effectively argued that Smith and Ricardo, holders of the labor standard, were both utilitarians, their view of social progress one that afforded greater happiness for society as a whole (Plamenatz, 1958, pp. 110–21).

Utilitarianism is a very broad, imprecise concept that covers a multitude of underlying theoretical positions. In the hands of Bentham, however, it necessarily leads to a modern utility standard of valuation.

Bentham's theoretical position

In his justly famous *Principles of Morals and Legislation*, Bentham sets forth his basic theoretical formulation:

Nature has placed mankind under the governance of two sovereign masters, pain and pleasure. It is for them alone to point out what we ought to do, as well as to determine what we shall do. On the one hand the standard of right and wrong, on the other the chain of causes and effects, are fastened to their throne.They govern us in all we do, in all we say, in all we think . . . The principle of utility recognises this subjection, and assumes it for the foundation of that system, the object of which is to rear the fabric of felicity by the hands of reason and of law. Systems which attempt to question it, deal in sounds instead of sense, in caprice instead of reason, in darkness instead of light . . .

The Principle of utility is the foundation of the present work . . .

By utility is meant that property in any object, whereby it tends to product benefit, advantage, pleasure, good, or happiness . . . or . . . to prevent the happening of mischief, pain, evil, or unhappiness to the party whose interest is considered: if that party be the community in general, then the happiness of the community; if a particular individual, then the happiness of that individual.

The interest of the community is one of the most general expressions that can occur in the phraseology of morals: no wonder that the meaning of it is often lost. When it has a meaning, it is this. The community is a fictitious body, composed of the individual persons who are considered as constituting as it were its members. The interest of the community then is, what? – the sum of the interests of the several members who compose it.

It is in vain to talk of the interest of the community without understanding what is the interest of the individual . . .

Has the rectitude of this principle been ever formally contested? It should seem that it had, by those who have not known what they have been meaning. Is it susceptible of any direct proof? It should seem not: for that which is used to prove everything else, cannot itself be proved: a chain of proofs must have their commencement somewhere. To give such proof is as impossible as it is needless. (Bentham, [1780] 1969, pp. 85–7)

Inexorably, Bentham's basis postulate leads him to a neoclassical standard of valuation:

All value is founded on utility . . . Value in use is the basis of exchange . . . (Bentham, 1954, vol. 3, pp. 83, 87).

Further, although this is not a necessary aspect of the utility theory of value itself, Bentham sets forth the principle of diminishing marginal utility:

1 Caeteris paribus, – to every particle of the matter of wealth corresponds a particle of the matter of happiness. Accordingly, thence,

2 So far as depends upon wealth, – of two persons having unequal fortunes, he who has most wealth must by a legislator be regarded as having most happiness.

3 But the quantity of happiness will not go on increasing in anything near the same proportion as the quantity of wealth: – ten thousand times the quantity of wealth will not bring with it ten thousand times the quantity of happiness. It will even be a matter of doubt, whether ten thousand times the wealth will in general bring with it twice the happiness. Thus it is, that,

4 The effect of wealth in the production of happiness goes on diminishing, as the quantity by which the wealth of one man exceeds that of another goes on increasing: in other words, the quantity of happiness produced by a particle of wealth (each particle being of the same magnitude) will be less and less at every particle; the second will produce less than the first, the third than the second, and so on. (Bentham, 1954, vol. 1, p. 113)

And to complete his argument in a consistent manner:

Money . . . we have already shewn to be the most accurate measure of the quantity of pain or pleasure a man can be made to receive. (Bentham, 1954, vol. 3, 437–8)

For Marx ([1869] 1906, p. 668), Bentham represented the point of view of the small businessman, a position shared by Halévy in his study of the so-called Philosophical Radicals (Halévy, 1934, pp. 264, 427). Why does this conclusion follow from Bentham's underlying general theory?

For Bentham, man is governed solely by the hedonistic principle of seeking pleasure and avoiding pain. And this utility-maximizing principle, even though it cannot be proved, is the only correct standard of evaluation: the attempt to establish a standard of right and wrong independent of the felicific calculus is held to be erroneous and nothing more than the effort of ideologists to impose their standards on the population (Bentham, [1780] 1969, pp. 91–2). That is, no objective standard exists by which ethical evaluations can be made. And why not?

For Bentham, the community is a 'fiction.' Rather than being comprised of classes held together by the underlying relations of society, the community is nothing more than a collection of individuals. Hence, social interest is nothing more than the sum of individual interests. One cannot, therefore, speak of any objective social interests existing at any point in time, but only of individual interests independent of fictitious society. And who is the best judge of such interests? Obviously, the individual.

Thus Bentham puts forward a standard of ethical evaluation based solely upon the subjective appraisal of the individual. This subjectivist, individualist perspective is that of the small businessman. In a competitive environment, the capitalist faces a hostile environment: workers as well as other businessmen are his enemies. The appearance is that of the individual standing alone, facing forces (the market) over which he has no control. Success in such an environment then seems to be based solely on the sagacity or luck of the individual. Since this is the case (or, at least, appears to be), the evaluation of what is good or bad rests solely on the subjective judgment of the individual, with money (gain or loss) as the measure of welfare.

When applied to economic valuation, such a point of view realizes itself in a utility theory of value. We observe that the modern version of utility theory rests on a calculation of pleasure and pain, of benefit and loss. Obviously, such a view is closely connected with and gives moral (and political) support to an economy which rests upon calculation (Horowitz, 1954, p. 30; Hunt, 1979, p. 113).

Thus, the subjectivist utilitarian approach of Bentham, reflective of the individualism developed within the context of capitalist society, necessarily generates a theory of economic valuation based on the subjectivist calculation of the individual as to pleasure/pain, benefit/loss – a hedonistic, utility theory of value. This standard, according to Bentham, is not provable through normal scientific testing because it rests on a subjective rather than an objective foundation. Hence it becomes an article of faith. Further, this capitalist standard is applied to the population as a whole.

There is one more feature of Bentham's general theory with which we want to deal. In the early stages of capitalist development, labor was viewed as the foundation of social progress and welfare (see above). From the standpoint of a *social* utilitarian thrust, then, the work effort would have been viewed as productive of pleasure. For Bentham, the opposite holds:

> *Aversion* – not *desire* – is the emotion – the only emotion which *labour* . . . is qualified to produce . . . In so far as *labour* is taken in its proper sense, *love of labour* is a contradiction in terms. (Bentham, 1954, vol. 3, p. 428)

Bentham, again, does nothing more than develop an argument based on the specific characteristics of capitalist society and applies this argument to the general case. In capitalist society, labor is not undertaken for the benefit of those performing the labor but for those hiring labor power to generate exchange value. In a sense, workers must be bribed to expend effort through the payment of a wage. (Of course, this is not a matter of choice; the conditions imposed by private ownership of the means of production demand such a relationship.) Hence work, as a general rule, appears to be painful, to produce disutility.

Such an argument carries within it two characteristics, one backward-looking, the other forward-looking. In the first instance, it is a repudiation of the older position of labor as the most important social resource and the means through which society advances. This, as we have argued, was part and parcel of the development of the labor theory of value. Second, this argument presages the development of the psychological labor cost theory of value, which was one aspect of the overt attack on the labor standard following Ricardo (see below). In both instances, however, we observe that Bentham, with his utility approach undertaken solely within the context of capitalist society, ideologically attempts to undermine the labor theory of value through a modernized version of the mercantile, feudal utility theory of value.

In sum, Bentham's general theory takes certain aspects of capitalist organization and generalizes those aspects into an ideological system that precludes investigation into that society. For Bentham, the economic calculations of the profit-maximizing businessman are the standard for all of society. And these standards are true for all of history, for all forms of social organization. In other words, all societies are essentially capitalist, and all people are businessmen (or, at a minimum, proto-businessmen). Hence the social relationships existing in any form of social organization are concealed behind the exchange values extant, and only surface phenomena can be examined.

The class perspective of Malthus

Malthus, more than any other major theorist of the period, reflects the changing circumstances surrounding the industrial revolution period. An analysis of his work indicates that he underwent two periods of development. In both cases, the arguments reflected the changing class relations during this time, and hence the changed class interests:

> Already his first work [*Essay on Population*], one of the most remarkable literary examples of the success of plagiarism at the cost of the original work, had the practical purpose to provide 'economic' proof, in the interests of the existing English government and the *landed aristocracy*, that the tendency of the French Revolution and *its adherents in England* to perfect matters was utopian. In other words, it was a panegyric pamphlet for the existing conditions, against historical development and, furthermore, a justification of the war against revolutionary France. His writings of 1815, on protective tariffs and rent, were partly means to confirm the earlier apology of the poverty of the producers, in particular, however, to defend reactionary landed property

against 'enlightened', 'liberal' and 'progressive' capital, and especially to justify an intended *retrogressive step* in English legislation in the interests of the aristocracy against the industrial bourgeoisie. Finally, his *Principles of Political Economy* directed *against* Ricardo had essentially the purpose of reducing the absolute demands of 'industrial capital' and the laws under which its productivity develops, to the 'desirable limits' 'favourable' to the existing interests of the landed aristocracy, the 'Established Church' (to which Malthus belonged), government pensioners and consumers of taxes. But when a man seeks to *accommodate* science to a viewpoint which is derived not from science itself . . . but from *outside, from alien, external interests*, then I call him 'base'. (Marx, [1905–10] 1968, pt II, p. 119)

At this point in the argument, we are concerned only with Malthus's first period, from the first *Essay on Population* [1798] to *The Nature of Rent* [1815]. While there is obviously a continuity between these works and his *Political Economy* and *Measure of Value* of 1820 and 1823, we can see a certain demarcation between the two sets, a demarcation established by the changes undergone by British society in that quarter-century. While Malthus always served the vested interests of landlords (to which class he belonged by virtue both of birth and of his official position in the Church of England), he accommodated himself to the facts of industrialization and the dominance of the manufacturing capitalists. In both periods Malthus stood against the lower classes.[1]

The theory of population

It is quite clear that Malthus developed his theory of population in response to certain ideas contained in the French revolutionary period and to the observed growth in poverty resulting from a capitalist industrialization process. Malthus himself tells us that the *Essay* was directed at the works of William Godwin, specifically his *Enquiry Concerning Human Justice* [1793] and 'Of Avarice and Profusion' [1797], and to a lesser extent the works of Condercet (Malthus, [1798] 1976, pp. 15, 57–65, passim).[2]

But these works were the product of social movement in France, symptomatic of the spirit of democracy and progress in the conduct of human affairs that infected the period leading to the great upheaval. The essence of this spirit was the supposed perfectibility of man, achieved through reason – if the human institutions preventing that potential from being achieved were eliminated. Among the institutions holding reason in check was the then-current class system based on property.

It should be noted that the writings of these optimists were highly popular during the period and were viewed by authority as extremely dangerous. It was not without reason that the British government passed the Aliens Act and the Traitorous Correspondence Act in 1793 and followed these with the suspension of habeas corpus in 1794. Godwin feared official persecution in the publication of his egalitarian, syndicalist views (Spiegel, 1971, p. 268), while others were tried, imprisoned or thrown out of the country.

For Malthus, such ideas – indeed, the French Revolution itself – were anathema:

> The real perfectibility of man may be illustrated, as I have mentioned before, by the perfectibility of a plant. The object of the enterprising florist is, as I conceive, to unite size, symmetry, and beauty of colour. It would surely be presumptuous in the most successful improver to affirm that he possessed a carnation in which these qualities existed in the greatest possible state of perfection . . . Yet although he may be aware of the absurdity of supposing that he has reached perfection; and though he may know by what means he attained that degree of beauty in the flower which he at present possesses, yet he cannot be sure that by pursuing similar means, rather increased in strength, he will obtain a more beautiful blossom. By endeavouring to improve one quality, he may impair the beauty of another . . . In a similar manner, the forcing manure used to bring about the French Revolution, and

to give a greater freedom and energy to the human mind, has burst the calyx of humanity, the restraining bond of all society; and however large the separate petals have grown, however strongly or even beautifully a few of them have been marked, the whole is at present a loose, deformed, disjointed mass, without union, symmetry, or harmony of colouring. (Malthus, [1798] 1976, p. 94)

The function of the *Essay* was to demonstrate a *natural* rather than social cause of poverty. In fact, for Malthus, his analysis was less a theory of population than a theory of poverty:

It has been said, that I have written a quarto volume to prove, that population increases in a geometrical, and food in an arithmetical ratio; but this is not quite true . . . The chief object of my work was to enquire what effects these laws, which I considered as established in the first six pages, had produced and were likely to produce on society.

That the principal and most permanent cause of poverty has little or no *direct* relation to forms of government, or the unequal division of property; and that, as the rich do not in reality possess the *power* of finding employment and maintenance for the poor, the poor cannot, in the nature of things, possess the *right* to demand them; are important truths flowing from the principle of population . . . And it is evident that every man in the lower classes of society, who became acquainted with these truths, would be disposed to bear the distresses in which he might be involved with more patience; would feel less discontent and irritation at the government and the higher classes of society, on account of his poverty; would be on all occasions less disposed to insubordination and turbulence; and if he received assistance, either from any public institution or from the hand of private charity, he would receive it with more thankfulness, and more justly appreciate its value. (Malthus, from the 3rd edn; cited in Rubin, [1929] 1979, pp. 295–6)

We are not concerned here with analyzing the hokum of the relation between geometric and arithmetic rates of growth, or with establishing that none of Malthus's ideas, including the concept of diminishing returns introduced in later editions of the *Essay*, were novel with him (Schumpeter, 1954, pp. 250–75). We do note, however, that the theory of Malthus, either in pure or adulterated form, has survived all criticism and is periodically resurrected as explanatory of social ills – particularly during periods of political duress (Meek, 1953, pp. 3–49). Hence, Malthus's argument provides an almost perfect example of a scientifically invalid theory which, because it provides useful results, continues to exist as an ideological support for the continued domination of a particular class. But why Malthus? From the point of view of his *Essay*, wherein lies the potential significance of his theory that makes it so useful in maintaining existing class relations?

The significance of Malthus lies in a non-social explanation of poverty, supported in his case by Divine Law, and in the argument that propertied systems of organization are both natural and necessary. These two general considerations give rise to both pessimism with regard to social improvement and fatalism in the acceptance of injustice.

For Malthus, class society was both necessary and natural; all conceived forms of organization seemingly antithetical to that based on property reduced themselves, in the final analysis, to a form similar to the relations existing in England:

It has appeared that a society constituted according to Mr. Godwin's system must, from the inevitable laws of our nature, degenerate into a class of proprietors and a class of labourers, and that the substitution of benevolence for self-love as the moving principle of society, instead of producing the happy effects that might be expected from so fair a name, would cause the same pressure of want to be felt by the whole of society which is now felt only by a part. It is to the established administration of property and to the apparently narrow principle of self-love that we are indebted for all the noblest exertions of human genius, all the finer and more delicate emotions of the soul, for everything, indeed, that distinguishes the civilized from the savage state; and no sufficient change has as yet taken place in the nature of civilized man, to enable us to say that he either is, or ever will be, in a state when he may safely throw down the ladder by which he has risen to this eminence.

If in every society that has advanced beyond the savage state, a class of proprietors and a class of labourers must necessarily exist, it is evident that, as labour is the only property of the class of labourers, every thing that tends to diminish the value of this property must tend to diminish the possessions of this part of society. The only way that a poor man has of supporting himself in independence is by the exertion of his bodily strength. This is the only commodity he has to give in exchange for the necessaries of life. It would hardly appear than that you benefit him by narrowing the market for this commodity, by decreasing the demand for labour, and lessening the value of the only property he possesses. (Malthus, [1798] 1976, p. 98)

Moreover, as Malthus notes, such forms of social organization benefit the lower classes. Those who hold property demand the labor power of the propertyless. Since the latter class possesses only labor power with which to earn its livelihood, it is benefited by the sale of this commodity to those who buy it. Hence, the greater the class of property-holders, the greater the demand for labor power and the greater the well-being of the working class.

The good parson erects a circular argument based upon prevailing institutional arrangements. Because property is natural, it is necessary – for without property-holders to effect the well-being of the propertyless, the lower orders would suffer abominably; there would be none to put their labor power to work. And all attempts to eradicate property as the foundation of society are doomed to failure because property is naturally ordered by God (Malthus, [1798] 1976, pp. 123–30). Therefore, regardless of superficial appearances, a harmony of interests exists between the classes by which the dominant classes protect and advance the interests of the lower classes.

Now, although a system such as that in the England of Malthus's time was (for Malthus) necessary, it was possible to ameliorate its harshest effects through reform. Reform, however, had its limits:

> In the same manner, though we cannot possibly expect to exclude riches and poverty from society, yet if we could find out a mode of government by which the numbers in the extreme regions would be lessened and the numbers in the middle regions increased, it would be undoubtedly our duty to adopt it. It is not, however, improbable that as in the oak, the roots and branches could not be diminished very greatly without weakening the vigorous circulation of the sap in the stem, so in society the extreme parts could not be diminished beyond a certain degree without lessening that animated exertion throughout the middle parts which is the very cause that they are the most favourable to the growth of intellect. If no man could hope to rise or fear to fall in society, if industry did not bring with it its reward and idleness its punishment, the middle parts would not certainly be what they now are.
>
> And though in every civilized state, a class of labourers must exist; yet one permanent advantage would always result from a nearer equalization of property. The greater the number of proprietors, the smaller must be the number of labourers; a greater part of society would be in the happy state of possessing property, and a smaller part in the unhappy state of possessing no other property than their labour. But the best directed exertions, though they may alleviate, can never remove the pressure of want, and it will be difficult for any person who contemplates the genuine situation of man on earth, and the general laws of nature, to suppose it possible . . .
>
> The great error under which Mr. Godwin labours throughout his whole work is the attributing almost all the vices and misery that are seen in civil society to human institutions . . . Were this really a true state of the case, it would not seem a hopeless task to remove evil completely from the world . . . But the truth is, that though human

institutions appear to be the obvious and obtrusive causes of much mischief to mankind, yet in reality they are light and superficial . . . (Malthus, [1798] 1976, pp. 122, 115, 66)

As Rogin has argued, Malthus was one of the great proponents of conservatism (Rogin, 1956, pp. 175–8). In its essence, Malthus's argument runs like this. Society has historically created various institutions to which people have accustomed themselves. Once those institutions are in place, they are not to be tampered with or the result will be harmful to society as a whole and to the lower orders in particular. Granted, change can take place within the established institutional framework, but any radical reordering of society is both unnecessary and positively injurious.

There were two main exceptions to this 'non-interference' argument: the Corn Laws, which Malthus defended; and the Poor Laws, which he wanted repealed. The latter were particularly abhorrent in the form of Pitt's bill, which guaranteed subsistence, as poor relief was to be financed out of property taxes and thus was a drain on the income of landlords. ('Observations on the Effects of the Corn Laws . . .,' 1814: Malthus, [1798] 1976, pp. 134–6.) Other than in these areas, the government should maintain a *laissez-faire* policy *once prevailing institutions were in place.* With the exceptions noted (which were favorable to the landlord class), this is obviously a status quo argument, designed to preserve the class interests of those benefiting from the social system.

Given such a position, no examination of the historical evolution of society is required, no extant institutions need be critically evaluated. Social institutions may be modified but they cannot be discarded, or, as with Malthus's position on the French Revolution, the result will be a 'deformed, disjointed, mass . . .' Hence, whatever exists is, in the main, proper (and, one should add, ordained by God). To propose change is improper.

We note that the argumentation of Malthus has neither scientific nor logical ground upon which to stand. It is unscientific because change is constant within society, and the then-present social relations and institutions were themselves the result of change. It is illogical because when change occurred, it could be defended on the same grounds as those which it replaced were defended – it exists. Thus, the only function the argument serves is one of irrational defense of existing relations, should those relations be pleasing to Malthus (and the landlords).

This class position of Malthus is replicated in his discussion of the motivation to produce children. Clearly, if the level of population were naturally determined, it would operate with equal validity within all classes and all sections of society. If 'people' were induced to breed to the limits of subsistence, then all people would be reduced to equally poor levels of income (unless, of course, one or more of the various 'checks' were functioning). Clearly this is not the case: by definition, poverty is not a characteristic of the wealthy. Thus, only the lower classes are subject to this 'law' or, at least, tend to be reduced to penury by the workings of this 'law.' Why is this? According to Malthus, it is because upper-class members are more intelligent, more provident and more far-sighted than their lower-class counterparts (Malthus, [1798] 1976, p. 34). The lower-class population, then, by imputation is stupid, tending to multiply itself to a level that results in its own poverty.

Such a position is in perfect harmony with Malthus's general theory of population. Since it is a naturally determined law (mandated by divine Will), it is not a social law. If the level of population were determined through social law, it would also be the product of the social relationships that comprise society. With Malthus, then, there is no need to examine such relationships (other than to implicitly take them as given), for his argument is independent of them: the poor are innately stupid. But, realistically, it is social relationships among people that both produce and determine what we term 'humans,' so the elimination of the social basis of population also eliminates consideration of population as human-determined. Society for Malthus, or at least the lower-class element of society, is nothing more than an ant hill, its members copulating or not, living or not, depending upon the available food supply, and tending to breed themselves to that limit of subsistence. In one fell swoop, then, Malthus develops an argument that 'solves' the two fundamental problems of the period. In proposing a naturally ordered society impervious to fundamental social change, the 'perfectibility' ideology of the French Revolution is rejected out of hand: the English upper classes are protected from the threat across the channel. Also, poverty is argued to be the result not of the class structure of society but of the natural fecundity of the poor themselves. Poverty is the fault of the poor rather than a social injustice. The victims themselves are to blame for their condition. As with Christian dogma, people 'sin' merely by being born.

On rent

Regarding the argument contained in *Nature and Progress of Rent*, one central point must be made: Malthus's position was an attempt to exonerate the landlords from the charge, levelled by Smith and others, that their income was the result of a class monopoly on land (Rogin, 1956, p. 178) and to defend the Corn Laws.

> Is it, then, possible to consider the price of the necessaries of life as regulated upon the principle of a common monopoly? Is it possible, with M. de Sismondi, to regard rent as the sole produce of labour, which has a value purely nominal, and the mere result of that augmentation of price which a seller obtains in consequence of a peculiar privilege: or, with Mr. Buchanan, to consider it as no addition to the national wealth, but merely as a transfer of value, advantageous only to the landlords, and proportionable *injurious* to the consumers? (Malthus, [1815] 1969, pp. 15–16)

Malthus argues his case by asserting a number of reasons (including that of diminishing returns) why rent is generated and paid as a portion of national income; but regardless of the specific reason, rent is not an income fixed by monopoly privilege, but rather a payment determined by natural law:

It may be laid down . . . that as a nation reaches any considerable degree of wealth, and any considerable fullness of population . . . the separation of rents, as a kind of fixture upon lands of a certain quality, is a law as invariable as the action of the principle of gravity. And that rents are neither a mere nominal value, nor a value unnecessarily and injuriously transferred from one set of people to another; but a most real and essential part of the whole value of the national property, and placed by the laws of nature, where they are, on the land, by whomsoever possessed, whether the landlord, the crown or the actual cultivator. (Malthus, [1815] 1969, p. 20)

In addition, rents themselves are a signal of social well-being:

We see then, that a progressive rise of rents seems to be necessarily connected with the progressive cultivation of new land, and the progressive improvement of the old: and that this rise is the natural and necessary consequence of the operation of four causes, which are the most certain indications of increasing prosperity and wealth – namely, the accumulation of capital, the increase of population, improvements in agriculture, and the high price of raw produce, occasioned by the extension of our manufactures and commerce.

On the other hand, it will appear, that a fall of rents is as necessarily connected with the throwing of inferior land out of cultivation, and the continued deterioration of the land of a superior quality; and that it is the natural and necessary consequence of causes, which are the certain indications of poverty and decline, namely, diminished capital, diminished population, a bad system of cultivation, and the low price of raw produce. (Malthus, [1815] 1969, p. 32)[3]

Malthus concludes his argument by addressing the question of taxation of rents, asserting that, not only do such taxes adversely affect the long-run interests of the nation as a whole, but the landlord class almost assuredly pays more than its fair share, contributing to the portion that should be paid by the agricultural capitalist (Malthus, [1815] 1969, pp. 52–61).

What Malthus defends, then, is the economic interests of the most regressive class in English society of the period – the landlords. Malthus argued that this class, far from being a drag on society and on capital accumulation (the prevailing contemporary opinion), was not only necessary to the maintenance of society, but beneficial to long-run economic growth. Although his theoretical rationale is developed later in his *Political Economy*, it is clear that Malthus is arguing from the position that high levels of consumption from the unproductive members of society are necessary for continued growth because consuming the whole of national output creates markets for new output and thereby stimulates the accumulation process. What we observe, then, is a shift from the point of view of the labor-theory-of-value theorists; the focus of economic activity is now on consumption rather than production. And in this regard, Malthus can be seen as contributing to the re-establishment of the utility theory of value as the dominant point of view, a view shared by the landlords.[4]

Malthus, then, represents nothing more than a throw-back to the feudal arguments of the previous social system – Divine Law (the foundation of natural law) as explanatory of social ills and an overt defense of the landlord class, a class that was a direct outgrowth of the older, feudal ruling class. His position that poverty was caused by over-population is nothing more than a recrudescence of the late feudal argument of exactly the same content and which was used for the same purpose – to fraudulently 'explain' poverty by blaming the poor themselves.

Say and the neoclassical perspective

Of the theorists examined here, I would hold that Jean Baptiste Say had the greatest direct influence on development of the neoclassical outlook. In addition to originating the 'French

School' of thought, his *Treatise* had widespread use in most European countries as well as in the United States, serving as *the* textbook in various institutions of learning throughout the nineteenth century:

> But no one has popularized economic science to the same degree as J. B. Say . . .
>
> The influence of J.B. Say contributed more than that of any contemporary writer, to extend in Europe a taste for political economy. His theories, so naturally applicable to political questions, were studied with ardor during the Restoration as a weapon of opposition and of war; and perhaps they owe a part of their success to the services they rendered in the parliamentary discussions of the period. (Blanqui, [1880] 1968, pp. 448-9)

There is little question that the principles established in the Treatise were influenced by the events surrounding the French Revolution, the growth of capitalist relations in France following the success of that event, and the general outlook of the labor theorists as set forth by Adam Smith. On the first cause, Blanqui states the following:

> The situation of France was very favorable for that study, after the storms of our revolution. Had not the people tried all systems and carried to their last results the most hazardous principles? Had they not had a near view of bankruptcy, the wasting of capital by war, the momentary destruction of commerce by the *maximum*, the blockade of the seas and that crowd of industrial and financial catastrophes with which the history of the time is wholly filled? The time had come to draw conclusions, and to sum up in one body of doctrine the theories which naturally arose from that mass of new and unheard of facts. It was necessary to explain this economic cataclysm unparalleled in the world, which appeared nevertheless as the precursor of a general renovation. This is what J. B. Say did, in publishing, under the consulate of Bonaparte, the first edition of his *Treatise on Political Economy*. From this book dates, in fact, in Europe, the creation of a simple,

strict and intelligent method of studying political economy, and the time has come for us to judge of it. (Blanqui, [1880] 1968, p. 443)

Although Say pretends to do nothing more than systematize the argument of Smith, he, in fact, launches an attack on every significant aspect of the general theory contained in *The Wealth of Nations*, particularly its examination of capitalist class relations:

> He is thought of as the theorist who put Smith's scattered principles in order. We shall try to demonstrate that Say put Smith's theory in order in the same way that a cautious spouse puts her husband's trousers in order when she turns them upside down and empties them of all their valuables. It is much safer that way. So Say 'purged' Smith of 'dangerous thoughts.' (Rogin, 1956, p. 209)

Indeed, Say represents the first systematic attack on the labor theory of value, and in the *Treatise* he presents an argument that is almost the exact opposite of that contained in *The Wealth of Nations*.[5] There are two major aspects and one minor aspect of this attack. To combat the labor theory of value and the analysis springing from that perspective, Say resurrects the utility theory as the basis of his argument. Coupled to this is his factor theory of production and distribution. The minor aspect of this attack (although it is inseparable from the two major conditions) is that he is the 'first to assign to the entrepreneur . . . a definite position in the schema of the economic process.' (Schumpeter, 1954, p. 555)

On the utility theory of value and its relation to the factor theory

The essence of Say's attack is the repudiation of the labor theory of value and the recrudescence of the utility theory as the starting point for a general analysis of economic relations:

To the labour of man alone he [Smith] ascribes the power of producing values. This is an error. A more exact analysis demonstrates . . . that all values are derived from the operation of labour, or rather from the industry of man, combined with the operation of those agents which nature and capital furnish him.

From this error Smith has drawn the false conclusion, that all values produced represent pre-exerted human labour or industry . . . from which position he infers a second consequence equally erroneous, *viz.* that labour is the sole measure of wealth, or of value produced.

The value that mankind attach to objects originates in the use it can make of them . . . To this inherent fitness or capability of certain things to satisfy the various wants of mankind, I shall take leave to affix the name of utility. Production is the creation, not of matter, but of utility . . .

Exchangeable value, or price, is an index of the recognised utility of a thing . . .

In fact, when one man sells any product to another, he sells him the utility vested in that product: the buyer buys it only for the sake of its utility, of the use he can make of it. (Say, [1803] 1827, pp. *xl*, 16, 2; as well, see pp. 235-44)

Say begins his argument not from the point of view of production but from that of consumption and exchange, the point of view of the merchant. We are here treated to a very old and at the same time quite modern theory of value, in which utility is the foundation of value, price is the measure of that value and is equal to value, and value is determined by demand in conjunction with the limits imposed by the conditions of supply. From this vantage point, Say eliminates an examination of the underlying social relations of production. Production is merely the generation of utility, which then serves to satisfy the subjective inclinations of those purchasing the products and for whom the commodities are produced.

In Say's analysis of utility and its relation to value, one can observe the connection to the subjective, individualist utilitarianism of Bentham. Say argues that the 'correct' valuation of a hypothetical commodity is determined by the price that a number of people agree on as representative of the utility that commodity conveys to the consumer ([1803] 1827, pp. 235-6). Value, then, is what people agree upon, and this subjective agreement determines the correct valuation. Hence, the *standard* of valuation is determined not by objective factors independent of one's perception, but by that perception itself. This is precisely the view of Bentham as set forth in his hedonistic calculation of moral right (see above).

Such a position leads (though not inexorably) to a factor productivity theory of production and distribution. Since all social relations have been eliminated from the base of the examination of the production process, the central point becomes the role that various factors of production play in the generation of output. Again, from the standpoint of the labor theorists, production was the result of social labor only, raw materials and machinery being the products of past labor. What Say argues is that universal laws of production exist in which the three factors of production combine to produce value. At the superficial level, this is obviously true. However, such a position does not distinguish between the production process contained in a slave society and that in a modern capitalist society: in all societies we observe the same 'triad' involved in production; hence, all societies are the same.

> The principal merit of this work consisted in having clearly defined the bases of the science. J. B. Say separated it from politics, with which the Economists of the eighteenth century had constantly confounded it, and administration, which the Germans thought inseparable from it. Thus reduced to more precise limits, political economy ran no further risk of being lost in the abstractions of metaphysics and the details of bureaucracy. J. B. Say rendered it independent by isolating it; and he proved that its study was as suitable for monarchies as for republics. (Blanqui, [1880] 1968, p. 443)

In Say's world, the process of combining the three factors of production in the most fortuitous manner is the key to the generation of a nation's wealth. This combination process requires 'judgment, perseverance . . . a knack of calculation . . . and a degree of risk' (Say, [1803] 1827, pp. 285-6). The individual who supplies these characteristics is the 'entrepreneur' (in the American edition, the 'adventurer' ([1821] 1827, p. 18)).

I do not propose to deal with this nebulous character here except to note the introduction of a new term that serves as a substitute for 'capitalist' (or other such words) and that appears to have various qualities not shared by the common lot of the population. At the same time, the concept had been established before Say. Smith, for example, had already argued against those who held that profits were a return to this 'entrepreneurial' activity (Smith, [1776] 1937, pp. 48-9). According to Say, it is this central organizer who is responsible for the 'setting in motion . . .' of the whole production apparatus and process ([1803] 1827, p. 285). What is significant here is that Say is placing at the central point of the production process an individual who makes the whole thing go, rather than examining, as did Smith and the Classicists in general, production as a *social* process and social organization in general.[6]

For Say, all three factors of production are viewed as equally significant and on the same social footing. Land, labor, and capital all 'labor', all perform 'productive service' (p. 26). Moreover, all labor is productive and all segments of society are productive (pp. 26-31). The proof of the first proposition is that work requires effort (trouble) and trouble requires some compensation. Since it requires compensation, it must contribute to production and is, therefore, productive.

What Say attacks here is Smith's distinction between productive and unproductive labor and his (and others') position that various classes in society, particularly the landlord class, contributed nothing to the economic process or well-being of society. For all of Smith's confusion on the subject, the meaning of his position is clear: he was addressing the question of the generation of surplus value and its distribution, specifying that productive labor was that giving rise to the surplus out of which profits, rents and the wages of unproductive labor were generated (Henry, 1975). But this clearly involves a view of the production process as based on exploitation.

For Say, all production generates values, and, therefore, all the factors contributing to that production are productive. Hence there is no exploitation in the production process as long as each factor receives an income proportionate to its contribution and all inputs (or their owners) are equally productive, all contribute to the well-being of society. What we see in such a position is not only a repudiation of the labor theory's implicit exploitation argument, but also a retreat from the previous capitalist position on landlords, clergy, bureaucrats, etc., as so many parasites on society – constituting a segment of society that should be radically reduced in size if not eliminated altogether. The French capitalists had won their revolution; it was now necessary to soften the attack of the Philosophers of the eighteenth century and forge the alliance with the weakened feudal elements to withstand the political thrust of the lower classes:

> Bourgeois society reproduces in its own form everything against which it had fought in feudal or absolutist form. In the first place therefore it becomes a principal task for the sycophants of this society, and especially of the upper classes, to restore in theoretical terms even the purely parasitic section of these 'unproductive labourers' . . .
>
> *Secondly*, however, a section of the agents of production (of material production itself) were declared by one group of economists or another to be 'unproductive'. For example, the landowner, by those among the economists who represented industrial capital (Ricardo). Others (for example Carey) declared that the merchant in the true sense of the word was an 'unproductive' labourer. Then even a third group came along who declared that the 'capitalists' themselves were unproductive, or who at least sought to reduce their claims to material wealth to 'wages', that is, to the wages of a 'productive labourer'. Many intellectual workers seemed inclined to share the scepticism in regard to the capitalist. It was therefore time to make a compromise and to recognise the 'productivity' of all classes not directly included among the agents of

material production . . . it had to be established that even from the 'productive' economic standpoint, the bourgeois world with all its 'unproductive labourers' is the best of all worlds . . . Both the *do-nothings* and their *parasites* had to be found a place in this best possible order of things.

Thirdly: As the dominion off capital extended, and in fact those spheres of production not directly related to the production of material wealth became also more and more dependent on it . . . the sycophantic underlings of political economy felt it their duty to glorify and justify every sphere of activity by demonstrating that it was 'linked' with the production of material wealth, that it was a means towards it; and they honoured everyone by making him a 'productive labourer' . . . (Marx, [1905-10] 1969, pp. 175–6)

For Say, surplus is the result of 'circumstance' – the selling price of a commodity happens to be more than the cost of its production (Say, [1803] 1827, pp. 51–2). Out of this 'surplus' comes savings, which, if *frugally* preserved, allows investment (productive consumption), which causes the advance of industry (pp. 52–9). Again, we observe that Say's theory takes the accumulation process out of the social process in general and places it solely in the hands of the individual. Again, the general theory of Say is not a social theory based on the underlying relations in production, but an individualist argument founded solely on the technical characteristics of any production process with the entrepreneur at the center. Further, Say's position is clearly the same as that put forward by the mercantilists.

Now, since all the factors of production contribute equally to the production of values, then each shares – and should share – in the distribution of those values based upon the contribution each makes (pp. 269–70). Say has no technical argument that assigns each factor its respective share, but, in attempting to demonstrate that each input is in some sense similar, he argues that wages, profits and rents are the respective payments for the *loan* of the inputs (p. 18), and that these income shares can *all* be viewed as the *profit* of the input as a measure of their respective contributions to aggregate value (pp. 269–70). Thus,

From all of which it is impossible to avoid drawing this conclusion, that the profit of capital, like that of land and the other natural sources, is the equivalent given for a productive service, which though distinct from that of human industry, is nevertheless its efficient ally in the production of wealth. (Say, [1803] 1827, p. 313)

In all this, Say assumes the existing property relations as given, and argues that these relations are good and salutary:

The origin or the justice of the right of property, it is unnecessary to investigate, in the study of the nature, and progress of human wealth. Whether the actual owner of the soil, or the person from whom he derived its possession, have obtained it by prior occupancy, by violence, or by fraud, can make no difference whatever in the business of the production and distribution of its product or revenue.

It is the province of speculative philosophy to trace the origin of the right of property; of legislation to regulate its transfer; and of political science to devise the surest means of protecting that right. Political Economy views the right of property solely as the most powerful of all encouragements to the multiplication of wealth, and is satisfied with its actual stability, without inquiring about its origin or its safeguards . . . Nor can property be said to exist, where it is not matter of reality as well as of right. Then, and then only can the sources of production, land, capital, and industry, attain their utmost degree of fecundity. (Say, [1803] 1827, pp. 245, 71)

This creates something of a problem in his distribution theory, for if incomes are the result of the contribution to output made by the various factors of production, how can one explain the fact that non-owned inputs (the sun, oceans, etc.) do not receive any payments:

Land, as we have above remarked, is not the only natural agent possessing productive properties; but it is the only one, or almost the only one, which man has been able to appropriate, and turn to his own peculiar and exclusive benefit. The water of rivers and of the ocean has the power of giving motion to machinery, affords a means of navigation, and supply of fish; it is, therefore, undoubtedly possessed of productive power. The wind turns our mill; even the heat of the sun cooperates with human industry; but happily no man has yet been able to say, the wind and the sun's rays are mine, and I will be paid for their productive services. I would not be understood to insinuate, that land should be no more the object of property, than the rays of the sun, or blast of the wind. There is an essential difference between these sources of production; the power of the latter is inexhaustible, the benefit derived from them by one man does not hinder another from deriving equal advantage. The sea and the wind can at the same time convey my neighbour's vessel and my own. With land it is otherwise. Capital and industry will be expended upon it in vain, if all are equally privileged to make use of it; and no one will be fool enough to make the outlay, unless assured of reaping the benefit. Nay, paradoxical as it may seem at first sight, it is nevertheless, perfectly true, that the man who is himself no shareholder of land, is equally interested in its appropriation with the shareholder himself . . . in Europe, where the appropriation is complete, the meanest individual, with bodily health, and inclination to work, is sure of shelter, clothing and subsistence, at the least. (Say, [1803] 1827, p. 317)

Say's argument is neither ingenuous nor convincing, but it does focus on a central point of this essay. Say tacitly admits that for resources to yield a return they must be privately owned, and it is this fact of ownership that allows them (their owners) to command income from their use. This effectively undermines his theory of distribution based on mere input productivity and takes us back to a Smithian world of social relationships and an exploitation theory of profits and rents. To resolve his dilemma (at least to his own satisfaction), Say has recourse to an illogical solution: inputs not privately owned can contribute to output without commanding a return because all are entitled to their use and this use in no way restricts the use another might have of them. Resources that are privately owned (land) are justly so because this private ownership restricts their use and through this restriction makes them productive. Hence, what exists exists, and this is right and fitting.

All the above taken together leads to the doctrine that existing society is one of harmonious relations:

> Certainly, if Political Economy discloses the sources of wealth, if it points out the means of rendering it more abundant, and teaches the art of drawing daily still more without ever exhausting it; if it demonstrates, that the population of a country may, at the same time, be more numerous and better supplied with the necessaries of life; if it satisfactorily proves that the interest of the rich and poor, and of different nations, are not opposed to each other, and that all rivalships are mere folly; and if from all these demonstrations it necessarily results, that a multitude of evils supposed to be curable, but even easy to cure, and that we need not suffer from them any longer than we are willing so to do; it must be acknowledged that there are few studies of greater importance, or more deserving the attention of an elevated and benevolent mind. (Say, [1803] 1827, pp. iv–v)

In this connection, it should be noted that the original function of 'Say's Law' was to demonstrate a harmony of interests among trading bodies (Rogin, 1956, pp. 214–5).

Say's general perspective, then, was diametrically opposed to that of the labor theorists. Rather than examining the social process of production and accumulation based on the social relationships extant, Say focuses on individualism with exchange as the central point of analysis. From such a position, the class analysis and inherent conflict among classes indicative of the classical view is abandoned and social harmony substituted. Again, we observe an argument similar to that of the feudal upper classes and one designed for the same end – the conscious concealment of, and apologetics for, existing social relations.

The general theory of lauderdale

While James Maitland, Lord Lauderdale, was not an original contributor to economic theory, he does represent a major figure in the ideological struggle against the labor theory of value and the conceptual perspective of the representatives of that theory during the period in question. A member of the Scottish aristocracy, Lauderdale was known politically for his reactionary position in Parliament (Paglin, [1967] 1973, pp. 20, 157–8), and for his 'bellicose attack on Adam Smith and the defenders of Smithian tradition' (Paglin in Maitland, [1804] 1966, p. vii).[7] The theoretical position of Lauderdale, the 'English Say' (Roll, 1956, p. 337), centered around the dissemination of the utility theory of value and, in conjunction with this, the argument that capital was productive of value and that profits, therefore, were not the result of exploitation. In all this, Lauderdale made no original contribution (Turgot and Say certainly serving as forerunners in both aspects of the argument), but he was the first British writer to set forth the 'triad' scheme of factor productivity (Schumpeter, 1954, p. 560). In both regards, he represents a leading figure in the frontal attack on the classical position.

It is a telling point that, in the preface to the second edition of his *Inquiry* [1818], Lauderdale, with some exaggeration, was able to claim that the main components of the Smithian view were defunct:

> Labour is now no longer regarded as a measure of value . . .
>
> The distinction betwixt productive and unproductive labour . . . is exploded . . .
>
> It is, by all, admitted, that capital derives its profits, either by supplanting a portion of labour . . . or, from its performing a portion of labour which is beyond the reach of the personal exertion of man . . . (Maitland, [1804] 1966, pp. xx–xxi)

When these opinions were first advanced by Lauderdale in 1804, they were treated with disdain, but they are now 'in most recent publications . . . assumed as indisputable and incontrovertible.' (Maitland, [1804] 1966, p. xx)

The point is not that Lauderdale was overblown in the estimation of his own impact on theory, but that such a claim could be made at all. In the main, he is correct: during the Industrial Revolution period, the labor theory of value was successively assaulted through both frontal and flank attacks until it fell into a decidedly minority position, Ricardo being the last great 'respectable' theoretician of this school.

The utility theory of value in its relation to the 'Triad'

We need not say much in addition to the argument surrounding Say. In the opening chapter of his *Inquiry*, Lauderdale argues the following propositions:

1 that 'nothing . . . possesses a real, intrinsic, or invariable value (Maitland [1804] 1966, p. 12);
2 that value is solely relative (p. 21);
3 that labor could not be the measure of value because its price is subject to change (p. 29);
4 that value is solely the result of 'man's desire' (p. 38);
5 that value depends on variations in supply and demand (p. 38) – that is, that value is equated to market price.

In all this, Lauderdale makes it clear that his theoretical opponent is Smith (p. 26); and, in developing his argument, he purposefully misrepresents his classical counterpart. It is not my intent to specifically detail Lauderdale's rendering of Smith's argument. Suffice it to say that Smith, while inconsistent and incomplete on many points, did not equate value with the price of labor as Lauderdale claims (pp. 27–37), and it is quite clear that either Lauderdale misunderstands the distinction between productive and unproductive labor, or he is purposefully lying about Smith's argument (p. 37). This, however, is an aside.

Essentially, Lauderdale develops an argument that is the very opposite of Smith's. Rather than beginning from the point of view of production, he argues from the consumption side. Wealth, then, is not the labor of the nation (or its product) but 'the abundance of the object of man's desires' (p. 152).

Since wealth is that which is consumed and is measured by the exchange value of commodities as determined by the subjective utility calculations of the consumer relative to supply conditions, all that is brought to market (exchanged) is wealth.

From this, Lauderdale maintains, it follows that the Smithian distinction between productive and unproductive labor is fallacious, because all labor provides a service and all labor is paid for that service (pp. 132–45). Thus, all labor contributes to the production of wealth.

With this, the point of Smith's argument concerning productive labor as that which produces surplus value is eliminated from consideration. In fact, not only is it eliminated, it is overridden – for if all labor is productive of wealth where wealth is merely the exchange value of commodities consumed, then the distinction between the portion of the working class that sells its labor power to capitalists for the purpose of accumulation and that portion whose labor power is not used for accumulation (but still sold) is obliterated. Hence, profits (or rents) cannot be a derivative income, cannot be the result of 'a transfer from the pocket of the labourer into that of the proprietor of stock' (p. 158).

But if profits (and rent) are not portions of surplus value, not the result of exploitation, then what is their source? Rents are the measure of the contribution that land makes to aggregate wealth, while profits are the measure of the contribution of capital.

Land is productive of wealth because, without it, food could not be grown (raw materials mined, etc.). Land therefore contributes to the production of exchangeable wealth and is entitled to a share of that wealth (pp. 122–30). Capital is productive either by replacing labor or by performing a function that humans are incapable of (pp. 154–206).

Now:

But the investigation in which we have been engaged, seems to preclude the necessity of entering into any detail on this subject; for if we have been successful in shewing that labour in all its varieties is more or less productive of wealth, it follows, that capital, the profit of which arises from performing, with great advantage to mankind, labour, which has already been proved to contribute towards wealth, must also be regarded as a source of wealth. (Maitland [1804] 1966, p. 206)

Thus:

Though these three original sources of wealth, in the various states of existence in which history displays man, contribute to his wealth in very different proportions, yet in every state of society in which he is known to exist, each, more or less, affords its share. (Maitland [1804] 1966, p. 121)

Let us restate the argument baldly. Commodities, including factors of production, are priced. Price is a measure of value that is equated to wealth in the aggregate. Since all labor power is priced and all labor power produces something, all labor power is productive (of wealth). Since all labor power is productive, the distinction between productive and unproductive labor and the classical source of surplus value disappears. Capital merely supplants labor; so, like all labor, it is also productive. Profits, then, are nothing but a measure of capital's productivity, just as wages are a measure of labor's contribution to wealth. Land, as the original factor of production, obviously makes its contribution, and rents are the standard of land's participation in the production process.

Thus, land, labor and capital are all productive of wealth and all receive (and are entitled to) a share of national income as determined by their respective contribution. Wages, profits and rents are eliminated as payments to the *owners* of factors of production; now they are merely payments to the inputs directly as determined by their respective productivities. With this perspective, the political issues of the ownership of the means of production, class analysis, the generation of surplus value – all the major issues dealt with by the labor theorists – disappear and are replaced by a mode of argument that specifies harmony in the production process where the factors of production combine to produce output and to share that output according to their respective contributions.

Conclusion

In October, 1808, in an article in the *Edinburgh Review*, James Mill noted, with curiosity and regret 'the great difficulty with which the salutary doctrines of political economy are propagated in this country.' Between 1776, the year in which Adam Smith published his *Wealth of Nations*, and 1817, the year in which Ricardo published his *Principles of Political Economy and of Taxation*, not a single complete treatise on political economy appeared in England. Adam Smith remained the only authority, and he was little heeded. (Halévy, 1934, pp. 264-5)

In a sense, the position taken by Halévy, though exaggerated, is correct. Prior to Ricardo, no economic work approached *The Wealth of Nations* in either depth of analysis or scope of inquiry. However, Halévy is incorrect in his estimate of the significance of the influence of the theorists here examined. While it is true that Bentham, Malthus, Say and Lauderdale were all inferior to Smith, their arguments, taken as a whole, seriously reduced the popularity of the point of view represented by Smith, a view that had been gaining favor in the previous century. And it would be the perspective of the anti-labor theorists that would surface as the prevalent outlook in the post-Ricardian period.

It is worthy of note that in this period the most prominent economists were all anti-classical. While pamphleteers abounded on both sides of every theoretical and practical issue (and during this period, the relationship between theory and practice was always quite close: Dobb, 1973, pp. 22–3), the principal thrust was away from the labor theory of value and its corollary aspects. And it was in this period that the basis was laid for what was to become the neoclassical theory of value and distribution.

Ignoring the specifics of the various arguments, what is observed as the general point of view characterized by the economists examined in this chapter? The first and overriding aspect is that of a utility theory of value. Such a theory establishes a point of departure, a mode of analysis, that abstracts from social relations contained within any form of organization. The utility theory of value takes as its basis the 'relationships between men and economic goods' (Robbins, 1952, p. 68), rather than those between humans. For the labor theorists, the exchange process was an aspect of capitalist society that *concealed* the relationships among people. The task, then, was to examine the underlying causes and connections of this process to reveal the fundamental laws of society. When one confines one's attention to the immediate facts of exchange, one is relegating economics to a superficial level of analysis.

But such a position has its uses. By confining the investigation to surface phenomena, one is arguing either overtly or tacitly the acceptance of those phenomena. In the marketplace, individuals approach each other as equals: each seller and each buyer has the same option to engage in the exchange process for any single commodity depending upon the inclinations of the individual in question. At this level of analysis, each economic unit is on the same footing as any other. If a bargain is struck, that bargain must satisfy the subjective notions of both parties, or else, quite simply, the exchange would not take place. Each entity is free to exchange or abstain from exchanging as he sees fit. Thus, while a seller might desire a higher price and a buyer a lower price, the fact that a price can be agreed upon and an exchange can take place is proof that the exchange process itself has generated a harmonious arrangement between the parties.

Such a position fulfils one of the express purposes of fraud: to conceal reality. By centering the argument on the exchange relationships, the utility theorists hide that which lies underneath exchange – the production relations resting on property. The former generates the notion of equality and freedom, while the latter displays inequality and coercion. Given utility (profit) maximization as the outlook of the capitalist, by applying this outlook to society as a whole, the utility theorists are promoting the idea that all in society are, in some sense, equal – that all have the same interests as the capitalist.

In the revolutionary period, the capitalists could objectively represent their interests as those of the non-ruling classes in general, because all those classes had a real interest in overthrowing the feudal order. By the time period surrounding the industrial revolution, this was no longer the case. The main classes of capitalist society had begun the process of division into antagonistic camps, and, with the dissemination of primitive socialist theory, it was feared that the working class could utilize such ideas to its own advantage. Hence, for the most observant (or most frightened) ideologists, it became necessary to replace the older, objective point of view with the fraudulent, subjective utilitarian approach.

The second aspect of the utility theory of value, and one closely connected with that of equality, is the argument that promotes a harmony-of-interests doctrine. Since the essence of the utility theory of value is the relationship between the individual and economic good and all have such a relationship, then all individuals are, in this sense, the same, and all have the same interests in maximizing utility. This individualist approach, centered around exchange and consumption, ignores class distinctions founded upon production relations, which are the basis for conflict.

Coupled to this is the factor theory, which holds that the production of value is the joint effort of land, labor and capital, with the three inputs seen in purely physical terms, each responsible for or contributing its respective share to the generation of those use values. Thus, cooperation or harmony exists in production, exchange and consumption.

This gives rise to the third political aspect of the utility theory of value, that which we term the 'universality principle.' A utility relationship between humans and goods exists in all societies and is fundamentally the same in all societies: People 'eat' and satisfy various requirements of consumption. In addition, raw materials, equipment and human labor are conjoined in the production process. What distinguishes types of social organization are the property relationships and the relations among classes founded on those property forms. In other words, capital is not capital in the universal sense of physical equipment but because of the precise relationship between the owner of that equipment and the propertyless workers who are coerced into exchanging their labor power. By confining analysis to mere superficial phenomena, the anti-classicists could advance the position that all societies were essentially identical – all produced with the assistance of the same three factors of production, and all consumed in order to satisfy utility ends. Hence the theories propounded on these bases were held to be universally applicable.

It was this 'trinity' doctrine, in conjunction with the utility theory of value, that Marx saw as the substance of what he termed 'vulgar economy':

> The form of revenue and the sources of revenue are the *most fetishistic* expression of the relations of capitalist production. It is their form of existence as it appears on the surface, divorced from the hidden connections and the intermediate connecting links. Thus the *land* becomes the source of *rent*, *capital* the source of *profit*, and *labor* the source of *wages* . . . the vulgar economists . . . translate the concepts, motives, etc., of the representatives of the capitalist mode of production who are held in thrall to this system of production and in whose consciousness only its superficial appearance is reflected. They translate them into a doctrinaire language, but they do so from the standpoint of the ruling section, i.e., the capitalists, and their treatment is therefore not naive and objective, but apologetic. The narrow and pedantic expression of vulgar conceptions which are bound to arise among those who are the representatives of this mode of production is very different from the urge of political economists like the Physiocrats, Adam Smith and Ricardo to grasp the inner connection of the phenomena.
>
> However, of all these forms, the most complete fetish is *interest-bearing capital* . . . (Marx, [1905–10] 1971b, p. 453)

All this gives rise to the position that the economic order examined was naturally determined (and, in Malthus's case, the result of Divine Will). Since all societies are essentially the same and were (or should be) conflict-free, there is no fundamental reason why society should undergo change of any substantive sort. Hence, the observed economic relations are naturally determined, and social institutions must adjust to laws that are independent of society. Obviously, then, the scope for human action in solving supposed ills is quite limited. One should therefore learn to accept those ills because little, if anything, can be done to remedy them.

We note that the seventeenth- and eighteenth-century labor theorists also put forward a natural law theory of social organization, which stemmed from developments in the physical sciences. Then, however, this approach was used primarily to combat the feudal fraud of Divine Law. The position taken by these theorists was that the natural workings of the economic order would eventually result in social well-being, ills being eventually remedied by the process of capital accumulation. The natural law theories of this period, when the capitalist class was both gaining ascendancy and consolidating its power, were progressive because they advanced the interests of the most advanced class in society. As observed, the natural law theorists of the labor theory school were optimistic as to the trend of society.

In the nineteenth century, however, the capitalist class was in the very early stages of defending its position against the potential revolutionary threat of the underlying population; natural law was now utilized to maintain their privileged position – at the expense of the rest of society. The natural law argument of the anti-classicists served the same function as the Divine Law argument of feudal theologians (indeed, for Malthus they were the same): to support existing class relations by claiming those relations to be immutable and rational.

It was, then, in the period between Smith and Ricardo that the basic elements of the neoclassical theory were put into place. Bentham, Malthus, Say and Lauderdale, representatives of a body of thought in general, were putting forth a view of society and of the laws governing that society which was antithetical to the prevailing view of the previous period and was, in essence, nothing more than a resurrection of the feudal position. This anti-labor theory argument would be elaborated and consolidated in the next two time periods, reaching its apex in the imperialist stage of development.

Notes: Chapter 4

1 In his first published work, *The Crises, A View of the Present Interesting State of Great Britain . . .* (1796), Malthus posited that only a return to government by 'country gentlemen' assisted by the 'middle classes' could save England from the perils of the political turmoil brought on by the French Revolution: see James, 1979, pp. 50–1. In the same piece, he openly attacked the Dissenters, who had previously served the country well during the Revolution of 1640 and the Restoration of 1688, but who were now a political liability and considered enemies of both State and Church.

2 James opines that the key individual with whom Malthus was debating was William Frend, his former tutor at Cambridge, who in 1783 published a pamphlet that resulted in his being locked out of his rooms and expelled from that institution: see James, 1979, pp. 47–8. Regardless of the personages at whom Malthus directed his argument, however, the key issue is the ideas those individuals represented; it was the ideas with which Malthus fundamentally disagreed.

3 We ignore the obvious contradiction in the above passage.

4 As well, Malthus's argument took the generation of profits out of the realm of production, and placed them in the realm of exchange, as profits could be created simply by giving more of social income to landlords: see Kregel, 1973, pp. 25-6.

5 The view that Say was nothing more than a systematizer of Smith still has currency: see Spiegel, 1971, p. 258.

6 For a critical examination of the concept of the entrepreneur, see Dobb, 1955b.

7 His landlord foundation was most pronounced in his views on free trade, which he favored except for agricultural protection, and in his attack on the Reform Bill of 1832, which reduced the electoral power of his class by giving more voting rights to the so-called middle class – non-landlord property holders: see Paglin, [1971] 1973, pp. 157-8.

CHAPTER FIVE

The dissolution of the labor theory of value and the rise to dominance of utility

It has long been held that 1830 represents the break with the classical perspective resting upon the labor theory of value.

The succeeding period, from 1820 to 1830, was notable in England for scientific activity in the domain of Political Economy. It was the time as well of the vulgarising and extending of Ricardo's theory, as of the contest of that theory with the old school. Splendid tournaments were held . . . The unprejudiced character of this polemic – although the theory of Ricardo already serves, in exceptional cases, as a weapon of attack upon bourgeois economy – is explained by the circumstances of the time. On the one hand, modern industry itself was only just emerging from the age of childhood, as is shown by the fact that with the crisis of 1825 it for the first time opens the periodic cycle of its modern life. On the other hand, the class-struggle between capital and labor is forced into the background, politically by the discord between the governments and the feudal aristocracy gathered around the Holy Alliance on the one hand, and the popular masses, led by the bourgeoisie on the other; economically by the quarrel between industrial capital and aristocratic landed property – a quarrel that in France was concealed by the opposition between small and large landed property, and that in England broke out openly after the Corn Laws . . . With the year 1830 came the decisive crisis.

In France and in England the bourgeoisie had conquered political power. Thenceforth, the class-struggle, practically as well as theoretically, took on more and more outspoken and threatening forms. It sounded the knell of scientific bourgeois economy. It was thenceforth no longer a question, whether this theorem or that was true, but whether it was useful to capital or harmful, expedient or inexpedient, politically dangerous or not. In place of disinterested enquirers, there were hired prize-fighters; in place of genuine scientific research, the bad conscience and the evil intent of apologetic . . . (Marx, [1869] 1906, pp. 18–19)

Marx, as one would expect, is correct in the main; but the position expressed above tends to minimize the growth of the general theory based on a subjectivist approach – a growth that had taken place in the period prior to Ricardo's *Principles* (Chapter 4) and was accentuated in the decade following the appearance of the third edition of that work.

The 1830s represent something of a culmination of previously established trends. On the one hand, we observe a striking shift away from a labor theory among all mainline economists. On the other hand – and which amounts to the same thing – the labor theory of value, insofar as it continued to be held by some reputable economists, was vulgarized and converted into something altogether different. Essentially, Ricardo was the last respectable economist to hold what might be called a pure labor theory of value. Beyond Ricardo, this point of view was taken over by that camp hostile to capitalist society – in particular, of course, the Marxists.

There were three principal factors in this development. Initially, the working-class movement, especially in England and France, took on an increasingly threatening organizational posture. While machine-breaking was still common, and indeed intensified during the 1820s (Berg, 1980; Hobsbawm and Rudé, 1975), we also observe the beginning of the development that would come to dominate the future of this class: militant unionism and its attendant socialist threat. While the Grand National Consolidated Trades Union was not organized until 1833 and the Chartist Movement was not formally launched until 1838, these were obviously the outgrowth of an established historical development.

This working-class threat was the result of the growth and consolidation of capitalist production relations, which were particularly accentuated during the industrial revolution. Both the growth and concentration of the working class, which made effective organization possible, and the hostility of this class to the conditions of its existence were the result of the historical tendency of capital. That is, the capitalists themselves were responsibile for laying the foundation for the threat to their existence.

Ancillary to this organizational movement on the part of a growing working class was the development and propagation of a perspective unique to this class – socialism. The 1820s saw not only the growth of Owenism, Fourierism and similar movements, but also the heightening of that tendency which was later termed 'Physical Force Chartism' (Thompson, 1968, p. 440).

The second significant factor was the take-over of the labor theory of value by theoreticians overtly hostile (though not necessarily consistently so) to the capitalist social order. In the 1820s, William Thompson and Thomas Hodgskin published works written within the tradition of the labor theory of value that were clearly anti-capitalist in their orientation.[1] While neither economist was socialist in the modern sense of the word, both opined that existing social relationships, standing on the exploitation of the producing classes, were detrimental to the well-being of the community. Both argued that a Lockean system of property relations, in which only direct producers would own productive equipment and produce for exchange but in an egalitarian arrangement, was morally and economically superior to that existing around them. Thompson went further, claiming that even in such an egalitarian, anarchical framework, greed and selfishness would continue to exist; thus a cooperative, Owen-type society would be ethically superior (Hunt, 1979, pp. 135–53).[2]

To the English writers, one should add the work of Sismondi. His *Political Economy* of 1815 attacked then-modern capitalism from the point of view of the petty producer. While Sismondi was not a socialist and set forth a faulty under-consumptionist critique of classical theory, he nevertheless was one of the first authorities to expose the class contradictions of capitalism (Rubin, [1929] 1979, pp. 335–45).

The main point, however, is that the labor theory of value was now taken over by critics of the social order, the so-called Ricardian Socialists, who pushed the general argument based on the labor theory to a point inconsistent with capitalism itself. While Smith and others may have carped about this or that feature of capitalism, they were nevertheless strong supporters of such a society. Now the same general theory was used to promote an ideological point of view antithetical to capitalism.

The third factor in this process was the addition of the chapter 'On Machinery' to Ricardo's third edition of his *Principles*. It is most likely incontestable (regardless of one's point of view) to state that Ricardo was the most influential economist of his period. Given his political associations, his personal prestige and his intellectual acumen, his theoretical work carried enormous weight. The great merit of Ricardo (and the cause of his posthumous undoing) was that he pursued his analysis regardless of where it led him. That is, he did not allow his preconceptions to compromise his scientific work.

Ricardo's ruthlessness was not only *scientifically honest* but also a *scientific necessity* from his point of view. But because of this it is also quite immaterial to him whether the advance of the productive forces slays landed property or workers. If this progress devalues the capital of the industrial bourgeoisie it is equally welcome to him. If the development of the productive power of labour halves the value of the *existing* fixed capital, what does it matter, says Ricardo. The productivity of human labour has doubled. Thus here is *scientific honesty*. Ricardo's conception is, on the whole, in the interests of the *industrial bourgeoisie*, only *because*, and *in so far as*, their interests coincide with that of production or the productive development of human labour. Where the bourgeoisie comes into conflict with this, he is just as *ruthless* toward it as he is at other times towards the proletariat and the aristocracy . . .

It is not a base action when Ricardo puts the proletariat on the same level as machinery or beasts of burden or commodities, because (from his point of view) their being purely machinery or beasts of burden is conducive to 'production' or because they really are mere commodities in bourgeois production. This is stoic, objective, scientific. In so far as it does not involve *sinning* against his science, Ricardo is always a philanthropist, just as he was in *practice* too. (Marx, [1905–10] 1968, pp. 118–19)

In the third edition [1821], Ricardo, previously arch-defender of the capitalist order because it met the scientific requirements of progress, argued that, upon further reflection, capitalism *may* prove regressive.

Ever since I first turned my attention to questions of political economy, I have been of opinion, that such an application of machinery to any branch of production, as should have the effect of saving labour, was a general good, accompanied only with that portion of inconvenience which in most cases attends the removal of capital and labour from one employment to another . . .

These were my opinions, and they continue unaltered, as far as regards the landlord and the capitalist; but I am convinced that the substitution of machinery for human labour, is often very injurious to the interests of the class of labourers.

My mistake arose from the supposition, that whenever the net income of a society increased, its gross income would also increase; I now, however, see reason to be satisfied that the one fund, from which landlords and capitalists derive their revenue, may increase, while the other, that upon which the labouring class mainly depend, may diminish, and therefore it follows, if I am right, that the same cause which may increase the net revenue of the country, may at the same time render the population redundant, and deteriorate the condition of the labourer. (Ricardo, [1821] 1970, pp. 386, 388).

At the same time, Ricardo modified his position on Owenism. Initially, he had dismissed this movement out of hand. By 1819, while obviously not a follower of Owen, he had come to the position that some of Owen's schemes were at least worthy of consideration, particularly that involving relief from technological unemployment through spade husbandry.

Essentially, 'Ricardo now dissociated himself from the popular middle-class (capitalist) dogma on machinery' (Berg, 1980, p. 72). Rather than continuing in the position that capital accumulation was a positive good for all classes, given their supposed underlying harmonious interests, Ricardo now began to address fundamental class antagonisms. And this change represents a fundamental shift in the whole thrust of the classical political economy resting on the labor theory of value. From its beginnings through Smith, the whole of the argument was an objective defense of capitalist economic relations. With Ricardo, the argument now begins to form a criticism of that order.

The three factors just noted were all aspects of the beginning of the transition from the competitive stage of capitalism to that of oligopoly. With the industrial revolution, the older, small-scale production units began to give way to the more centralized facilities one is accustomed to in today's economy. Along with this process came the centralization of the working class, a class which, if organized, could stand in opposition to the capitalists as a ruling class. Workers were now replacing the more reactionary landlord class as the principal social enemy of the unfettered rule of the bourgeoisie. Further, the long contest between the capitalist and feudal elements in England and France was nearly over. True, there were still some battles to be waged, notably those over parliamentary representation and the Corn Laws in England, but the main contests were historically settled. Essentially, the revolutionary, progressive work of the capitalist order was coming to an end. Now, given its entrenched position, the capitalist class was entering its conservative phase.[3]

With the emergence of the working class as an organizational force, theories addressing solutions to the problems facing it, namely poverty and non-extant political rights, began to take hold. The post-industrial revolution period was one of those great historical periods in which ideas took on social significance. Economists and their theories were not viewed as irrelevant or arcane, but were the subject matter of much debate. Moreover, the working class, given its growing economic significance and organizational strength, began the process of formulating its own theories – theories that would ostensibly eliminate or at least alleviate its social condition. Thus, any theory that favored or seemed to favor this class would, from the standpoint of capitalist ideologists, stand in disrepute.

In essence, the labor theory of value had begun to outgrow its capitalist constraints. From the point of view of objective, scientific inquiry, the social system was showing signs of distress, of retrogression. Capitalism was beginning to be criticized on the basis of the same theory it originally promoted as advantageous to its growth and consolidation. In addition, the most significant reputable economist of the period, one who unabashedly held the labor viewpoint, had shown signs of abandoning his previously staunch, pro-capitalist position. To counteract these trends, the objective point of view had to be attacked and undermined. With the growth in the 'social disturbances' of the 1820s and, in particular, the 1830s, the spread of socialist theory, and the growth of a pro-working-class labor theory of value, this attack on the labor theory was intensified.

The significance of the 1820s in this attack and in the early dominance of the subjectivist approach can be witnessed in the attitudinal shift regarding worker education. Previous to this decade, the education of the working class could largely be ignored, but by 1830 this situation had markedly changed (Meek, 1967, p. 69). We now observe an outpouring of popular literature directed specifically to the working class and to educating it toward an acceptance of capitalist relations as natural, mutually beneficial, and promoting the interest of workers (Routh, 1977, pp. 81–97; Webb, 1955).

In the 1820s we also observe the burgeoning of various

Mechanics Institutes, which were for the most part organized by employers and members of the liberal intelligentsia, both to educate workers to their 'true interests' and to add a measure of discipline to the work-force (Berg, 1980, pp. 145–78). Problems did arise with various institutes – such as that of London, where Thomas Hodgskin and Robert Owen lectured – but on the whole these social mechanisms of education served their primary purpose of attempting to placate their audience through a liberal dose of pro-capitalist political economy.

> The institutes became a centre for a burgeoning industry in popular political economy. Most of this work was middle-class propaganda of the crudest kind. Francis Place was a keen advocate of this political economy, and Brougham produced a series of lectures for use in provincial institutes. Thomas Chalmers believed that . . . political economy had a definite role in the Institutes as he 'was not aware of a likelier instrument than a judicious course of economical doctrine for tranquilizing the popular mind and removing from it all those delusions which are the main cause of popular disaffection'.
>
> Political economy was a 'sedative to all sorts of turbulence and disorder'. Further, the attention drawn by Chalmers to the affinity between 'the taste for science' and the 'taste for sacredness' became the principle behind the cooperation of the church and the mechanics institutes at a much later date. Political economy within the institutes taught moral virtue, and the church was quick to follow in this role. . .
>
> Many of the other speakers to the Mechanics Institutes spoke of political economy in the context of concern over machine breaking . . . The Newcastle upon Tyne Institute heard lectures, in May 1825, and again in May 1826, 'on the utility of machinery, in promoting the comfort and happiness of the working classes of society'. . . Place, as always, was very clear about the social meaning of the movement.
>
> 'The Mechanics Institute is one, if not the most important, of our institutions. The better sort of working people

134

have received a portion of instruction and whether this
can be described as either good or bad it cannot be undone
. . . if the people had remained in their former ignorance,
the burnings now so rife among the farmers would be as
rife among the manufacturers. The knowledge obtained
by the manufacturing people in the North has led many
to the conviction of the fact that machinery is not and
has not been their enemy.' (Berg, 1980, pp. 163, 165–6)[4]

In the third decade of the century, the locus of economic
theory was not the development of alternative argument but
the criticism of Ricardo, focusing on the labor theory of
value. Best known for this criticism was the work of Samuel
Bailey, who attacked Ricardo's theory of value from a purely
relativist, exchange point of view (Bailey, [1825] 1967, pp.
1–45). In addition, but only incidentally, he set forward utility
as the ultimate standard of valuation, denoting '[the] effect
produced on the mind' as the basis for value (p. 180).

As is well known, by 1831 the Political Economy Club,
a most influential organization of the period, was able to
reach the following (rather contradictory) conclusion about
Ricardo:

He is one of the first who has treated the subject of
Taxation, and he always reasons out his propositions,
whether true or false, with great logical precision and to
their utmost consequences; but without sufficient regard
to the many modifications which are invariably found to
arise in the progress of Society. One of the errors of
Ricardo seems to have been to have followed up Malthus'
principles of population to unwarrantable conclusions . . .
First of all, it is contended that the interest of the Landlords
does in fact coincide with those of the other classes; and
then we see that in Ireland, where rent is absorbing
everything, in consequence of the immense competition
for land, a system of Poor Laws is likely soon to equalize
the division. (cited in Meek, 1967, p. 68)

At the same time, Ricardo's ostensible followers – James
Mill, McCulloch and DeQuincey – were insufficient to the

task of defending Ricardo from the onslaught, if defending him they were. All of which led Schumpeter to the following proposition, supportive of his general anti-Ricardian position:

> We have already seen that the core of the school consisted of only four men besides Ricardo himself. By this I mean that James Mill, McCulloch, and DeQuincey were the only unconditional adherents and militant supporters of Ricardo's teaching who gained sufficient reputation for their names to survive. West . . . stood apart . . .
> None of the three added anything substantial, and the touches they did add – James Mill and McCulloch especially – were mostly of doubtful value. They did not even succeed in summing up Ricardo correctly or in conveying an idea of the wealth of suggestions to be found in the latter's *Principles* . . . It was not their fault that Ricardo's system failed from the first to gain the assent of a majority of English economists – and not only, as the Ricardians tried hard to believe, of the dunces and laggards. This was owing to its inherent weaknesses. Nor was it their fault that the system was not made for a long career. But it was their fault that defeat came so quickly. Ricardo died in 1823. In 1825, Bailey launched his attack that should have been decisive on the merits of the case. Actually it was not, for schools are not destroyed so easily. But the decay of the Ricardian school must have become patent shortly after, for in a pamphlet published in 1831 we read that 'there are some Ricardians still remaining.' In any case, it is clear that Ricardianism was then no longer a living force. (Schumpeter, 1954, pp. 476–8)

The 1820s debate was largely confined to the rather academic limits of Ricardo proper: its thrust was the destruction of the objective theory of value and its corollaries rather than the erection of a new, counter-classical theory. There were, of course, developments on the latter front, such as Malthus's *Principles of Political Economy* [1820] and *The Measure of Value* [1823]. In both works Malthus demonstrated his continued allegiance to the landlord class, but he adopted a more modern, pro-capitalist position relative to the earlier *Essay*. At the same time, he advanced a cost of production theory of value (Malthus, [1823] 1957, pp. 1–19; [1820] 1951, pp. 50–122) while ostensibly holding to the labor standard.[5] This alteration allowed him to develop a defense of the propertied classes through a theory of distribution directed specifically against the exploitation theory that follows from the labor theory of value, and of which Malthus was keenly aware (Malthus, [1820] 1951, p. 76).

> [These] three conditions . . . must necessarily be fulfilled in every society, in order to obtain the continued supply of by far the greaₗₑⱼ part of the commodities which it wants; and the compensation which fulfils these conditions, or the ordinary price of any exchangeable commodity, may be considered as consisting of three parts: that which pays the wages of the labourers employed in its production; that which pays the profits of the capital, including the advances to the labourers by which such production has been facilitated; and that which pays the rent of land, or the compensation for the use of those powers attached to the soil which are in the possession of the landlord; the price of each of these component parts being determined exactly by the same causes as those which determine the price of the whole.
>
> The price which fulfills these conditions is precisely what Adam Smith calls the natural price; and when a commodity is sold at this price, he says it is sold for precisely what it is worth. (Malthus, [1820] 1951, p. 77)

In the 1830s, however, there was a qualitative change in the nature of the attack on the labor theory of value. Now attention was paid directly to the threat posed by the working class and to the development of an alternative argument which, if properly disseminated among that class, could effectively undermine the threat to capitalist rule.

Concentrating our attention on some representative economists of the period (including some of Schumpeter's 'also-rans'), we observe a commonality among the various theories deemed important during the period. Obviously, there were differences among the authorities as to the specifics of the argument (as there still are), but a general pattern demonstrates itself.

On the education of the working class

The first problem addressed was the recognition that the working class was becoming increasingly conscious of its class role in the production process, and the necessity to educate this class to accept a subservient role in society and to adopt a view of the social order that argues for stability. The general issue is set forth by Longfield and Scrope.

> Opinions are every day assuming greater weight in society. It is daily becoming more important, that the notions which are generally entertained should be correct, since they now lead so directly to action . . . Opinions, whether true or false, will no longer remain inactive; they both immediately affect legislation, and exercise immense influence on a class of people formerly removed beyond the reach of such discussions, but whose notions and consequent conduct are now of the greatest importance as well to their own comforts as to the peace and prosperity of their country. I allude to the labouring orders, both agricultural and manufactural. It is no longer a question, whether these men shall think or not, or what degree of influence their opinions ought to exert over their conduct; they will follow the path where they conceive their interests to point, and it only remains to be considered, in what manner a true sense of their real interests may be most effectually brought home to them . . . The people will no longer be guided by the authority of others.
>
> All reflecting people now concur in this, that the comforts and happiness of the labouring classes depend almost entirely upon their own conduct; and this opinion is equally consistent with either doctrine respecting the policy or impolicy of poor laws . . . It depends in some degree upon every person present, whether the labourer is taught that his interest will be best promoted by prudence and

industry, or by a violent demolition of the capital destined to his support. Unhappily the moral sense of right and wrong is very feeble among those classes at the present period, and the conduct of the labourer will be principally decided by what he conceives to be the cause of his distress, and that again will be very much influenced by the pains which each of you, gentlemen, take to learn and disseminate the true doctrines of Political-Economy, and the arguments by which they can be supported. Let the labourer be taught to know, and the proof is simple and easy to be understood by all, that the wages of his labour cannot be determined by the wishes of his employer, that they are even as independent of the decrees of the legislature as they are of his own will, and that they are ultimately entirely dependant upon the prudence or improvidence, the industry or idleness, of the labouring classes themselves. Let them be taught to trace out accurately the entire set of consequences that would result from each law that they might feel most inclined to call for, and they will at the same time see how inevitably their wild legislation would ensure their own destruction, and how small a part of their present weal or woe is 'that part which laws or kings can cause or curve.' (Longfield, [1834] 1971, pp. 16–19)

The prevailing want of the present day seems to be want of correct information as to the true interests of society. The progress of popular education has already infused a *mind* into masses heretofore but passive instruments in the hands of those who were the exclusive possessors of knowledge. *The people* now read; the people reason; the people think for themselves. What do they read? What are their thoughts? From what principles do they reason? These are questions of deep import. For the answers to them must determine the ultimate result of the revolution, hitherto a tranquil and bloodless, but yet a complete revolution, which has long since commenced, and is in active progress throughout Europe. By education the people are everywhere acquiring knowledge; and knowledge *is* power . . . Those whose daily labour wins their daily bread, with whom comforts are scarce, and necessaries not abundant; whose very means of existence are in the highest degree precarious, – this class no sooner begins to read, to think, to reason, and to inquire, than their reading, their thoughts, their reasoning, and their inquiries run into channels of vital interest to themselves, and immediately connected with their own position. They ask themselves, they interrogate each other, they consult all publications to which they have access, upon the to them all-important question, 'How it happens that their condition is so depressed – their position so precarious? Whether this state of things is necessary, and, if so, why? If not, then how it may be ameliorated? For to tolerate it any longer than appears to them unavoidable, assuredly they will not submit . . .

The danger in an inquiring age like the present, when institutions have ceased to be respected because they are established, and venerated because they are ancient, – when the people have begun to think and to reason on such subjects, and are no longer contented with what is, without satisfying themselves whether it ought to be, – the danger lies in the general ignorance of the public as to the true principles of public welfare, and in the general suspicion that the discordance of existing institutions from these principles is far greater than it really is, – a suspicion which is generated by the unwillingness of legislators to refer their conduct to first principles, and nourished by those who are ready at all times to imbue the multitude with opinions which may dispose them for violence and plunder. (Scrope, [1833] 1969, pp. viii–ix, 31)

Senior, in his 'Three Lectures on the Rate of Wages,' indicates the significance of the working-class demonstrations of 1829–30 for the necessity of developing a general theory amenable to the long-run interests of capital in containing this class:

The following Lectures contain little that is not well known to many of my readers, and still less that is peculiarly and exclusively appropriate to the present emergency.

They were written and delivered in a period of profound tranquility; but we are now in a state which may require the exertions of every individual among the educated classes, and many may have to assist in executing, or even in originating, measures for the relief of the labouring population, who are not yet sufficiently familiar with the principles according to which that relief is to be afforded. (Senior, [1837] 1966, p. iii)

Further, Senior demonstrates his knowledge of the nature of minority class rule and the importance of the diffusion of principles designed to deflect lower classes in their attempt to gain political power:

the apparent interest of the lower classes is the other way. They grossly miscalculate the number and value of the prizes in the lottery of life, they think that they have drawn little better than blanks, and believe those who tell them that if all the high lots were abolished everybody might have a hundred-pound prize.

As long as this is the political economy of the poor, there seems to be only three means of governing a densely peopled country in which they form the large majority. One is to exclude them from political life. This is our English policy . . . Another is the existence among them of a blind devotion to the laws and customs of the country . . . A third plan is to rely on military power – to arm and discipline the higher and middle classes, and to support them by a regular army trained to implicit obedience. (Senior, 1871, vol. I, pp. 150–2)

On the whole, the anti-labor theorists of the period were aware of and disconcerted by the fact that the working class was developing its own theoretical position on the nature of society – a position that was antagonistic to the interests of established society. It is also evident that previously established authority was no longer capable of maintaining order, that changes had to be made, particularly in regard to the economic education of the working class. Following Senior, if the working class would no longer heed authority

141

(on the basis of fraud), the ruling class would have to resort to force as its primary instrument of domination. Hence, the development of a (correct) 'political economy of the poor' was vital in order to maintain the status quo.

This political economy had one overriding goal: it was to convince the lower classes that their interests were best served within the framework of constituted society (capitalism), and that economic laws prevented these classes from achieving goals so mischievously set forward by individuals such as Hodgskin or Owen. That is, the new political economy was not to be developed on a scientific basis, but with a political end in mind – educating the working class to an anti-worker, pro-capitalist position. It might be noted that one of the strongest proponents of this position, Bishop Whately, argued that workers were equivalent to the 'savages' in the colonies, and that their education should be equivalent to that which attempted to 'civilize' those peoples – acceptance of England's colonial domination (Whately, [1832] 1966, pp. 76–89).

The attack on socialism

The fear of socialist theory disseminated among and accepted by the reading working class is easily discernible in the works of the economists of the period. Scrope, for example, seems to have developed his arguments specifically in response to the works of Owen (Scrope, [1833] 1969, passim). Essentially, socialism in its pre-Marxist varieties was 'in the air', and the anti-classicists demonstrated a marked concern with these doctrines and set forth their arguments specifically in response to such seditious ideas – demonstrating that such false notions, if implemented, could only result in a deterioration for that class which espoused them:

> The inequality of conditions amongst men in the advanced state of civilized society is chiefly occasioned by the inequality of their possessions of wealth or property; and inequality of property is again chiefly occasioned by the constant and unavoidable operation of two great causes; – first, *by the difference of application or industry, and*

142

of parsimony or saving, between one person and another; and, secondly, *by the devolution of fortunes upon individuals;* or, in other words, *by the inheritance of the savings of persons deceased in all time past falling to particular individuals or families, and not to others* . . .

Nor is it possible to conceive any thing more just, or more reasonable and unchallengeable, than this inequality; or any right more sacred to things external, than that which arises in the manner just described, to the accumulations of capital by whomsoever they have been made, and to whomsoever they have been fairly or voluntarily bequeathed.

Yet it has been said by no less eminent a person than Mr. Godwin, that 'it is a gross imposition that men are accustomed to put upon themselves, when they talk of the property bequeathed to them by their ancestors. The property is produced by the daily labour of men who are now in existence. All their ancestors bequeathed to them was a mouldy patent, which they show as a title to extort from their neighbours what the labour of those neighbours have produced.'

It has been one of the chief objects of this work to demonstrate the fallacy of the argument contained in the above passage. . . (Read, [1829] 1976, pp. 120–2)

Such must be the fate of the labourer in every country where disorder prevails, and life and property are insecure. Give him arms and discipline, and he may acquire power and imagine himself free, for he will cease to obey the laws, but be ruled by some demagogue with a rod of iron. His imaginary freedom will consist in being governed by laws hastily framed by a dishonest and ignorant legislature, and administered by a corrupt and passionate tribunal with remorseless severity. But even if the habits which lead a demagogue to success were such as naturally produced calm reflection, freedom from passion, integrity, and wisdom, still, while anarchy and turbulence prevail, immutable necessity ordains that the labourer shall suffer this part of the hard condition of the slave. He must encounter severe toil, and receive scanty wages. From this state of degradation and slavery, order and obedience can alone relieve him . . . (Longfield, [1834] 1971, p. 242)

The attack on the labor theory of value

It was clearly recognized by the anti-classical economists that the fundamental economic basis to socialist propaganda rested on the labor theory of value. If value was the result of labor expended, then it seemed to follow that labor was entitled to the full measure of the output generated. Hence a significant part of the educational program begun during the period surrounded the dissuading of the working class from accepting the doctrines taught by Hodgskin and other pro-working class economists, a doctrine that finds its roots in the authority of Smith and Ricardo. In response to a long quote from Hodgskin, Read demonstrates that the basis for such a mistaken notion is found in Smith:

Dr. Smith himself was not . . . wholly free from error in his treatment of the question between the labourers and capitalists. He does not indeed treat that question directly, but, speaking of 'the circumstances of the lower ranks of the people,' – of 'servants, labourers, and workmen of different kinds,' – he says incidentally, 'it is but equity that they who feed, clothe, and lodge the whole body of the people should have such a share of the produce of their own labour as to be themselves tolerably well fed, clothed, and lodged'; meaning evidently, from the context, that the labourers alone feed, clothe, and lodge 'the whole body of the people,' – an error which, though incidental . . . is not the less likely, if unnoticed, to be attended with bad effects, and is by far the most important oversight that is to be discovered in the *Wealth of Nations*. For this position would seem to imply that capital is of no use, and affords no assistance in the work of feeding, clothing, and lodging the people – a position which, if put in this shape, would at once have shown the importance of the fallacy which lurked in that apparently harmless sentence . . . And yet to admit these obvious truths is wholly to give up the portentous doctrine that the labourers alone feed, clothe, and lodge the whole body of the people, and at once to destroy the inference which must otherwise have been founded upon it, to the prejudice of the capitalists. To talk of equity as demanding that the labourers should receive a *'share* of the produce of their own labour' will never be satisfactory; why should they not receive the whole of its produce? The error lies in supposing that labour produces all, – that the whole of the produce of labour and capital arises from the exertions of the labourers, independently of the capital with which they work, and are assisted. (Read, [1829] 1976, pp. xxxii–xxxiii)

The same theme is taken up by Longfield and Scrope, among others.

. . . I felt it necessary to occupy some of your time in endeavouring to prove that labour, although frequently a useful and convenient measure of value, is not on that account to be considered the only real one. It is a convenient measure because it admits of being directly compared with all important commodities, but the arguments employed to prove it the only real measure are I think entirely inconsistent with every notion that we are accustomed to entertain of the meaning of the term value . . . Labour therefore is not a 'real,' in the sense of being an invariable, measure of value. Indeed it is utterly impossible that there can exist any invariable measure of value as long as the prices of different commodities vary in relation to each other. (Longfield, [1834] 1971, pp. 42–4)

Smith and his followers have insisted much on everything having a *real* value, which they define to consist of the quantity of *labour* required to produce it; and they accordingly call labour the natural standard or measure of value. But it is indispensable for a standard measure to be something both definite in its nature, and as nearly as possible invariable itself in value . . .

But what can be more vague and indefinite in its meaning, or more variable in its value, than labour? . . .

145

It has, however, been urged by these writers that the exchangeable value of anything will always depend on the quantity of labour necessary to procure or produce it, and on this ground it is proposed as the best measure of the value which it composes. One would have supposed that the commonest facts might have sufficed to prevent the promulgation of so false a position . . .

The fact is, that all these attempts to identify value with labour, or to distinguish *real* from relative value, are founded in a gross misconception of the nature of value, which, as we have said above, like length, weight, bulk, or any other quality susceptible of measurement, has essentially a relative only, not a positive meaning. (Scrope, [1833] 1969, pp. 166–7)

None of these economists treated the labor theory fairly, but falsified the position put forward by Smith and others, in particular with regard to their position on productive equipment. No major labor theorist ever argued that such 'capital' was useless, or that it did not add to the efficiency of the worker. What they did argue was that such equipment was the result of past labor. This, of course, leads to the logical conclusion that those who actually produce and have produced in the past (as an historical class) *do* have a claim to the results of their efforts, and it points to the weakness of mere property rights as a source of income. Hence the relation between the labor theory of value and socialism (or communism) developed into an issue precisely during the period when prevailing propertied institutions were increasingly seen as a drag on progress and as the underlying cause of poverty.

It should be noted that this connection continued to be a major area of contention throughout the nineteenth century (even after the political contests of the period in question had been largely forgotten). For example, H. S. Foxwell refused to deliver a presidential address to the Royal Economic Society on Ricardo's theory because he feared that his attack on that great economist would have been too violent, given Ricardo's view of the conflict of class interests based on a labor theory of value (Keynes, 1936, p. 592).[6]

The substitution of an alternative theory of value and distribution

Given the common, concerted attack on the labor theory of value and the theory of distribution that flows from it, it was necessary to substitute an alternative point of view. During this period the utility theory of value increasingly became the dominant theory of value, but it was not the only position adhered to. We also observe the labor cost, cost of production, and supply–demand approaches. In all cases, though, the alternative theory emphasized a subjectivist approach to valuation. Also, and in keeping with this, all the distribution schemes erected stressed the right of propertied income as reflective of capital's and land's contribution of production – a productivity approach.

> The term value . . . does not express a quality inherent in a commodity. It expresses . . . a feeling of the mind . . . (Lloyd, [1833] 1968, p. 31)

> What we have advanced on the elements of value makes it evident that the value (or selling price) of an article at any time and place is determined by the proportion of the demand to the supply at that time and place. (Scrope, [1833] 1969, p. 185)

> Of the three qualities which render any thing an article of Wealth, or, in other words, give it Value, the most striking is the power, direct or indirect, of producing pleasure, including under that term gratification of every kind, or of preventing pain, including under that term every species of discomfort . . . *utility* . . . being generally used to express the quality of preventing pain or of indirectly producing pleasure, as a means . . .
> The causes which determine the reciprocal values of commodities, or, in other words, which determine that a given quantity of one shall exchange for a given quantity of another, must be divided into two sets: those which occasion the one to be limited in supply and useful . . . and those which occasion those attributes to belong to the other. In ordinary language, the *force* of the causes which

give utility to a commodity is generally indicated by the word *Demand*; and the weakness of the obstacles which limit the quantity of a commodity by the word *Supply*.

Thus the common statement that commodities exchange in proportion to the force or weakness of the causes which give utility to them respectively and to the weakness or force of the obstacles by which they are respectively limited in supply. (Senior, [1836] 1965, pp. 6, 14)

Although he is a bit outside our time-spectrum, the work of Richard Jennings should be mentioned. In his *Natural Elements of Political Economy* [1855], Jennings attempted a complete general theory of economic relations based purely on subjectivist psychological notions. That this effort had its antecedents in the post-Ricardian attempts to undermine the labor theory of value cannot be doubted.

In regard to distribution, two main themes stand out in the arguments of the period: that property is deserving of a return based upon its contribution to output, and that wages are determined by forces akin to those of natural law and workers, therefore, are in some sense deserving of what they get and can do nothing of substance to alter their situation. Quite obviously, this was in response to socialist propaganda, which argued that the working class should and could obtain a larger share of total output, if not lay claim to the whole of production.

In whatever proportions the several classes of labourers, capitalists, and landowners contribute their quota to the production of wealth, in that proportion have they clearly an equitable title to share in the wealth produced. (Scrope, [1833] 1969, p. 227)

Having given a general outline of the three great classes among whom all that is produced is distributed, and of the general laws which regulate the comparative values of different products, we now proceed to consider the general laws which regulate the proportions in which Landlords, Capitalists, and Labourers share in the general distribution, or in other words, which regulate the proportions which Rent, Profit, and Wages bear to one another . . .

We have followed the established nomenclature which divides society into Landlords, Capitalists, and Labourers; and revenue into Rent, Wages, and Profit. And we have defined Rent to be *the revenue spontaneously offered by nature or accident*; Wages, *the reward of labour*; and Profit, *that of abstinence*. (Senior, [1836] 1965, p. 128)

My principal object, however, has been to draw attention to the elementary proposition, that *the rate of wages depends on the extent of the fund for the maintenance of labourers, compared with the number of labourers to be maintained* . . . It must also follow that the rate of wages can be raised, or, what is nearly the same, the condition of the labouring classes improved, only by either increasing the fund for their maintenance, or diminishing the number to be maintained. (Senior, [1831] 1966, pp. iii–iv)

The position that all classes were productive of value and, therefore, were deserving of income was pushed to the extreme in the defense of the most reactionary and useless class of the period, the landlords.

In general, however, it may be affirmed, that most men of all ranks and classes are engaged during the greater part of their lives in useful labour of some sort or other, and either do something which contributes to production directly, or assist in the administration of public affairs – of justice and government; which last-mentioned occupation is indeed peculiarly the province of this third class of persons, a great proportion of whom is always found employed in this way . . . The landlords are indeed the natural nobles and magistrates of the country; and all offices of a public nature, as well as the cultivation of the arts and sciences, though free to all in a free country, belong in a more especial manner to the class of capitalists who can command the leisure and other means so conducive, and even, generally speaking, indispensable to the successful or advantageous prosecution of such avocations. Nor are those to be condemned who follow none of these pursuits.

149

They injure no one who, possessing the means, seek only in an innocent manner to attain happiness; and if they arrive at their object without any other particular employments, they will by no means be unprofitable members of the community. They will not have lived in vain. Nay, as it is human happiness which is the great end and aim of all our earthly labours, and as the happiness of individuals, it follows as a necessary consequence, that such members or persons as arrive at that end by the shortest road are, as members of the community simply taken, the most profitable of all. (Read, [1829] 1976, pp. 45–6)

There is a very evident advantage accruing to society from the existence of an independent and wealthy class of persons, disengaged from the necessity of constant personal attention to their affairs, and therefore enabled to give up their time gratuitously to literary and scientific studies, of the performance of public, but unpaid duties. It is from this class that the ranks of our legislature and magistracy, our authors and men of science, must be recruited. And it is moreover, from the elevation of mind and manners, the refinement and intellectual polish which leisure and easy circumstances enable this class to attain, that much benefit descends to all the other classes, in the example afforded them of a higher taste for the comforts and decencies of life, and a higher standard of enjoyment than the gratification of mere animal wants. (Scrope, [1833] 1969, p. 179)

Clearly, in the interests of class harmony, even the struggle against the landlords had to be overridden. This class, in contradistinction to the position set forward by Smith and Ricardo, had to be elevated to an exalted status.

The defense of property

Bound up with the rejection of the labor theory of value and the various theories of distribution was the overt defense of property rights, which had been coming under increasing attack during the period.[7] While private property had always needed a rationale, the situation in the post-industrial revolution period was quite different from that in the capitalist revolutionary epoch.

Earlier, given the progressive nature of the capitalist economic organization, the pro-property argument was largely in accord with the facts of society: because capitalist property arrangements were conducive of rapid economic progress, property could be defended as beneficial to the community as a whole. Now, however, the situation had changed. Rather than promoting the social good, property was seen as a drag on progress and the basis of social injustice. Given the facts of the post-Napoleonic depressions and the apparent growth in poverty, such a position not only had merit (at least superficially), but was increasingly accepted by the underlying population as explanatory of its social ills. The defense of property relations erected during the period was, in distinction to that of the revolutionary period, not in accord with the actualities of the economic organization of society of the time, and attempted to cover over the changes that had taken place since the early, petty forms of capitalist society.

This defense was based largely on a Lockean view of property rights developed during the revolutionary stage of capitalist development – specifically, the proposition that individuals had a legitimate claim to property to the extent that the property could be worked by the labor of the property-holder (Locke, [1690] 1924, pp. 129–41). Locke and others developed a theory of property rights applicable to the petty mode of production in which small producers worked upon their own means of production using primarily their own labor power. Now, however, we observe the same argument applied to a full-fledged capitalist society in which collectivized property arrangements had superseded the individualized relations of the previous century. The hiring of propertyless workers on a large scale invalidated the older, Lockean, theory and justification. Where it was acknowledged that modern property arrangements no longer fit the Lockean model, adjustments to that model were developed that reached the same conclusions regarding the social benefits of property. With Scrope, for example, the argument was tendered that property would accumulate through the normal exchange relations: those who had sufficient income would buy more property from those willing to sell it. Since this must necessarily be a mutually advantageous arrangement, social welfare was thus increased.

Moreover, in the post-industrial revolution period, the argument was developed that property was an arrangement that both put an end to social conflict and was the primary vehicle through which economic development was fostered. In other words, property rights generated the directly opposite results of those claimed by Owens, Hodgkins and others.

The second great natural right, coequal perhaps with that of personal freedom, is *the equal right of all mankind to the common bounties of the Creator* . . . The earth, the air, the waters, and all their produce, must be common property; of which each individual has a right to make such use as shall not prejudice the rest of mankind in a greater degree than it benefits himself . . . Whatever limitation, therefore, is established to the right of man to use or consume any natural productions, can be justified . . . only by proof that such limitation is necessary for the general welfare . . .

In the same way as it is clearly perceivable by reason that the right of individuals to personal freedom of action must be limited by regard for the general good, so is it with respect to their right to the use of the desirable productions of nature. Without such limitation practically enforced, there must arise perpetual strife between individuals anxious to use the same thing, the same fruit or wild animal, for instance; and the will of the stronger prevailing, the equal rights of the weaker party would be overthrown. The continual recurrence of such contests must be completely destructive of the general happiness; and, therefore, for limiting and determining the right of individuals to the *sole* use or consumption of natural products: One simple rule of this sort appears to have been universally adopted by every fraction of the human family, in every quarter of the globe, and from the first traces we possess of their history. And it is this; that what a man obtains from nature *by his own exertions* becomes *his property*. (Scrope, [1833] 1969, pp. 16–17)

Wherever wealth increases to any great degree, it must necessarily be accumulated into masses or capitals of considerable magnitude in the hands of individuals; and where wealth of other descriptions is possessed in large quantities or capitals, distinct from the land, there the land must be possessed in large quantities or capitals also, because there will always be found the means or ability to purchase it in large quantites . . .

It has, however, been said, that God gave the earth in common to mankind, and that 'the land is the people's farm,' which ought to be enjoyed as common property, and as the natural and equal inheritance of all; but it is to be remembered, that in every country where the land is fully appropriated, it will always be found that it has been improved and ameliorated by human labour and capital . . . Those persons by whose *capital*, or by whose *labour* and *saving* they have been produced, or the persons to whom they have consigned their rights, must surely be allowed to have a preferable claim. Were this indeed not conceded, none of those properties, nor any others of the kind, would ever be produced at all . . .

Those individuals by whose labour and saving, or capital, wealth is first produced and accumulated upon the land, must be allowed the exclusive right to it, else they would never accumulate such wealth; and they must also be allowed the right to sell, bequeath, or bestow it on whom they please. It is only the bare uncultivated earth, where it is unappropriated and unimproved by labour, to which an equal and common right can be pretended . . . (Read, [1829] 1976, pp. 104–7)

The harmony of interests doctrine

The general position put forward during the period regarding the nature of society did not ignore classes altogether (as did the later neoclassicists), but held that there was harmony among the classes and individuals. This, of course was in direct contradiction to the argument set forth in Ricardo, and usually explicitly set forth in Smith[8] and the other labor theoreticians of the period. Also, the harmony of interests thesis responded to the radical theoreticians and to the objective facts of capitalist society.

> In the natural state of the relation between the capitalist and the labourer, when the amount of wages to be paid, and of work to be done, are the subjects of a free and open bargain . . . The connexion between him and his master has the kindliness of a voluntary association, in which each party is conscious of benefit, and each feels that his own welfare depends, to a certain extent, on the welfare of the other . . . (Senior, [1831] 1966, pp. ix–x)

> This inquiry will, I think show that the great body of the present owners of property have no reason to dread the discussion of such questions; for that their real interests are not opposed to, but, on the contrary, are identified with those of society at large; and that they may, therefore, safely, and without apprehension, meet their adversaries on the fair field of argument, and rest their cause on the firm foundation of the first principles of natural justice. (Scrope, [1833] 1969, p. 32)

> And by wise provision of nature, the more indispensable any commodity is to human subsistence of happiness, the more strict and absolute is the limit within which our consumption of it is confined . . . By this provision the riches of the wealthy are prevented from interfering with the maintenance of the poor. The richest individual, whatever quantity of corn or other food he may possess or be able to purchase, is not able to consume more than the poor man . . .
> And the nature and reason of man leading him to exchanges, he will dispose of that surplus which he cannot use himself to some one who in exchange for it can give him something that can contribute to his enjoyment . . .
> Thus in an exchange there must be two persons and at least two things concerned; that portion of any commodity which any one possesses and does not intend to consume is called the supply; the disposition to give something in

exchange for it may be called the demand. An exchange of equivalents is advantageous to both parties . . . At first sight it would appear, and many reasonings have proceeded upon the supposition, that the three principal classes have interests directly adverse to each other . . . But the fact is not so. The parties to every contract have, just at the time of making it, an interest opposed to each other, each being desirous to get as much, and to give as little, as he can. But the competition of others prevents this adverse interest from operating to the detriment of either, and previous to the contract, all parties have a common interest that the articles which are the subject of the exchange should be produced in the best and cheapest manner. (Longfield, [1834] 1971, pp. 44–5, 223)

While there were a number of crude arguments relating to harmony of interests during the period,[9] the more significant economists established their premise in one of the facts of capitalist society – exchange. Focusing on the exchange relation, which follows from the utility theory of value, the argument could be pressed that any exchange implies a voluntary, equal relationship, or the exchange simply would not occur. Hence, as goods are exchanged, it follows that all parties to the exchange process must have a commonality of interests. Of course, the fundamental exchange relationship is between workers and owners of capital, and this cannot be a free and equal exchange given that workers must be propertyless by definition – a fact that connotes coercion in the sale of their labor power. For the anti-classicists, this particular, basic exchange relationship was either ignored or, in the case of Senior, treated as merely the same as the exchange of finished commodities.

Quite obviously, the economists could not totally ignore the class conflict that was raging about them and which prompted their arguments in the first place. At this historical juncture, the conflict was too open, too widespread and too significant to be dispensed with merely by ignoring it. However, given the supposed harmony that should prevail, how then to explain the problem? The solution was that of blaming ignorance, fraud, corruption and malcontents for the prevailing conflict.

> Ignorance, rather than fraud, we believe to be the main root of the evil . . . It is to the ignorance then of both governors and governed, as to the just direction of their collective resources, and the true principles of economical policy; to the blundering stupidity of power, rather than to its knavery and wickedness, that we must trace the defective arrangements, and consequently imperfect operation of the mechanism of most existing societies. (Scrope, [1833] 1969, pp. xiv–xv)

The object of conflict, then, becomes not society itself but an outside force that imposes itself upon society. If the problem is ignorance, then correction can be accomplished through education; if it is fraud, corruption, and malcontents, the issue can be dealt with squarely by relieving society of those who practice such evils. In any case, the root cause of social distress is not society but a non-social force that creates havoc in an otherwise smoothly functioning, harmonious arrangement. This is the so-called Devil's thesis, which places the focal point of analysis on external rather than internal forces and which serves, therefore, to shift attention away from an examination of those internal forces that, potentially at least, could be the source of the social ill.

The subjectivist approach

A most important aspect of the fundamental change in economic analysis during the period was the substitution of a subjectivist approach for the objective theory of the classicists which rested on the labor theory of value. For the proto-neoclassicists, the basis of analysis was found not in the empirical examination of society, but in various principles established by the theoretician himself. That is, the starting point was not in the underlying production relations, but in mental constructs which then determined the course of analysis to be followed. The most significant theoretician in this regard was Richard Jennings, who set forward a totally psychological theory of economic behavior in his *Natural Elements of Political Economy*. However, all of the major theorists of the period had a subjectivist foundation for their analyses.

> If Economists had been aware that the Science depends more on reasoning than on observation, and that its principal difficulty consists not in the ascertainment of its facts, but in the use of its terms, we cannot doubt that their principal efforts would have been directed to the selection and consistent use of an accurate nomenclature. (Senior, [1836] 1965, p. 5)

> The principles of Political Economy must obviously be deduced from axioms relative to the conduct and feelings of mankind under particular circumstances, framed upon general and extensive observation. But neither the feelings nor the conduct of a being like man, endowed with mental volition, and infinitely varying degrees of sensibility, can with anything like truth, be assumed as uniform and constant under the same circumstances. Hence the highest degree of certainty which can belong to the principles of Political Economy will amount only to moral probability, and must fall short of the accuracy that characterizes the laws of the physical sciences. (Scrope, [1833] 1969, p. 41)

> I trust Gentlemen, that you will attend to the difference between a proof founded on an abstraction, and one founded upon a supposition. The former cannot but lead to truth, although its application may be a matter of some difficulty; the latter may lead to truth or falsehood, according as the supposition upon which it is founded is or is not conformable to the reality of things. The doctrines respecting rent, to which I called your attention this Term, are founded on a supposition which I attempted to shew was verified by experience. The theory of profits which I attempted to prove on Tuesday, is founded partly upon facts lying within the knowledge of all, and partly upon abstract reasoning. The theory of wages which I explained today, is founded upon mere abstract reasoning, and

cannot be false in any time or country. (Longfield, [1834] 1971, p. 220)

The theory synthesized

During the post-Ricardian, post-industrial-revolution period, we observe the formation of what was to become the neoclassical theory. Moreover, during this period this perspective became dominant: Ricardo was the last respectable classical, labor-theory-of-value economist. It is also observable that the prevalent theory was the opposite of that of the classical model and the opposite of that required by scientific criteria. For Marx, this was the period in which 'vulgar' economics takes the front seat, caused by the social development of capitalism itself and the attendant growth in scientific theory:

> The position is quite different as regards *vulgar political economy*, which only becomes widespread when political economy itself has, as a result of its analysis, undermined and impaired its own premises, and consequently the opposition to political economy has come into being in more or less economic, utopian, critical and revolutionary forms. For the development of political economy and of the opposition to which it gives rise keeps pace with the *real* development of the social contradictions and class conflicts inherent in capitalist production. Only when political economy has reached a certain stage of development and has assumed well-established forms – that is, after Adam Smith – does the separation of the element whose notion of the phenomena consists of a mere reflection of them take place, i.e., its vulgar element becomes a special aspect of political economy. Thus, *Say* separates the vulgar notions occurring in *Adam Smith's* work and puts them forward in a distinct crystallized form. *Ricardo* and the further advance of political economy caused by him provide new nourishment for the vulgar economist (who does not produce anything himself): the more economic theory is perfected, that is, the deeper it

penetrates its subject-matter and the more it develops as a contradictory system, the more is it confronted by its own, increasingly independent, vulgar element, enriched with material which it dresses up in its own way until finally it finds its most apt expression in academically syncretic and unprincipled eclectic compilations.

To the degree that economic analysis becomes more profound it not only describes contradictions, but it is confronted by its own contradiction simultaneously with the development of the actual contradictions in the economic life of society. Accordingly, vulgar political economy deliberately becomes increasingly *apologetic* and makes strenuous attempts to talk out of existence the ideas which contain the contradictions. (Marx, [1905–10] 1971b, p. 501)

Marx's judgment is partially confirmed by Hayek almost a century later. In *The Counter-Revolution of Science* (Hayek, 1955), the orthodox Austrian specifically argues that, for economics as a social science to be rational, it must adopt the opposite perspective and method of natural science: that is, it must be subjectivist, individualist, ahistorical and accidental ('purposiveless').

The dominant theory propounded during the post-industrial-revolution period was all of a piece. While the general argument was not as well consolidated as it became in the Imperialist stage (see below, Chapter 6), it displayed an internal consistency reflective of a general point of view.

The starting point of this perspective was the theory of value. Based on utility, the argument focuses on exchange relationships as primary, thus ignoring, or relegating to secondary status, the underlying production relations. This, then, presents a superficial picture of the economic order and studiously omits discussion and analysis of the fundamental relationship in capitalist society – that of the capitalist and working classes. By concentrating on exchange (the consumptionist or mercantilist point of view) and ignoring the social relations of production, the proto-neoclassicists are able to present a view of society which is apparently egalitarian: since the exchange of goods is freely entered into – one can choose to buy or sell without coercion – it appears that such relations are based on equality between the buyer and seller. And so they are, in any individualist sense. However, the basic exchange relationship is that of the capitalist and worker where, given the existence of property rights, a propertyless class is coerced into selling labor power to a propertied class. The price at which this labor power is sold is immaterial: whether it is high or low does not alter the basic underlying factor of coercion, of *inequality*.

From their position on equality in the exchange relationship, economists can then construct a theory of distribution based on a non-exploitative argument. And to be consistent, such a theory must contain an argument in which the incomes of the propertied classes are in some sense deserved. Were this not the case, the egalitarian basis of the purchase of commodities would be suspect, given that the income used for said purchases would have been somehow generated on an inegalitarian base. This leads to the conclusion (which is in fact an assumed starting point) that capitalist society is harmonious.

If there is equality in both distribution and exchange, then all segments of society have the same objective interests in both the total output generated and the manner in which that income is distributed. Moreover, given the subjectivist, axiomatic foundations of the argument, all societies are seen as essentially the same. Given that individuals in all societies consume, and obviously consume on the basis of utility (or goods simply would not be produced for consumption), then all societies display the same general characteristics. All societies are the same; they are all similar to the caricature of capitalism erected by the economists of the period. This, then means that the nature of capitalist society does not have to be examined at all: it is merely a universal, natural system.

All of this leads to a defense of the established order. If society is an historical constant, if its laws are universal in nature and scope, then it is a social order that displays constancy. Its laws are not socially determined but naturally ordered. And, if this is the case, society itself cannot be modified to change those laws – at least, not to any significant extent. Hence what exists is natural, and nothing can be done to ameliorate the situation.

The last point to be made is the political nature of the anti-Ricardian onslaught. Schumpeter argues that:

> the antagonism to the West-Ricardian schema that all of these [proto-neoclassicists] display was primarily scientific and not political: Read's hostility to the Ricardian socialists may have set him against the Ricardian theory of value, but for the rest I cannot find *motivating* political antagonisms between these writers and the Ricardians. (Schumpeter, 1954, p. 489)

In a minor sense, Schumpeter is correct: one does not find an overt political confrontation between the dead Ricardo and the now-respectable economists. The labor theory of value can be argued without direct reference to the underlying perspective it represents, and these debates can be quite lofty and thus arid. However, enough has been brought forward to demonstrate that these economists were full of politics and conscious of the class issues of the period. The labor theory of value was directly connected to the issues of the period – not merely in the sense that it was taken up by the so-called Ricardian Socialists, but more fundamentally in that it provided a general theory which was unpleasant from the point of view of the dominant class. As a result, this theory became a focal point of politics at the highest level – that of the ongoing contest among the classes. And in this sense, no matter how dry or arcane the debate seems, it seethes with politics, and hence with conscious motivation.

On James Mill and J. R. McCulloch

In the period under review, the development of capitalism, particularly in England and France, had reached the point where the class cleavage between the capitalist and working classes became primary. In the eighteenth and early nineteenth centuries, the struggle for progress was waged primarily by the capitalists (in particular the manufacturing interests) against the landlords. Now, however, that battle was, for all practical purposes, over. An objective investigation of the social order now demanded placing oneself in the interests of either capitalists or workers. Previously, if one placed oneself in the capitalist camp, one was fighting for progress – against reaction. Now, the consolidation of the capitalist order had been achieved and it was apparent that this class itself was becoming reactionary – it wanted to stabilize the status quo rather than promote further change.

Theoretically, Ricardo represents the watershed. The labor theory of value had previously assisted capitalists in developing their society. Now, however, this objective point of view was beginning to ally itself with the working class, the antithesis of capitalism. Hence, any economist who presented a consistent labor theory of value also became a critic of the social order and a potential theorist of the destruction of that order. Those who perceived themselves as having an interest in the preservation of that order necessarily had to abandon the labor theory even though they may well have continued to place themselves in the Ricardian camp. The two most prominent theoreticians of this type were Mill and McCulloch.

Mill attempted to present the Ricardian theory as an abstract, logically consistent body of doctrine. In doing so, he 'rid' Ricardo of the contradictions that Ricardo himself had worried over for the last five years of his life. But, since these were the same contradictions presented by capitalist society itself, Mill also succeeded in ridding capitalism of its contradictions. That is, he presented capitalist society as a harmonious arrangement, much like the proto-neoclassicals of the period did.

Mill was the first to present Ricardo's theory in systematic form, even though he did it only in rather abstract outlines. What he tries to achieve is formal, logical consistency. The *disintegration* of the Ricardian school 'therefore' begins with him. With the master, what is new and significant develops vigorously amid the 'manure' of contradictions out of the contradictory phenomena. The underlying contradictions themselves testify to the richness of the living foundation from which the theory itself developed. It is different with the disciple. His raw material is no longer reality, but the new theoretical form in which the master had sublimated it.

It is in part the *theoretical disagreement of opponents of the new theory* and in part the *often paradoxical relationship of this theory to reality* which drive him to seek *to refute* his opponents and *explain away* reality. In doing so, he entangles himself in contradictions and with his attempt to solve these he demonstrates the beginning *disintegration of the theory* which he dogmatically espouses. On the one hand, Mill wants to present bourgeois production as the absolute form of production and seeks therefore to prove that its real contradictions are only apparent ones. On the other hand, [he seeks] to present the Ricardian theory as the absolute theoretical form of the mode of production and to disprove the theoretical contradictions, both the ones pointed out by others and the ones he himself cannot help seeing. (Marx, [1905–10] 1971b, pp. 84–5)

The position taken by Marx on James Mill (and on John Stuart) is that Mill was an honest but incompetent (relative to Ricardo) economist who was inundated by the anti-Ricardian environment surrounding him. With McCulloch, however, the evidence is somewhat different. While both Mill and McCulloch vulgarized Ricardo, the basis of McCulloch's bastardization is his opportunism.

Initially, McCulloch does not hold a labor standard. First, he introduces a psychological (subjectivist) 'toil and trouble' measure of labor rather than the objective labor hours of previous labor theorists. Second, his theory of value is of a relative sort in which value is determined in exchange for labor or other commodities. In this regard, then, McCulloch does not differ from the orthodox economists against whom he is ostensibly contending.

That an article may have value, it is indispensable that some expenditure of labour, or, which is the same thing, some sacrifice of toil and trouble, should be required for its acquisition, and that it should be capable of being appropriated or enjoyed by one individual or more, to the exclusion of others . . .

Exchangeable value being the power which a commodity has of exchanging for other commodities, or for labour, it follows that the exchangeable value of no single commodity can vary without occasioning a simultaneous variation in the exchangeable value of those with which it is compared. (McCulloch, [1864] 1965, pp. 233, 235)

More important than this, however, is McCulloch's adamant defense of property rights and his attempt to demonstrate a commonality of interests within the framework of a capitalist social order. His reaction to Ricardo's chapter on machinery is indicative of his overriding concern with established property relations:

Before you began to describe to your readers the disadvantages attending the diminution of gross produce by the introduction of machinery, it would have been well had you inquired whether in point of fact such diminution ever did actually take place, or whether it was at all likely that it could take place – Your argument is to be sure hypothetical; but the hypothesis will be thrown aside, and all those who raise a yell against the extension of machinery, and ascribe to it that misery which is a mere necessary consequence of the oppressiveness of taxation, and of the restraints on commerce will fortify themselves by your authority! If your reasoning . . . be well founded, the laws against the Luddites are a disgrace to the Statute book . . . (McCulloch to Ricardo, June 5, 1821; in Ricardo, 1952a, pp. 384–5)

Moreover, in his *Principles*, McCulloch sets forth a defense of private property no different in substance from that of the proto-neoclassicists ([1864] 1965, pp. 25–36).

Ricardo himself criticized McCulloch for his position on the supposed harmony of interests doctrine under capitalist society:

'The interests of individuals is never opposed to the interests of the public' [McCulloch].

In this I do not agree. In the case of machinery the interests of master and workmen are frequently opposed. Are the interest of landlords and those of the public always the same? I am sure you will not say so. (Ricardo to McCulloch, May 7, 1822; in Ricardo, 1952b, p. 194)[10]

Thus, McCulloch, while parading under somewhat Ricardian banners, repudiates the substance of the classical theory and, in reality, appears as an orthodox economist in his general point of view. As long as it was opportune to hold Ricardian positions, McCulloch did so. When these positions became troublesome, indeed dangerous, he modified his view. At the same time, since he was identified as a Ricardian discipline, he could not openly repudiate that honest investigator.

McCulloch is simply a man who wanted to turn Ricardian economics to his own advantage – an aim in which he succeeded in a most remarkable degree . . . Since McCulloch first obtained a professorial chair in London on account of Ricardian economics, in the beginning he had to come forward as a Ricardian and especially to participate in the struggle against the landlords. As soon as he had obtained a foothold and climbed to a position on Ricardo's shoulders, his main effort was directed to expounding political economy, especially Ricardian economics, within the framework of Whiggism and to eliminate all conclusions which were distasteful to the Whigs. (Marx, [1905–10] 1971b, pt IIIb, pp. 171–2)

Conclusion

The post-Ricardian, post-industrial-revolution period coincided with Bernal's 'Heyday Stage' (1830–70), in which natural science made the advances that laid the foundations for modern science. It was during this stage that the physical sciences reached something of a zenith under capitalist production relations. In a sense, this was true in social science as well, primarily through the work of Marx, Engels and

Morgan, among others. However, the economic content of this achievement was now relegated to a minority, underground position. Essentially, in the post-Ricardian period, respectable economics ceased being scientific, adopting an increasingly subjectivist, individualist perspective.

This should not be surprising. The social sciences are always more sensitive to the political movement of society itself than are the natural sciences. The physical sciences are potentially threatening to the maintenance of existing social relations but, because the scope of these investigations is nature rather than society, any causal relationships between theories of natural science and society are indirect and (usually) obscure. This is obviously not the situation regarding the social sciences.

In addition, the development of industry itself promoted growth in the physical sciences (in particular, physics and chemistry), both by supplying to science the necessary tools through which new developments could be undertaken, and by making further demands on scientists in these areas. With the development of modern industry, however, came the organized working class, which now posed the major threat to the continuation of capitalist society. Hence, while science continued to be promoted in the physical realm, those who studied society recoiled from investigating objective conditions within society and increasingly adopted a position of apologia.

It should be noted, though, that, while the social sciences are understandably more prone to directly reflecting actual conditions within society, when a major theoretical discovery in the realm of nature has an observed relationship to existing social relations, that advance is subject to the same considerations outlined in regard to economics. The attack on and vulgarization of Darwin's discoveries indicates the significance of this position.

In general, the dominant economic theory propounded during the period was the opposite of that which the reality of capitalist society offered for analysis and which science demands: class harmony as opposed to conflict, a subjective rather than objective perspective. The foundations of this anti-scientific trend was the subjectivist theory of value, which was necessarily implemented as the focal point in the attack on the labor theory of value. In addition to eventually forming the basis for the general theory itself, this approach allowed the defense of existing property relations under the heading of natural, eternal, universal law.

It is noted that the eighteenth-century classicists defended property in addition to setting forth a natural law approach to the analysis of society. However, a fundamental difference exists between those who argued from the objective point of view and the subjectivists. In the Revolutionary and Transitional States, the thrust of the argument of the pro-capitalist economists was against a religious apologia for feudal society and the establishment of criteria by which society could be judged rational or irrational. Thus, a function served by the older approach was to free thought of religious encumbrances (at least to an extent) and to form a basis for scientific judgment. That is, the natural law basis was scientific in its orientation. For the proto-neoclassicists, the opposite function was served: to befuddle intellectual inquiry in the interests of preserving the social relations then extant. The former theoreticians were progressive and scientific, the latter conservative and unscientific.

The fundamental issue was society itself. In the eighteenth century, capitalism was indeed progressive, eliminating or reducing the social constraints established by feudal society. In the nineteenth century, faced with the threat of an organized working class and having, for the most part, secured its victory over its feudal opposition, the capitalist class was interested in preserving its social place; and this meant preserving the social relations that allowed it to do so. Hence, in undergoing its transition from a small- to a large-propertied class, and thereby laying the basis for its regressive features, the capitalists changed from a progressive, liberating force to one of conservatism. The dominant ideology changed along with the capitalists.

An idea or act may be progressive or reactionary, depending upon the social circumstances in which it is fostered. At one historical juncture, translating the Bible into a common language was a revolutionary, liberating act because it allowed the lower classes to form their own opinion of scriptural doctrine independent of the feudal, clerical officials. Quite obviously, the common opinion often differed markedly from that of the officials. In the present period, such an effort to popularize the Bible could no longer serve a progressive purpose, but could only assist in preserving modern religious doctrine.

In fact, one observes an interesting feature of the universalist, natural law argument of the proto-neoclassicists: contrary to the structure of the classicists, the theory merges with and supports the dogma of religion. Whately's admonition that the function of economists was to seek laws in conformity with Divine Will is evidence of this point, but the most complete theory in this context was set forth by Bastiat.

The most complete, systematic argument against science was set out not in England, but in France. There is good social reason for this. With the advent of the French Revolution, capitalist relations, which had been developing for the past several centuries, burst forth in hothouse fashion. But, because French capitalism came to dominance at a more advanced stage than it did in England, it also contained its antithetical social system – socialism – to a higher degree. That is, the working class in France was more developed in the Revolutionary Stage than that of England at a comparable time.

Moreover, the criticism of society, begun by the rationalists, carried over into the capitalist epoch and turned against the capitalists themselves. Now, however, this criticism took the form of socialist criticism (no matter how weak or theoretically unsound) of Sismondi, Proudhon and Fourier. The response to this was a political economy, the Say–Bastiat School, which spoke directly to the class conflict openly displayed in France, and of which Bastiat was 'the most superficial and therefore the most adequate representative of the apologetics of vulgar economy' (Marx, [1869] 1906, p. 20).

In France the appearance of capitalism is marked at once by a strong critical current which has the recent memory of the Revolution to feed on. The protectionism of the revolution were such powerful currents that economic liberalism had at once to be more intransigent and less

168

realistic than it had been in its native country. (Roll, 1956, p. 302)

Bastiat, more than any other representative of the period, presents the general theoretical position which would eventually become dominant, that of the shallow (superficial) emphasis on surface phenomena where those phenomena are seen as permanent fixtures of the social organism. Concentration on such superficial relationships means ignoring the underlying social relations that make capitalism a distinct social organization. That is, Bastiat does not analyze capitalism at all: he merely delivers various assertions that are held to be of universal significance.

Bastiat cannot be considered a great or original thinker. Certainly, Schumpeter's position that he was 'the most brilliant economic journalist who ever lived' (Schumpeter, 1954, p. 500) is apt. However, as a summary economist, and one who lived in revolutionary times and participated in the governance process, Bastiat shows a symmetry, a unity, that represents the best attempt of the period in consolidating the anti-Ricardian tradition.

The central point of Bastiat's theoretical system is that society displays an underlying harmony of interests, which contrasts, of course, to the position taken by the Ricardians and the Socialists:

All men's impulses, when motivated by legitimate self-interest, fall into a harmonious social pattern. This is the central idea of this work, and its importance cannot be overemphasized. (Bastiat, [1850] 1964a, p. xxi)

Moreover, this harmony is God-ordained:

For certainly, if humanity is inevitably impelled toward injustice by the laws of value, toward inequality by the laws of rent, toward poverty by the laws of population, and toward sterilization by the laws of heredity, we cannot say that God's handiwork is harmonious in the social order, as it is in the physical universe; we must instead admit, with heads bowed in grief, that He has seen fit to establish His social order on revolting and irremediable discord.

You must not believe, my young friends, that the socialists have refuted and rejected the theory that, in order to avoid offending anyone, I shall call the theory of discord. On the contrary: despite their protests, they have accepted it as true; and, for the very reason that they accept it as true, they propose to substitute coercion for freedom, an artificial social order for the natural social order, and a work of their own contrivance for the handiwork of God . . .

The central idea of this work, the harmony of men's interests, is a *simple* one. And is not simplicity the touchstone of truth? The laws governing light, sound, motion, seem to us all the more true because they are simple. Why should the same thing not be true of the law of men's interests?

It is *conciliatory*. For what can be more conciliatory than to point out the ties that bind together industries, classes, nations, and even doctrines?

It is *reassuring*, since it exposes what is false in those systems that would have us believe that evil must spread and increase.

It is *religious*, for it tells us that it is not only the celestial but also the social mechanism that reveals the wisdom and declares the glory of God . . . (Bastiat, [1850] 1964a, pp. xxviii–ix)

Bastiat's argument is based on an individualistic view of society in which each entity is a free agent ([1850] 1964a, pp. xxx, 45) and comes together with other agents for the purpose of exchange. For Bastiat,

Exchange *is* political economy. It is society itself, for it is impossible to conceive of society without exchange, or exchange without society. (Bastiat, [1850] 1964a, p. 59)

And the foundation of exchange, in which is the basis of society and the harmony of interests doctrine both naturally and divinely ordered, is utility ([1850] 1964a, pp. 26–7, 221).

Bastiat clearly recognizes the political significance of this theory of value.

> From the viewpoint of political economy society is exchange. The primary element of exchange is the notion of value, and consequently the connotations that we give to this word, whether true or erroneous, lead us to truth or error in all our social thinking, (Bastiat, [1850] 1964a, p. 100)

From this general theoretical point of view, Bastiat goes on to attack socialism ([1848–50] 1964b, passim), defend property and the propertied classes ([1850] 1964a, pp. 154-283; [1848–50] 1964b, pp. 97-115), and generally defend the prevailing order of things. In Bastiat, to repeat, one finds the most general, systematic account of what was to become the neoclassical theory, theory for which the basis was laid in the post-Ricardian period but which did not become consolidated until the 1870–1900 period, Bernal's Imperialist Stage.

Notes: Chapter 5

1 T. Hodgskin, *Labour Defended Against the Claims of Capital* [1825]; *Popular Political Economy* [1827]: W. Thompson, *An Inquiry into the Principles of the Distribution of Wealth* . . . [1824]; *Labour Rewarded, The Claims of Labour and Capital Conciliated* [1827].

2 In his thorough and illuminating study of the popularizers of this period, Noel Thompson argues that the principal theoretical weakness of the so-called 'Ricardian Socialists' (who were neither Ricardian nor Socialists) was that of basing their argument on exchange rather than production. This accounted for inconsistencies and contradiction which, in the final analysis, brought them to a capitalist position: see Thompson, 1984, pp. 219–28.

   This point is most interesting in that it has already been argued (Chapter 4) that the essence of the anti-scientific trend is the development of theory based on consumption or exchange as the starting-point for analysis.

3 It should be emphasized at this point that social periods are never cleanly demarcated. One cannot date the 'end' of the progressive period or the 'beginning' of the conservative stage. Rather, as a result of the changes wrought by capitalist development, one epoch

is gradually replaced by another until the characteristics of the latter dominate society.

4 Understandably, not all representatives of the ruling class were as enthusiastic (or intelligent) about the need for such an educational program. For example, Giddy, a member of Parliament and President of the Royal Society, stated:

> However specious in theory the project might be, of giving education to the labouring classes of the poor, it would in effect be found to be prejudicial to their morals and happiness; it would teach them to despise their lot in life, instead of making them good servants in agriculture, and other laborious employments to which their rank in society had destined them; instead of teaching them subordination, it would render them factious and refractory, as was evident in the manufacturing countries; it would enable them to read seditious pamphlets, vicious books, and publications against Christianity; it would render them insolent to their superiors; and in a few years the result would be that the legislature would find it necessary to direct the strong arm of power towards them, and to furnish the executive magistrate with much more vigorous laws than were not in force. (cited in Kuczynski, 1967, p. 109)

5 In his notes on Malthus's *Principles*, Ricardo observes that, not only did Malthus abandon the labor theory of value, but, at one point, he adopted a utility theory: Ricardo, 1957, pp. viii, 24–5, 56–67.

6 In an attack on the position put forward here, Hollander, 1980, has argued that the textual analysis of both the 'Ricardian Socialists' and the anti-Ricardians demonstrates that the proto-neoclassicists were not motivated by their social attitudes toward the labor theory and the class conflicts surrounding them. While he does make some specific points regarding particular individuals and particular theoretical observations, I find much of his argument off the mark. Surely, enough has been evidenced to illustrate that there was a *general* awareness of the issues involved and a *general* attempt to develop a counter-argument to the labor theory and the ideological and organizational working-class threat.

7 One measure of the success of this counter-attack was the diminishing influence (and theoretical sophistication) of the anti-property forces in England as the period wore on. There are, no doubt, various reasons for this. One that must be taken into account is the effect that the early neoclassicists had on economic thinking in general which forced the absorption of their views into the general theory of the critics themselves. Thus, the anti-property ideology became increasingly diluted in its attack, having adopted much of the argument which it ostensibly was debating.

8 The reader is reminded of Smith's contradictory position on class harmony and class conflict; see Chapter 3 above.

9 Of all the crudities of the period, one candidate for the least scientific treatise is Bishop Whately. In his *Introductory Lectures on Political Economy* [1832], this religious official informed his Oxford students that the whole task of economic theory was to develop argumentation in conformity with God's rules of behavior.

10 See McCulloch's *Principles*, in which he not only argues the harmony-of-interests proposition but also demonstrates his fear of a malcontented working class: ([1864] 1965, pp. 117–41).

CHAPTER SIX

The consolidation of 1870–1900 and the rise of monopoly capital

It has been demonstrated that all the essential qualities of neoclassical theory were laid prior to 1870. Simply, there was no 'marginal revolution' in this period. Rather, what is observed during the last third of the nineteenth century is a consolidation, systemization and institutionalization, in which the subjectivist theory developed a monopoly position within economics. Obviously, dissenters remain, but these have been held to be outside the pale and, as long as capitalist society is able to maintain some measure of success, not worthy of serious consideration.[1]

Even though there was no 'revolution' in economic theory during the period, an argument is still needed to explain the transformation that did take place, for 'Why they [Jevons, Menger, Walras] were successful where their predecessors had failed is a question that has been much debated but defies definite conclusion' (Spiegel, 1971, p. 513).[2]

Neoclassical theoreticians have proven incapable of solving the riddle of the period. Basically, the argument has been reduced to that of an idea whose time had come (Blaug, 1973). There is good reason for this. Given the subjectivist (utility) base of the theory, a universalist, non-social perspective is generated. As the theory is ostensibly independent of time and place, and thus is capable of examining economic relations independent of time and place, the theory itself is independent of social foundation. It is an aspect of natural law that has always existed and has merely awaited sufficiently astute minds to comprehend it. Hence, while obviously forerunners existed and a gradual comprehension

174

of the theory accumulated, it was not until the triumvirate of the 1870s that the historically constant truth was translated into a humanly discernible ideological structure. Thus, no explanation of the period is really required. All one must do is posit the appearance of 'Great Men,' independent of society itself, who take center-stage in the study of ideas (see Chapter 1) – that is, if the neoclassical historian is consistent with neoclassical theory.

What we observe, then, is a gradual realization of truth, which reaches culmination following the accumulation of knowledge and, more important, with the appearance of intellectuals holding sufficient mental powers who are capable of comprehending the inner mysteries of the theory. Once established, the theory then takes on a life of its own, with further improvements and modifications occurring as a matter of course. The period 1870–1900, then, was nothing more than an intellectual watershed that saw the domination of the utility theory of value realized.

There *is* one basis for this domination discussed by neo-classical theorists that does touch upon society itself. Stigler has argued that the adoption of the utility theory of value was consonant with the professionalization of the discipline (Stigler, 1941, p. 10; 1973). For Stigler, this merely means that, with professionalization, the riff-raff were excluded from the discipline and the more intelligent, politically neutral, economists came to a position of dominance. As Blaug points out, though, this raises the further questions as to why economics became professionalized during the last quarter of the century, and why it should seize upon the utility theory of value (Blaug, 1973, p. 12). As will be discussed below, there is substance to Stigler's point (though not that which Stigler himself suggests), and the questions raised by Blaug can be addressed within the context of social change itself.

To explain the dominance of neoclassical ideology during the period in question, one must place this dominance within a social context. To repeat the argument contained in Chapter 1, any idea must have a social foundation and thus must be a product of society itself. To focus on 'great thinkers' is to place those intellectuals outside society and to deny their training and role within society. As well, if ideas are to have social import, they must be disseminated through society, given the social mechanisms of communication open to those ideas at the time.

In his survey of reasons offered for the dominance of the neoclassical approach, Blaug essentially dismisses any theory that places society and social change in the forefront of the explanation (Blaug, 1962, pp. 281–3). Specifically, 'the idea that modern economics has no other raison d'etre than to provide an apologetic for capitalism is too farfetched to be entertained' (p. 238).[3]

In addition to the supposed differences in political attitudes among the major theoreticians of the period (about which more later), Blaug raises the issue of differences in the level of development and structures of society in the three countries of neoclassical domination, Austria, France and England. Hence there can be no direct relationship between society and changes therein and the theory. Essentially, 'all crypto-Marxist explanations in terms of changes in the structure of production, or in the relationship between social classes, tend to strain our credulity' (Blaug, 1973, p. 3).

I disagree. I do concur, though, that a full and complete Marxist explanation has yet to systematically explain the transition in convincing terms that place this development squarely within a fundamental social context. Blaug's point is correct only in that some details have been omitted in this explanation. Let us review the major specific developments of the period that have been cited as reasons for the 'marginal revolution,' then attempt to place these within a more general development within capitalist society.

The first consideration is that of the growth in modern, large-scale unionism on a (industrialized) world scale. Coupled to this was the development of the various socialist organizations and the establishment of the International Workingmen's Association (the First International) in 1864, the express purpose of which was to facilitate the organization of workers as a class, regardless of their national origins (Foster, 1956, pp. 63–113). From a capitalist point of view, such an historic development would be perceived as a significant threat, particularly given the overtly anti-capitalist leadership of much of this working-class movement.

Second, in 1871 the Paris Commune was established. Begun as a national defense of Paris against the invading Prussians, the city, almost by default, came under the control of Parisian workers who, out of sheer necessity, established the first working-class state (Lissagary [1886] 1967; Marx and Engels, 1971). That this incident represented a watershed in the working-class movement can be witnessed by the convulsion it sent through the capitalists (who responded by organizing both French and Prussian troops to drown it in blood), and by the fact that the Commune served as the model for later Marxist analysis of the 'dictatorship of the proletariat' (Lenin, [1917] 1977).

Third, in 1873 the capitalist world entered the period known as the Great Depression. Though spasmodic recoveries occurred in the 1880s, this cyclical downturn lasted until the mid-1890s (Dobb, 1963, pp. 300–19). While there surely had been cyclical activity prior to this period, this depression, in both length and severity, represented a fundamental departure from previous bouts of such disturbances and indicated a break with the more progressive, more optimistic, past. Now, so it appeared, capitalism had entered into a period where it was doubtful that it could continue to 'deliver the goods.'

The last point is that of the publication of Marx's *Capital* in 1867. In it, the labor theory of value reached its culmination and had clearly shifted its class nature from a defense of the capitalist social order (as with Smith and the earlier labor theorists) to one of attack – a shift, as argued above, that was begun by Ricardo.

Now, none of the above points in themselves are sufficient to provide a social explanation for the neoclassical domination of this period. Initially, all the basic neoclassical theoretical argumentation had been developed prior to 1870. Even if one confines oneself to the great subjectivists of the early 1870s, we find that their theoretical positions had been established in the previous decade. Jevons, for example, argued his case in 1862 before the British Association for the Advancement of Science. This was, of course, before any of the events listed above occurred, and (along with at least the work of Menger) could not, therefore, have been influenced by the Commune, the mass labor organizations, or the Great Depression. As well, the publication of *Capital* cannot be seen as of immediate import in itself, particularly given that it came out in German and had almost no direct influence in English academic circles. Only for Menger could this have been of significance.

But a listing of potential specific causes misses the point. All the above developments were features of a fundamental transition within capitalist society itself, and it was this transition that laid the social basis for the domination of the neoclassical theory. As well, it is necessary to remind the reader that it took some time for this theory to acquire its monopoly position within the discipline. The dating of the major works of the leading ideologists is incidental; the important point is that, in the ensuing thirty years, this theoretical perspective was promoted to a position of ideological dominance (Howey, 1960; 1973). Jevons, Menger and Walras did not take economics by the proverbial ears and mold it to their liking by sheer dint of intellectual vigor. Rather, their works fell on fertile soil – although cultivation was still required.

During the period in question, capitalism completed[4] its transformation from the competitive stage of development to that of oligopoly or monopoly capitalism.[5] The social system was now regressive and, therefore, had entered its revolutionary epoch.

Under conditions of oligopoly, capitalists maximize profits by restricting output in order to raise prices to 'what the traffic will bear.' To borrow Veblen's felicitous phrase, they engage in industrial 'sabotage' or 'a conscientious withdrawl of efficiency' (Veblen, [1923] 1967, pp. 205–28). Thus, a contradiction is established between business (or property relations) and industry (production and technology), or between the production of profits and the production of use values, a contradiction that was not evident under conditions of competition (see Chapter 2). Basically, one class – capitalists – organizes to restrict the economic well-being of the community as a whole in order to advantage itself.

Given this contradiction, then, the social order as a whole demonstrates its inability to advance human welfare to the level that unfettered technology would allow. In fact, given the restriction of output, capitalists must also restrict the flow of output-maximizing technology (Lilley, 1965, pp. 180–91; Blackett, 1935). I am not arguing that under monopoly capital output or technology is not increased – that is obviously not so – but merely that the social system acts as a brake on that increase. This is evident given the facts of large and sustained levels of unemployment, unused capacity, and long and severe periods of stagnation. In addition, a great deal of output and technology is directed toward anti-social activities, principally war (Bernal, 1967, pp. 165–90).[6] Essentially, given the potential of modern technology and large-scale producing organizations, there is no technological reason for hunger or inadequate shelter, medical care and the like. Yet, these are constants of the modern capitalist world, particularly notable in those colonial areas controlled by the large capitalist organizations of the advanced countries.

By the second half of the nineteenth century, then, capitalism had reached the end of its social usefulness. It had reached that stage of development in which it began its transformation into a different type of social organization altogether:

> At a certain stage of development, the material productive forces of society come into conflict with the existing relations of production . . . From forms of development of the productive forces these relations turn into their fetters. Then begins an era of social revolution. The changes in the economic foundation lead sooner or later to the transformation of the whole immense superstructure. In studying such transformations it is always necessary to distinguish between the material transformation of the economic conditions of production, which can be determined with the precision of natural science, and the legal, political religious, artistic or philosophic – in short, ideological forms in which men become conscious of this conflict and fight it out. Just as one does not judge an individual by what he thinks about himself, so one cannot judge such a period of transformation by its consciousness, but, on the contrary, this consciousness must be explained from the

179

contradictions of material life, from the conflict existing between the social forces of production and the relations of production. No social order is ever destroyed before all the productive forces for which it is sufficient have been developed, and new superior relations of production never replace older ones before the material conditions for their existence have matured within the framework of the old society. (Marx, [1859] 1970a, p. 21)

One can now place the specific points outlined above into this general context and make social sense of them.

With the concentration of the means of production, labor power was also concentrated. Workers were brought together, shared the same experiences, and agitated to improve their conditions, continuing and intensifying a process that began with the industrial revolution. They acted on the basis of what they thought would be effective in bringing about amelioration – their theory.

Marx was able to write *Capital* only when the subject of his inquiry, capitalism, had reached a level of development in which it showed its regressive features as well as displayed the social forces that could lead to its elimination. Had Marx lived in the eighteenth century, he would, at best, have been able to produce a *Wealth of Nations*. *Capital* was a product of mature capitalism – when the transformation from competitive to monopoly capitalism was well underway.

However, it was not the appearance of *Capital* in 1867 that effected a fundamental shift in the theory of the working class, but the fact that Marxism, as a body of theory, was increasingly 'in the air,' and organizations were developing that operated under the banner of socialism.[7] And, as the practical point of Marxist theory is the elimination of capitalist social relations, to the extent that these large and potentially powerful working-class organizations adopted Marxist theory, they proved a significant threat to the very existence of capitalism.

Also, the experience of the Paris Commune, which, though not led directly by Marxist theory, partially demonstrated the correctness of that theory, showed that socialism was a practical possibility and not just the theoretical result of idle speculation by intellectuals who had no firm grasp of the realities of social existence (the Utopians).

And, coupled to the growth of working-class organizations and working-class theory, the onslaught of the Great Depression gave evidence of the fact that capitalism, as a social system, was moribund and no longer suitable as a mode of existence for the majority of humankind.

This transition to monopoly capital was a world phenomenon, affecting all areas, including those now labeled 'underdeveloped',[8] and was not dependent upon the specific social features of any particular country. Hence Blaug's argument that the various differences in economic development or social structure of England, Austria and France 'proves' that no underlying social change could have been the root cause of the neoclassical domination is off the mark. A given social system will always display peculiarities in different regions; but its basic or essential characteristics remain the same. In the second half of the nineteenth century, England, Austria and France joined the other capitalist countries in undergoing the world transition to monopoly capitalism, though at different rates of development and displaying different characteristics.[9]

Monopoly capital and science

The transition to monopoly capitalism was made possible by the growth of science and the resulting growth in technology under the epoch of competition. Given the marked lack of social obstacles, the rapid technological change under conditions of competition, and the necessity to understand and control the economic environment, science – both natural and social – was promoted. With continuous change in the level of technology, small-scale producing units eventually gave way to modern, large-scale facilities. Industries characterized by a large number of small producers were transformed into those of a few, large firms; and, with this transition, the science that brought about this development had to be repudiated.

'Science is predominately a transforming and not a conserving influence . . .' (Bernal, 1967, p. 385). The fundamental task of science is to seek solutions to problems, both of a practical, short-run sort and of the large, 'riddle of the universe' variety. And in order to facilitate the implementation of these solutions, science necessarily promotes the elimination of those factors that stand in the way of the solution. Thus, science promotes change based on an understanding of how and why things work the way they do.

Capitalists, like all minority ruling classes, oppose change once they have established themselves as the dominant class. Under conditions of competition, change could not be readily controlled; on the contrary, change – within the capitalist framework – was allowed a relatively large amount of freedom. But change brought about the growth and consolidation of the working class, the growth and consolidation of working-class theory and, finally, the growth and consolidation of monopoly capitalism. Now, further change was not only dangerous, it was suicidal to capitalists; and, given the enormous influence of a relatively small and well organized segment of the community, change could be prevented, or at least channelled into safe directions – or so it was thought.

> Unless society can use science, it must turn anti-scientific, and that means giving up the hope of the progress that is possible. This is the way that Capitalism is now taking, and it leads to Fascism. The other way is complete Socialist planning on a large scale; this would be a planning for the maximum possible output and not a planned restriction of output. I believe that there are only these two ways . . .
> (Blackett, 1935, p. 139)

In the natural sciences, the effect of this development was not as direct or as obvious as in the social sciences. Science, insofar as it could be utilized in profit-making ventures, was still required. However, it was now absolutely necessary to present the appearance that science had no materialist base. That is, science was useful, but it could not delve into the substance of things or demonstrate provable causal relationships. It was, in other words, useful in solving practical, short-run problems, but it could not address the fundamental questions of existence. Science (rather, some scientists) retreated to the

182

position espoused by the feudal idealist reactionary Berkeley in 1710 (see Chapter 2). Leading this philosophical charge, under the cover of a modern form of idealism – positivism – was Ernst Mach (see Chapter 2; Bernal, 1971, vol. 4, pp. 1093–4; Caudwell, 1939).[10]

The essence of this retreat, as indicated in the case of Haeckel (Chapter 2), was to 'reconcile' science and religion, or materialism with idealism:

> The conformist tendencies of scientists in recent times are well exemplified by the development of the relations between science and religion. It is not a hundred years since the struggle between science and religion was the central conflict of the intellectual world. A scientist was practically synonymous with an atheist, or at least an agnostic. Now we are assured, on both sides, that the struggle between religion and science has been resolved by discovering there is nothing incompatible between the two, while eminent scientists vie with bishops in supporting mystical views of the universe and of human life. The difference is not in the least due to the invalidation of the arguments used in the earlier controversies, but rather to the fact that in the middle of the nineteenth century religion was really trying to interfere with the growing sciences of biology and geology. The scientist did not wish to be thought irreligious, but he was then faced with the awkward choice of appearing so or denying the plain meaning of his work. The moment that denial was no longer formally demanded of him the scientist of the later period was only too willing to return to religion and, with it, to general social conformity. The change was particularly marked after the Russian Revolution because it was then that the importance of religion as a counter-revolutionary force was again fully appreciated. The same state of affairs had occurred at an earlier period, at the end of the eighteenth century. At that time science and deism of the Voltairian type were closely, and it seemed inevitably, associated. When, however, the French Revolution showed that deism was definitely dangerous for the existing order of things, science for a while fell under the

same ban, which was not lifted until it was found possible in the early part of the nineteenth century to combine a science which knew its place with proper attachment to Church and King. (Bernal, 1967, pp. 389–90)

The long struggle of science against religion, which began in the modern world with the stage of revolutionary capitalism, had come full circle. The social system that initially fostered the materialist outlook (with severe restrictions, to be sure) had now reached the level of development where materialist ideology was a decided liability to its continuation. Hence idealism, always lurking in the wings and always promoted along with materialism, was now elevated to a position of dominance, and the older, previously discredited, arguments of the feudal opponents of capitalism were brought forth to defend the now moribund social system.[11]

The impact on the social sciences, economics in particular, was even more significant. Quite obviously, social science is more directly sensitive to the social order than physical science. Conversely, society itself must take a greater interest in those areas of inquiry that are occupied by the study of society. Specifically, given that any social order organizes to protect itself, it must necessarily guard against the intrusion of social theory inimical to its maintenance.

It has been seen that economic theory began to turn away from a materialist, objective theory of value in the period between Smith and Ricardo, and that this development intensified considerably in the post-Ricardian period, while the natural sciences were continuing to make great strides forward. In the 1870–1900 period, these anti-scientific trends were consolidated, systematized and established in a privileged, monopoly position in the halls of academe.

For good reason. Consider the social effects of an objective investigation into the relation between the economic order and various economic effects of that order. Poverty, for example, is the absence of sufficient food, clothing, shelter. The production of these necessities is controlled by businessmen, who, under conditions of monopoly capital, organize to restrict output in order to maintain artificially high prices. This is particularly evident during periods of depression when food, for example, is physically destroyed while people literally starve (a social crime that has now become the norm). The elimination of poverty, then, calls for the expansion of output beyond that desired by those who control production, placing the profit-maximizing privilege of large capitalists in jeopardy. In the final analysis, the elimination of poverty would call for the elimination of the cause of poverty: capitalism itself. The defense of the social order thus calls for an ideology that conceals this point or develops an argument that offers an alternative, idealist defense of poverty – fraud.

Note that the same charge could not have been made under conditions of competitive capitalism. Poverty certainly existed then, and to some extent it was the result of the organization of the social order. But, given the output-maximizing tendencies of competition, an honest inquiry would not call for the elimination of capitalism, but rather for reform or modification within the existing social framework. We observe that the first calls for radical transformation did not begin until the period of the industrial revolution, the point at which the transition to monopoly capital began.

What is observable is that major conflicts and debates occurred in all branches of science and philosophy during the period in question. And, in each case, the scientific advances of the previous three centuries were either dismissed out of hand (in the social sciences) or, as in the natural sciences, vulgarized and/or provided with an idealist theoretical foundation, the very antipode of science (Bernal, 1971, vols 3,4, passim).

Darwin's work met with violent religious opposition – by clerics and scientists who wanted to maintain religion as an ideological system – and then was vulgarized in order to undermine its revolutionary and atheistic implication (Gould, 1979, 1982, passim; Hull, 1973). The work of Herbert Spencer served to further bastardize evolutionary theory, particularly in the supposed application of one of Darwin's principles – survival of the fittest – to human society, where it was used to defend the privileges of the dominant class.

Counterposed to the macro, evolutionary Darwinian theory was the genetic theory which utilized the individualist perspective as a foundation for its general theory. In doing so, it promoted ideology both mechanically determinist and 'accidental' at the same time. That is, the genetic pattern determines a stable existence interrupted periodically by chance occurrences that cannot be predicted (Monod, 1971).[12]

We have already noted the fundamental shift in physics (Chapter 2). Here, readers are merely reminded that the essence of this shift was the rejection of a materialist base to physics and the substitution of one founded on idealism (Lenin, [1908] 1970). Chemistry underwent the same development.

In anthropology, the materialist, evolutionary work of Lewis Henry Morgan *et al.* came under attack by Lowie, Boaz, Graebner and, not surprisingly, a Catholic contingent led by Wilhelm Schmidt, S.V.D. While in technical disagreement on seemingly every fundamental point (much as the various branches of neoclassical economics), these anti-Morganites had a common ground in waging war on the general evolutionary views of the materialists (Briffault, 1927; White, 1959).

In philosophy in general, dominance was won by the various idealist schools – positivism, pragmatism, etc. – and, in each case, a return to fundamental Berkeleyite principles was enshrined as the basis of the attack on materialism (Cornforth, 1947, 1950; Lenin, [1908] 1970; Wells, 1954).

To these and other developments in history, psychology, political science and so on, one must add the work of Eduard Bernstein and others, who, under the facade of Marxism, bastardized every fundamental principle established by Marx and Engels (Bernstein, [1898] 1967; Lenin, [1917] 1977). Such 'revisionists' engaged in distortion and sins of omission. Further, and *not* incidentally, Bernstein rejected the labor theory of value and substituted, albeit in modified form, a utility theory of valuation (Bernstein, [1898] 1967, pp. 28–39). That is, Bernstein embraced the essence of neoclassical theory itself. [13]

Essentially, in the period during which the transition to monopoly capitalism took place, capitalism, as a reactionary social system, necessarily waged war on science, which demands progress. One area within which this war was waged was that of economic theory. The labor theory of value was now decidedly driven underground and the utility theory emerged triumphant.

The ideological perspective of the neoclassicists

The major neoclassical economists of the 1870–1900 period did not develop their ideas in a vacuum. In examining the general political perspective of the class position that lay at the bottom of their theory, what is observed is a common outlook that (regardless of individual variations) necessitated the type of economic theory embraced. Since their economic analysis is well known, I shall, for the most part, ignore this aspect of their work and focus on a general argument concerning the relation of the utility theory of value to fraud, a relation demanded by the transition to monopoly capital.

Jevons was overtly (and, I think, proudly) an anti-democrat. In 1866 he wrote:

My Introductory lecture to the course of Cobden lectures, has brought some little criticism from the Radicals upon me. I am often troubled and now more than ever to know how to reconcile my inclinations in political matters. What side am I to take, one – the other – or can I take both? I cannot consent with the radical party to obliterate a glorious past – nor can I consent with the conservatives to prolong abuses into the present. I wish with all my heart to aid in securing all that is good for the masses, yet to give them all they wish and are striving for is to endanger much that is good beyond their comprehension. I cannot pretend to underestimate the good that the English monarchy and aristocracy, with all the liberal policy actuating it, does for the human race, and yet I cannot but fear the pretensions of democracy against it are strong and in some respects even properly strong. This antithesis and struggle perhaps after all is no more than has always more or less existed but is now becoming more marked. Compromise perhaps is the only resource. Those who rightly possess the power in virtue of their superior knowledge must yield up some that they may carry with them the honest but uncertain will of those less educated but more numerous and physically powerful. (Jevons, 1972, p. 208)

Jevons was writing at a point in English history when democracy, still within the framework of capitalist relations, seemed to be threatening. There was great agitation for the enlargement of the franchise by the working class, and it seemed most unlikely that this class voice could be simply ignored. The problem was to appear to yield to popular demand while retaining – indeed, making more secure – extant class privilege. The Reform Bill of 1867 accomplished this end by extending voting rights to a relatively small section of the working class – the better paid, highly skilled, more conservative section – while continuing to deny such rights to the vast majority which could not yet be trusted with such power because it had not yet been brought sufficiently under the ideological control of the upper classes (Smith, 1966, passim).

In the above quote, Jevons reflects the confusion and fear of the upper classes in their political confrontation with 'the mob.' It is understood that the past will no longer serve the present goals of the ruling segments of society, that some modification must be made in the existing political arrangements, but it is unclear what this is to be. The trick is for those with 'superior knowledge' to persuade their inferior, but potentially more powerful, countrymen to continue to play the same game with some small changes in the rules.

Jevons's fear of and contempt for the working class was largely the result of that class's supposedly incorrect understanding of political economy. With a correct theory to guide its actions, it would then understand the limitations imposed upon it by economic law and would considerably moderate its demand for what it considered justice. In fact, Jevons's little primer, *Political Economy* [1878], was designed for the express purpose of attaining such an end:

In preparing this little treatise, I have tried to put the truths of Political Economy into a form suitable for elementary instruction . . . There can be no doubt that it is most desirable to disseminate knowledge of the truths of political economy through all classes of the population by any means which may be available. From ignorance of these truths arise many of the worst social evils – disastrous strikes and lockouts, opposition to improvements, improvidence, destitution, misguided charity, and discouraging failure in many well intended measures. More than forty years ago Miss Martineau successfully popularised the truths of political economy in her admirable tales. About the same time, Archbishop Whately was much struck with the need of inculcating knowledge of these matters at an early age. With this view he prepared his 'Easy Lessons on Money Matters,' of which many editions have been printed. In early boyhood I learned my first ideas of political economy from a copy of these lessons . . . But it is evident that one condition of success in such efforts is the possession of a small text-book exactly suited to the purposes in view. (Jevons, [1878] n.d., pp. 5–6)

To be effective, and in keeping with Whately's admonition, this educational program had to commence quite early in order to 'impress upon them the simple truths concerning their social position before the business of life has created insuperable prejudices' (Jevons, 1886, p. 4). That is, working-class children must be taught correct political economy prior to the education they will receive later in the actual world of modern economic relations.

Jevons's educational program carried over into his attitude toward and analysis of the 'labor question,' specifically in his position on trade unionism, in which he held to the still common opinion that such organizations were bad for the individual worker because they restricted individual freedom:

The best example which I can give . . . of the evils and disasters which may accompany progress is to be found in trade unions and the strikes they originate and conduct. Of these I may say, in the words of a recent article of the

'Times,' that 'every year sees these organizations more powerful, more pitiless, and more unjust. Such atrocities as that reported from Sheffield are but the extreme cases of a tyranny which is at this very moment paralysing the large part of the trades of the country.' We wish every working man to be not only free, but privileged; but to this end he must have intelligence and education, else he is not free but in name . . . He must learn to see that in the trade unions, in which he chiefly places his hopes at present, there is no true individual freedom, but that he is entirely at the mercy of the prevailing opinions of his fellow-workmen, often in fact of a few leaders of the union. (Jevons, 1886, pp. 10, 12)

From the individualist utility perspective, Jevons reaches the above conclusion logically and can consistently attack unions from this point of view. Since *any* organization necessarily places both restrictions and responsibilities on its members, individuals are not then free to do as they may like. But since unions in this sense are no different from, say, a Boy Scout troop, Jevons's specificity in his remarks makes it clear that the function of his proposed educational program is to dissuade workers from organizing rather than to attack organization in general. After all, on the same grounds he could have attacked capitalism or the organizations of capitalists. He did not and could not, because he was not opposed to democracy for this class.

Further, in his *Political Economy*, written specifically to popularize neoclassical theory, Jevons launches a frontal attack on working-class organizations, devoting the largest single section of that work to an analysis of trade unionism. Here, he argues that:

It is sad, again, to see thousands of persons trying to improve their positions by means which have just the opposite effect, I mean by strikes, by refusing to use machinery, and by trying in various ways, to resist the production of wealth. Working men have made a political economy of their own: they want to make themselves rich by taking care not to produce too much riches . . .

Political economy teaches us to look beyond the immediate effect of what we do, and to seek the good of the
whole community, and even of the whole mankind . . .
It is certain that if *people do not understand a true political
economy, they will make a false one of their own.* Hence the
imperative need that no one, neither man nor woman,
should grow up without acquiring some comprehension
of the science which we are going to study. (Jevons, [1878]
n.d., pp. 10–11)

In the same work we learn that unions either cannot or
should not regulate the hours of work (the eight-hour day)
(p. 63), increase wages (pp. 64–5), prevent scab labor during a
strike (p. 67), or regulate the pace of work (the speed-up) (pp.
71–3). All these, and other, points are made consistently on
the basis of a utility theory of value, by which individualist,
unfettered competition produces socially desirable results
through the inexorable workings of supply and demand.

Essentially, though, the issue is that of morality, and in this
regard unions are simply an 'evil' (Jevons, [1882] 1968, p. 32).
The primary question is not the unjust economic effects of
such organization; it is how to rid society of such a distinctly
menacing development, or – and this is the point of Jevons's
educational program – how to tame it so that it no longer
generates pernicious effects.

In keeping with this position on unions, Jevons argued
(again, consistently on the basis of the utility theory of
value) that then-modern capitalist society was a society of
class harmony. This, of course, was contrary to what was
seemingly observed in the actual workings of the world
(Jevons, [1882] 1968, passim). Private property and capital
'are jealously guarded by the legislator, not so much for
the benefit of a small exclusive class, but because capital
can hardly be accumulated and employed without vivifying
industry, and diffusing comfort and subsistence through the
whole body of society' (Jevons, 1883, pp. 107–8).

According to Jevons, observed conflict is the result of
erroneous thinking, not an outcome of the actual state of
affairs that exists in class societies. Thus, the role of the state
is to act as the guarantor of this harmony, preventing any

section of the populace from acting in an anti-social fashion. It is now time that 'all class rancour, and all needless reference to former unfortunate occurrences, should be laid aside. The economic errors of trade unions after all are not worse than those which pervaded the commercial, if not governing classes a generation ago' (Jevons, [1882] 1968, p. viii).

What problems do exist are caused not by fundamental social relations extant within a particular form of society, but by the workings of natural (economic) law over which individuals or classes have no control:

> When we are able to understand why the labourer gets so little at present, we shall see, perhaps, how he might manage to get more, but in any case we shall see that it is due *in great part to the laws of nature*. (Jevons, [1878] n.d., p. 49)

Thus, for example, rather than examining cyclical fluctuations as a product of a capitalist economic system – a social phenomenon – Jevons promoted the notion of sunspots – a natural phenomenon – as lying at the foundation of these cycles.

All the above (and more) follows directly from Jevons's attack upon and repudiation of the labor theory of value (Jevons, [1871] 1970, pp. 184–7) and his adamant defense of the utility perspective:

> The conclusion to which I am ever more clearly coming is that the only hope of attaining a true system of economics is to fling aside, once and for ever, the hazy and preposterous assumptions of the Ricardian school. Our English economists have been living in a fools paradise. The truth is with the French school . . .
>
> When at length a true system of economics comes to be established, it will be seen that that able but wrong-headed man, David Ricardo, shunted the car of economic science on to a wrong line. . . There were economists, such as Malthus and Senior, who had far better comprehension of the true doctrines . . . but they were driven out of the field by the unity and influence of the Ricardo–Mill school.

It will be a work of labour to pick up the fragments of a shattered science and to start anew, but is a work from which they must not shrink who wish to see any advance of economic science.

There are valuable suggestions towards the improvement of the science contained in the works of such writers as Senior, Cairnes, Macleod, Cliffe-Leslie, Hearn, Shadwell, not to mention a long series of French economists from Baudeau and Le Trosne down to Bastiat and Courcelle Seneuil; but they are neglected in England because the excellence of their works was not comprehended by David Ricardo, the two Mills, Professor Fawcett and others who have made the orthodox Ricardian school what it is. Under these circumstances it is a positive service to break the monotonous repetition of current questionable doctrines, even at the risk of new error. I trust that the theory now given may prove accurate; but, however this may be, it will not be useless if it cause inquiry to be directed into the true basis and form of a science which touches so directly the material welfare of the human race. (Jevons, [1871] 1970, pp. 67–8, 72, 261)

Jevons's task, as he sees it, is to rid economics of the lingering effects of classical theory (vulgarized though it was by this time), erect the 'true,' utility theory, and utilize this theory to combat the social evils of the day – in particular, the working-class movement. Thus, Jevons himself sees a direct relationship between the utility theory of value and the defense of the capitalist order. What was necessary at the time was to consolidate this theory, purge the remaining Ricardian arguments from the doctrine, then disseminate it through the educational system.

Of the three 'revolutionaries' of the early 1870s, Menger was the most consistent and adamant subjectivist, a tradition continued by the Austrian economists' variation on the neoclassical theme. It was his task, self-appointed to be sure, to address specifically the collectivist, socialist theory that was spreading on the Continent. The argument contained in *Problems of Economics and Sociology* [1883], while separated from his *Principles of Economics* by twelve years, presents a defense of the subjectivist, individualist, accidentalist perspective upon which *Principles* is based. But it is more than a defense. As Hayek has pointed out, the whole of *Problems* is a polemic directed against the German Historical School of economists (Hayek, 1934, pp. 405–6). Hence, the approach mandated by the adoption of the utility theory of value is seen to run directly counter to that of the collectivist, historical, social approach.

The German Historical economists, led by Schmoller, were not Marxists or socialists. Rather, they supported government intervention within the framework of capitalism to moderate such a society in order to allow it to function more smoothly and to ameliorate its harshest effects. From a staunchly individualist point of view, however, collectivists of any stripe are made to appear equally dangerous: witness the standard lumping of fascists and socialists as equivalent under ostensibly different political facades (Hayek, 1944, passim). In any case, *Problems* presents the archetypal position of neoclassicism and can be seen as a methodological supplement to, and intellectual defense of, *Principles*.[14]

> The historical school of jurists utilizes the above notion to arrive at the thesis that law is something above the arbitrariness of the individual, is even something independent of the arbitrariness of the temporary generation of the national body. They state that it is an 'organic' structure which cannot and must not be arbitrarily shaped by individuals . . . From this thesis the above school now further derived consequences which are in part extremely practical. It concluded that the desire for a reform of social and political conditions aroused in all Europe by the French Revolution really meant a failure to recognize the nature of law, state, and society and their 'organic origin.' It concluded that the 'subconscious wisdom' which is manifested in the political institutions that came about organically stands high above meddlesome human wisdom. It concluded that the pioneers of reform ideas accordingly would do less to trust their own insight and energy than to leave the reshaping of society to the 'historical process of development.' *And it espoused other such conservative*

basic principles highly useful to the ruling interests [emphasis added].

The notion of an analogous conservative orientation in the field of economy was fairly obvious. And a historical school of economists comparable to the historical school of jurists, which would have defended existing economic schools and interests against the exaggerations of reform thought in the field of economy, but expecially against socialism, would have fulfilled a certain mission even in Germany and prevented many a later setback.

But nothing was further from the thoughts of the historical school of economists in Germany than the idea of an analogous conservative orientation in the field of economy . . . On the contrary, its proponents, in a practical respect, lined up even a short time ago almost completely with the liberal policy-makers of progress in the field of economics, until no small part of them most recently offered the rare spectacle of a *historical* school of economists with socialistic tendencies. (Menger, [1883] 1963, pp. 91–2)

Essentially, the failure of the German economists was that of deviating markedly from the historical school of jurists, who developed the proposition that law was above society, a 'natural,' universal phenomenon. Such a view was most useful in combating social movements for reform, thus preserving then-extant vested interests.

In contradistinction to the historical economists, Menger opined that the task of proper economists was to develop general laws, applicable to all times and places, which could then be modified to account for specific, institutional differences among various economic organizations:

The development of economic phenomena and the necessity of taking this fact into account in the realistic theory of economic phenomena are beyond all doubt. No one to any extent familiar with theoretical investigations will, however, claim that we are to strive for the solution of the above problem, for instance, by creating just as many economic theories as there are developmental stages

of economic phenomena . . . The road which the theoreticians in the field of economy have to take to solve
the above problem can . . . only consist in our taking
as the basis of our presentation a specific state of the
economy, especially significant with respect to the time
and place, and merely pointing out the modifications
which result for the realistic theory from differently constituted developmental stages of economic phenomena and
from different spatial conditions. (Menger, [1883] 1963,
pp. 107–8)

This universality principle, defended through an invalid
comparison to physical laws – which *are* independent of
society – is, of course, an aspect of Menger's general economic theory as found in *Principles*. We note here that this
principle was directed specifically against those economists
who argued that different societies had different economic
relations, and thus different economic laws of motion.

Coupled to the universality principle is the individualist view of social organization. Menger's position is overt
and clear on this point: 'National' (aggregate) relations are
'fictions'; the so-called 'national economy' is nothing more
than the summation of individual (atomistic) units, and it
is only the individual units that can be examined scientifically:

What the national economists designate with the expression 'national economy,' national economy in the common
sense of the word, is *by no means a juxtaposition of isolated
individual economies*. The latter, rather, are closely tied
together by traffic with one another. But just as little is
what they so designate a *national economy* in the above
strict sense, or per se *one economy* at all. It is really, on
the contrary, a complex or, if one wishes, an *organism
of economies* (of singular and common economies), but,
we repeat, it is not itself an economy. To make use of
a popular image, there is here the same relationship as
e.g. in a chain which presents a unit consisting of links,
without, however, being a link itself. It is the same as
in a machine which presents a unit made up of wheels,

and so on, without being a wheel itself. (Menger, [1883] 1963, p. 194)

This, of course, follows directly from the subjectivist, individualist utility theory of value:

> not only the *nature* but also the *measure* of value is subjective. Goods have value *to* certain economizing individuals and this value is also *determined* only by these individuals. (Menger, [1871] 1981, p. 146)

From this point of view, then, Menger can logically attack social reform and defend existing property relations. For Menger, social phenomena and institutions are not the result of 'intended,' or planned, conscious actions – which would require group or collective action – but arise through the (usually unconscious) acts of individuals motivated by self-interest. Thus, social motion is individualist and, therefore, accidental. Following one strand of thought from Adam Smith, this individual behavior results in the unintended advancement of the common good:

> That social structure, too, which we call the state, has been the unintended result of efforts serving individual interests, at least in its most original forms.
>
> In the same way it might be pointed out that other social institutions, language, law, morals, but especially numerous institutions of economy, have come into being without any express agreement, without legislative compulsion, even without any consideration of public interest, merely through the impulse of *individual* interests and as a result of the activation of these interests . . .
>
> We already alluded above to the fact that a large number of the phenomena of economy which cannot usually be viewed as 'organically' created 'social structures,' e.g., market prices, wages, interest rates, etc., have come into existence in exactly the same way as those social institutions which we mentioned in the preceding section. For they, too, as a rule are not the result of socially teleological causes, but the unintended result of innumerable

efforts of economic subjects pursuing *individual* interests. The theoretical understanding of their nature and their movement can thus be attained . . . by reducing them to their elements, to the *individual* factors of their causation, and by investigating the laws by which the complicated phenomena of human economy under discussion here are built up from these elements. (Menger, [1883] 1963, pp. 157–9)

This, then, is a direct attack on, and a rebuke of, those who attempted to promote social reform through collective action. The socialists or historical economists of a socialist bent were operating contrary to the laws of human nature, and since they were attempting to unsettle those laws, their activities could only result in practice deleterious to the well-being of society.

Property relations, for Menger, were merely an extension of his position on the individualist, subjectivist perspective that follows from the utility theory of value. Specifically, property was nothing more than exchange relations based on individual utility calculations. Those who held property did so on the basis of individualist, non-social, rationale:

In an isolated household economy . . . this joint purpose of the goods necessary for the preservation of human life and welfare is apparent since all of them are at the disposal of a single economizing individual. The harmony of the needs that the individual households attempts to satisfy is reflected in their property . . .

The entire sum of goods at an economizing individual's command for the satisfaction of his needs, we call his *property* . . .

In this struggle of survival, the various individuals will attain very different degrees of success. But whatever the manner in which goods subject to this quantitative relationship are divided, the requirements of some members of the society will not be met at all, or will be met only incompletely. These persons will therefore have interests opposed to those of the present possessors with respect to each portion of the available quantity of goods. But with this opposition of interest, it becomes necessary for society to protect the various individuals in the possession of goods subject to this relationship against all possible acts of force. In this way, then, we arrive at the economic origin of our present legal order, and especially of the so-called *protection of ownership*, the basis of property.

Thus human economy and property have a joint economic origin, since both have, as the ultimate reason for their existence, the fact that goods exist whose available quantities are smaller than the requirements of men. Property, therefore, like human economy, is not an arbitrary invention but rather the only practically possible solution of the problem that is, in the nature of things, imposed upon us by the disparity between requirements for, and available quantities of, all economic goods. (Menger, [1871] 1981, pp. 75–76, 97)

Since property (or the class relations that stand behind property) is the result of mere scarcity, this institution could not be the source of social problems or discontent. In fact, property was developed to assure some semblance of order and harmony. Agitation directed against property or property-holders is thus misplaced, though this agitation demands the development of law (and other apparatuses of the state) to protect owners. Further, as property is merely the holding of exchange values, then all members of society are property-holders to some extent. The issue is not one of classes, then, but merely of unequal distribution of property among members of the community, who all have the same interest in holding property.

More important, Menger's position on the universality and natural qualities of property and exchange placed him squarely in opposition to *known* and scientifically validated data concerning the actual development of these social institutions. His conjectural, a priori 'history' may have been a suitable temporary substitute in Smith's period, but by the 1870s, the work of Tylor, Morgan and others had clearly and unequivocally demonstrated that property, exchange and other features of what was to become capitalist society had a relatively short history; for most human existence, these 'natural,' 'universal' categories were done without quite nicely. In short, Menger fabricates a theory of the origins of various institutions to suit his ideological purposes – one that was known to be false at the time.

Walras's political perspective is evidenced in the introductory chapters of *Elements* [1874]. Superficially, Walras appears as the most moderate, most reasonable of the major economists of the period, a fact made even more ironic given that the general equilibrium model in his following chapters is the most trenchant, abstract and rigorous argument of the three economists. In these chapters, Walras, somewhat ingeniously, lays out a philosophical argument that necessarily results in a conclusion defending capitalist property relations. This follows, again, from the adoption of the utility theory of value, which establishes exchange as the basis for analysis.

In defining economics, Walras begins by seeming to attack the position, taken by Say and others, that economics is a natural science, examining supra-societal laws. In doing so, he recognizes that such a characterization has served the political function of defending capitalist institutions against the charges of socialists:

> according to Say, it is entirely a *natural* science. From Say's definition it would seem that the *production, distribution,* and *consumption* of wealth take place, if not spontaneously, at least in a *manner* somehow independent of the will of man . . .
>
> What has proved so pleasing at the same time so misleading to economists in this definition is precisely its characterization of the whole of political economy as a natural science pure and simple. Such a point of view was particularly useful to them in their controversy with the socialists. Every proposal to redistribute property was rejected *a priori* and practically without discussion, not on the grounds that such plans were contrary to economic well-being or to social justice, but simply because they were artificial arrangements designed

to replace what was natural . . . (Walras, [1874] 1954, pp. 54–5)

Walras then argues that man, contrary to the older French economists (and others), is a social animal, differentiated from the lower species by his ability to arrange social forms in different ways:

Unfortunately, convenient as this point of view is, it is mistaken . . . Man is a creature endowed with reason and freedom, and possessed of a capacity for initiative and progress. In the production and distribution of wealth, and generally in all matters pertaining to social organization, man has the choice between better and worse and tends more and more to choose the better part. Thus man has progressed from a system of guilds, trade regulations and price fixing to a system of freedom of industry and trade, i.e. to a system of *laisser-faire, laisser-passer*; he has progressed from slavery to serfdom and from serfdom to the wage system. The superiority of the later forms of organization over the earlier forms lies not in their greater naturalness (both old and new are artificial, the newer forms more so than the old, since they came into existence only by supplanting the old); but rather in their closer conformity with material well-being and justice. The proof of such conformity is the only justification for adhering to a policy of *laisser-faire, laisser-passer*. Moreover, socialistic forms of organization should be rejected if it can indeed be shown that they are inconsistent with material well-being and justice. (Walras, [1874] 1954, p. 55)

Walras goes on to divide the universe into two categories: natural phenomena and social phenomena. The latter is further divided into two sub-categories: applied science and moral science, which are defined in the following terms:

a fundamental distinction must be drawn in the realm of human phenomena. We have to place in one category those phenomena which are manifestations of the human will, i.e. of human actions in respect to natural forces. This category comprises the relations between persons and things. In another category we have to place the phenomena that result from the impact of the human will or of human actions on the will or actions of other men. This second category comprises the relations between persons and persons. The laws of these two classes of phenomena are essentially different . . .

Translating this distinction into appropriate definitions, I call the sum total of phenomena of the first category *industry* and the sum total of phenomena of the second category *institutions*. The theory of industry is called *applied science* or *art*; the theory of institutions *moral science* or *ethics*. (Walras, [1874] 1954, p. 63)

The question then becomes: From the point of view of economics as one area of inquiry, which of these three categories is appropriate for analysis?

At this juncture, it is crucial for Walras to specify the base upon which the remainder of his work rests. On this point, he is unequivocal in delineating his 'pure theory of economics.' Lesson 3 begins as follows:

By *social wealth* I mean all things, material or immaterial . . ., that are scarce, that is to say, on the one hand, useful to us and, on the other hand, only available to us in limited quantity. (Walras, [1874] 1954, p. 65)

Walras thus establishes scarcity and, from this, value and exchange, as the basis of all economic inquiry, including that of applied science (industry or production) and ethics (institutions):

useful things which exist only in limited quantity are capable of being appropriated and actually are appropriated . . . those who do this reap a double advantage: not only do they assure themselves of a supply which can be reserved for their own use and satisfaction; but . . . they are also in a position to exchange the unwanted remainder for other scarce utilities which they do care to consume . . . For the present we . . . note that *appropriation* (and consequently the *ownership of property*, which is legalized appropriation, or appropriation in conformity with justice) is applicable to all of social wealth and nothing but social wealth.

We have just intimated that useful things limited in quantity are *valuable and exchangeable*. Once all things that can be appropriated . . . have been appropriated, they stand in a certain relationship to each other, a relationship which stems from the fact that each scarce thing, in addition to its own specific utility acquires a special property, namely that of being exchangeable against any other scarce thing in such and such a determinate ratio . . . Such is the phenomenon of value in exchange, which, like the phenomenon of property, applies to all social wealth and nothing but social wealth.

Useful things limited in quantity are *things that can be produced and multiplied by industry* . . . Taking the definition of social wealth given above, as the sum total of scarce things, we may now state that *industrial production*, that is, *industry*, like appropriation and value in exchange, is applicable to all social wealth, and nothing but social wealth. (Walras, [1874] 1954, pp. 66–7)

Thus:

Value in exchange, industry and property are, then, the three generic phenomena or the three orders or groups of specific facts which result from the limitation in quantity of utilities or the scarcity of things. All three are bound up with the whole of social wealth and nothing else . . . From what point of view shall we study it? Shall we do it from the point of view of value in exchange, that is, from the point of view of the influences of purchase and sale to which social wealth is subject? Or shall we do it from the point of view of the conditions which favour or hinder the increase in quantity of social wealth? Or, finally, shall we do it from the point of view of property, the object of which is social wealth, that is to say, from the point of view of the conditions which render the appropriation of social wealth legitimate or illegitimate? We must make up our minds. Above all, we must be exceedingly careful not to study social wealth from all three points of view at once or from any two of them simultaneously . . . (Walras, [1874] 1954, p. 68)

The important point in all this, given Walras's delineation of economics outlined above, is that use value and exchange, which form the basis for the discipline, are natural phenomena and equivalent, therefore, to the natural sciences:

Thus any value in exchange, once established, partakes of the character of a natural phenomenon, natural in its origins, natural in its manifestations and natural in essence . . .

It must be evident to the reader from the previous discussion that I do not claim that this science constitutes the whole of economics. Force and velocity are also measurable magnitudes, but the mathematical theory of force and velocity is not the whole of mechanics. Nevertheless, pure mechanics surely ought to precede applied mechanics. Similarly, given the pure theory of economics, it must precede applied economics; and this pure theory of economics is a science which resembles the physico-mathematical sciences in every respect. (Walras, [1874] 1954, pp. 69, 71)

It is true that human action is not unimportant or incapable of effecting certain modifications in this natural state of affairs, but such actions are necessarily of a secondary nature:

This does not mean that we have no control over prices. Because gravity is a natural phenomenon and obeys natural laws, it does not follow that all we can do is to watch it operate. We can either resist it or give it free rein,

204

whichever we please, but we cannot change its essence or its laws. It is said we cannot command nature except by obeying her. This applies also to value. (Walras, [1874] 1954, p. 69)

The initial task, then, of the economist is the construction of a theory of the ideal type, from which all other analysis and conclusions will follow, including those pertaining to industry (applied science) and institutions (ethics or social economics):

the pure theory of economics ought to take over from experience certain type concepts, like those of exchange, supply, demand, market, capital, income, productive services and products. From these real-type concepts the pure science of economics should then abstract and define ideal-type concepts in terms of which it carries on its reasoning. The return to reality should not take place until the science is completed and then only with a view to practical applications. Thus in an ideal market we have ideal prices which stand in an exact relation to an ideal demand and supply. And so on. Do these pure truths find frequent application? . . . We shall see . . . that the truths of pure economics yield solutions of very important problems of applied economics and social economics, which are highly controversial and very little understood. (Walras, [1874] 1954, pp. 71–2)

It must be noted at this point that Walras's 'pure' model, which forms his point of departure, is that of an idealized, competitive capitalist society. Given exchange based on utility as a foundation for subsequent analysis, he quickly reached a capitalist standard whereby whatever followed would be evaluated.

Having established exchange as the basis for his pure (natural law) economics, Walras then demonstrates why industry and institutions are subsidiary to and follow from this natural exchange foundation. Industry is the organization of the production of scarce goods and services, which are then exchanged (Walras, [1874] 1954, p. 73). In the process of organizing society to produce exchange values, income is distributed. Given the division of labor in modern production, it is important to distribute income with some sense of equity in mind; without equity, social disorder would prevail, and that is to be avoided at all costs (p. 75). In any case, production and distribution are both capable of being influenced by man and, therefore, cannot be part of natural science (exchange); and both are subsidiary to exchange (pp. 75–6).

Property relations (or the circumstances of the appropriation of scarce, useful things) are, again, not natural but social phenomena:

> Property consists in fair and rational appropriation. While appropriation by itself is an objective fact, pure and simple, property, on the other hand, is a phenomenon involving the concept of justice; it is a right. Between the objective fact and the right, there is a place for moral theory. This is an essential idea, which must not be misconstrued. It is entirely beside the point to find fault with the natural conditions of appropriation or to list the different ways in which men have distributed social wealth in different places and at different times throughout history. It is, however, very much to the point to scrutinize these various systems of distribution from the standpoint of justice, originating in the moral personality of man, or from the standpoint of equality and inequality; to inquire in what respects all past systems were, and all present systems still are defective, and to describe the only good system. (Walras, [1874] 1954, p. 78)

It would appear, then, that Walras admits underlying social relations into his theoretical structure, if only in a secondary role. And it is this social mechanism of appropriation that gives rise to the question of morality:

> Thus the mode of appropriation depends on human decisions, and according as those decisions are good or bad, so will the mode of appropriation be good or bad. If good, there will be a mutual coordination of human

206

destinies; justice will rule. If bad, the destiny of some will be subordinated to the destiny of others; injustice will prevail. What mode of appropriation is good and just? What mode of appropriation does reason commend as compatible with the requirements of moral personality? This is the problem of property. (Walras, [1874] 1954, p. 77)

Walras then reduces the question of just appropriation to that of communism versus individualism (capitalism), and this forms the basis of social economics:

> Which is right, communism or individualism? Are not both of them both right and wrong at the same time? We do not need to decide this dispute here . . . All I had in mind was to make clear what exactly is the object of the problem of property considered from the broadest and most comprehensive point of view. This object consists essentially in establishing human destinies in conformity with reason and justice. Appropriation being in essence a moral phenomenon, the theory of property must be in essence a moral science . . . If any science has for its object to render to each what is properly his, if, therefore, any science espouses justice as its guiding principle, surely it must be the science of the distribution of social wealth, or, as we shall designate it, social economics. (Walras, [1874] 1954, pp. 78–9)

At this point, there are two considerations of import. First, in Walras's scheme of things, social relations are not the focal point of theory. Nor can they be. Given the utility theory of value as the foundation of the argument, exchange appears as a natural, universal phenomenon. Thus, the property relations that exist, or have existed, cannot occupy center-stage because they are separable from this point – even though private property relations underlie the very necessity of exchange. The real issue is whether industry (applied economics), which aims at the increase of wealth, is in conflict with social economics, which deals with the question of justice:

The theory of property defines the mutual relations established between man and man with respect to the appropriation of social wealth, and determines the conditions of the equitable distribution of social wealth within a community. In this connection, men are considered in the capacity of moral personalities. The theory of industry, on the other hand, defines those relations between man and things which aim at the increase and transformation of social wealth, and determines the conditions of an abundant production of social wealth within a community. Here men are considered in the capacity of specialized workers. The conditions determined by the theory of property are moral conditions deducible from the premise of justice; while those determined by the theory of industry are economic conditions deducible from the premise of material welfare. In the one case as in the other we are dealing with social conditions, or with guiding principles for the organization of society. But are these two orders of consideration in conflict with each other? If, for example, both the theory of property and the theory of industry agree, on grounds of justice, in repudiating slavery or in repudiating communism, then all is well. Suppose, however, that one of these condemns slavery or advocates communism on grounds of material welfare. Then there would be a conflict between moral science and applied science. Is such a conflict possible? If it appears so, what should be done? (Walras, [1874] 1954, p. 79)

The second point is that Walras does, in fact, reach a conclusion on this question:

We shall come back to this problem later and then give it the attention it deserves. It is a question of the relation of ethics to economics which was hotly debated by Proudhon and Bastiat, among others, around 1848. In his *Contradictions economiques* Proudhon argues that there is a conflict between justice and material wellbeing. Bastiat in his *Harmonies economiques* defended the opposite thesis. I think that neither proved his point. I shall take up Bastiat's proposition again and defend it in a different way. (Walras, [1874] 1954, pp. 79–80)

This is a necessary conclusion. Given the subjectivist, individualist utility theory of value as a foundation, individuals appear to enter into exchange relations as equals. Since they choose whether or not to enter into such arrangements, they would do so only if it appears to be advantageous to them. The fact that exchange takes place, then, is proof that it is mutually advantageous and must, therefore, commend itself on the basis of justice as perceived by the individuals involved.

With the general equilibrium model Walras went on to develop, he attempted to prove that under a perfectly competitive, *laissez-faire* regime, the socially optimum, just results would necessarily be achieved. From his underlying, pro-capitalist, political perspective, Walras created a model that would demonstrate the results he viewed as desirable:

Freedom [of competition] procures, within certain limits, the maximum utility, and, since the factors which interfere with freedom are obstacles to the attainment of this maximum, they should without exception be eliminated as completely as possible. Of course, economists have been saying all along that they advocate laisser-faire, laisser-passer. Unfortunately, it must be said that up to the present economists have been less concerned with establishing proofs for their arguments in favour of *laisserfaire, laisser-passer* than they have been with using them as weapons against the socialists, new and old, who for their part are equally negligent in establishing proofs for their arguments in favour of State Intervention. I am well aware that in saying this I shall outrage a few susceptibilities. Nevertheless, I should like to ask: How could these economists prove that the results of free competition were beneficial and advantageous if they did not know just what these results were? And how could they know these results when they had neither framed definitions nor formulated relevant laws to prove their point? My own argument has so far been a priori. (Walras, [1874] 1954, p. 256)

It must be noted that Walras was cognizant of the limitations of his argument. He notes, for example, that his theory does not hold in the case of natural monopolies. Also, and this contrary to Wicksell's observation (Wicksell, 1934, p. 74), Walras was aware that his conclusion rested on a given distribution of income and that changes in the initial income endowments would alter the optimum results (Walras, [1874] 1954, p. 257).

Walras claims that his argument is silent on the question of social justice (in contradiction to what he argues in his Introduction). I think that such an assertion is vacuous, and it is here that Wicksell's point has merit. Walras asserted that his theory was incapable of distinguishing among possible income distributions and, thus, was silent on the question of social justice (which is linked to the question of distribution). However, this declaration was of a passing nature in the context of the work as a whole; more important, it is not the central point. What Walras attempted to demonstrate was that competitive capitalism generated the best, optimal results with any distribution of income. And it is capitalism, not distribution, that Walras defends. Thus, capitalism, compared with other forms of social organization, is just. There may be various degrees of justice within such a framework, but the system itself is morally defensible.

Like Menger (and Jevons), Walras develops his theoretical argument not on the basis of known information concerning the development of modern property relations but, rather, on a conjectural, a priori basis; he merely asserts, for example, that scarcity is the basis of exchange, etc., then develops an abstract argument founded on such a principle. All three 'revolutionaries' do nothing more than knowingly create an idealized structure in striking contradiction to *known* facts.

One could reproduce the same general position taken by Jevons, Menger and Walras through an examination of the work of any major neoclassical theoretician of the period. Since the neoclassical theory, based on a utility theory of value, represents a general ideological perspective, any economist holding such a theory must, if consistent, reach the same general conclusions as the substantial or essential social questions facing the discipline.[15]

Rather than running through the gamut of the major economists, I shall add only one to those chosen for illustration:
Marshall.

Marshall was the most significant of the 1870–1900 economists. He wrote toward the end of the period, after the
Walrasian–Mengerian–Jevonian triumph had been established, and was thus able to digest the arguments set forth,
eliminate incorrect or unseemly positions, and better systematize that which had gone before. In other words, Marshall was
in an historical and intellectual position to provide a consistent
and systematic account of this body of theory. Moreover,
Marshall was known as one of humane sentiments, exhibiting
a marked tendency toward reform and, in particular, toward
the amelioration of poverty; and his *Principles* bears the closest
resemblance to reality of all the major neoclassical works of his
day. Marshall, then, provides the singularly best case study
for the argument developed here.

Our starting point is Marshall's view of change. As is well
known, Marshall adopted a supposedly 'evolutionary' view
of the economic process, but his version was that of the
vulgarized Spencerian form of this theory:

> The doctrine that those organisms which are the most
> highly developed . . . are those which are most likely to
> survive in the struggle for existence is itself in process of
> development . . .
>
> The law of 'survival of the fittest' states that those
> organisms tend to survive which are best fitted to utilize
> the environment for their own purposes. Those that utilize
> the environment most, often turn out to be those that
> benefit those around them most; but sometimes they are
> injurious.
>
> Conversely, the struggle for survival may fail to bring
> into existence organisms that would be highly beneficial:
> and in the economic world the demand for any industrial
> arrangement is not certain to call forth a supply, unless it
> is something more than a mere desire for the arrangement,
> or a need for it . . .
>
> In the ruder stages of human life many of the services
> rendered by the individual to others are nearly as much

due to hereditary habit and unreasoning impulse, as are those of the bees and ants. But deliberate, and therefore moral, self-sacrifice soon makes its appearance; it is fostered by the far-seeing guidance of prophets and priests and legislators, and is inculcated by parable and legend. Gradually the unreasoning sympathy . . . extends its area and gets to be deliberately adopted as a basis of action: tribal affection, starting from a level hardly higher than that which prevails in a pack of wolves or a horde of banditti, gradually grows into a noble patriotism; and religious ideals are raised and purified. The races in which these qualities are the most highly developed are sure, other things being equal, to be stronger than others in war and in contests with famine and disease; and ultimately prevail. Thus the struggle for existence causes in the long run those races of men to survive in which the individual is most willing to sacrifice himself for the benefit of those around him; and which are consequently the best adapted collectively to make use of their environment . . .

This influence of heredity shows itself nowhere more markedly than in social organization. For that must necessarily be a slow growth, the product of many generations . . . In early times when religious, ceremonial, political, military and industrial organization were intimately connected and, were indeed but different sides of the same thing, nearly all those nations which were leading the van of the world's progress were found to agree in having adopted a more or less strict system of caste: and this fact by itself proved that the distinction of castes was well suited to its environment and that on the whole it strengthened the races or nations which adopted it. For since it was a controlling factor of life, the nations which adopted it could not have generally prevailed over others, if the influence exerted by it had not been in the main beneficial . . .

. . . progress may be hastened by thought and work; by the application of the principles of Eugenics to the replenishment of the race from its higher rather than its lower strains, and by the appropriate education of the faculties of either sex: but however hastened it must be gradual and relatively slow. It must be slow relatively to man's growing command over technique and the forces to nature . . . And it must be very much too slow to keep pace with the rapid inflow of proposals for the prompt reorganization of society on a new basis. In fact our new command over nature . . . places greater responsibilities on those who would advocate new developments of social and industrial structure. For though, institutions may be changed rapidly; yet if they are to endure they must be appropriate to man: They cannot retain their stability if they change very much faster than he does. Thus progress itself increases the urgency of the warning that in the economic world, *Natura non facit saltum*. (Marshall, [1890] 1964, pp. 201–4, 207)

The point of including this extended quotation is not to quibble with the specific elements in Marshall's view, to debate whether the development of patriotism or religious sentiments were advances in human organization. Rather, it is to illustrate Marshall's 'evolutionary' view, which, taken as a whole, can be seen to support then-extant relationships. Combining the survival-of-the-fittest dogma with that of the genetic transmission of those qualities best suited for a given environment, Marshall develops a general theoretical framework in which his argument unfolds. Countering the socialist demand for a radical transformation of existing society, he argues that 'Nature contains no leaps': change unfolds continuously and gradually and does so on the basis of environmental suitability.

In itself, this does not deny the possibility of a gradual transformation into a non-capitalist social organization. But Marshall's change is within a given environmental (capitalist) context. A thoroughly evolutionary view is inconsistent with the (individualist) utility theory of value (Hunt, 1979, p. 283). As has been argued above, the Benthamite utilitarian base of the neoclassical theory of value is nothing more than a philosophical picture of competitive capitalist relations and a justification of those relations. What Marshall's view of change admits of is change within those relations only. Moreover, as cited above, whatever changes do take place

must be, on the whole, beneficial or they would not have
occurred (or, at least, they would have remained in place).

This proposition can be illustrated by reference to Marshall's
position on competition and the issue of the tendency toward
monopolization, which, as pointed out above, was one of the
distinguishing features of the period:

> here we may read a lesson from the young trees of the
> forest as they struggle upwards through the benumbing
> shade of their older rivals. Many succumb on the way,
> and a few only survive; those few become stronger with
> every year . . . seem as though they would grow on for
> ever, and for ever become stronger as they grow. But
> they do not. One tree will last longer in full vigour and
> attain a greater size than another; but sooner or later age
> tells on them all . . . the taller ones gradually lose vitality;
> and one after another they give place to others, which,
> though of less material strength, have on their side the
> vigour of youth.
>
> And as with the growth of trees, so was it with the
> growth of businesses as a general rule before the great
> recent development of vast joint-stock companies, which
> often stagnate, but do not readily die. Now that rule is
> far from universal, but it still holds in many industries
> and trades. Nature still presses on the private business
> by limiting the length of the life of its original founders,
> and by limiting even more narrowly that part of their lives
> in which their faculties retain full vigour. And so, after a
> while, the guidance of the business falls into the hands of
> people with less energy and less creative genius . . . it is
> likely to have lost so much of its elasticity and progressive
> force, that the advantages are no longer exclusively on its
> side in its competition with younger and smaller rivals.
> (Marshall, [1890] 1964, pp. 263–4)

Though mindful of and responsive to the existence of
non-competitive oligarchic business organizations, Marshall
nevertheless attempts to rescue the competitive model from
the world of reality – through a supposed application of
evolutionary theory. In fact, his analogy of the life-cycle of

forests indicates that his theory is not evolutionary at all, but merely an example of quantitive change with no fundamental transformation of a qualitative nature. For the latter, he would have to consider the development and disappearance of forests (capitalism) as a whole. What Marshall presents is a life-cycle continuum in which this cycle repeats itself *ad infinitum*. Business firms grow and die, the result of their own internal weakness induced by growth itself; they are then replaced by younger, more vigorous firms; and so on. The primary reason for this cyclical development is entrepreneurship. This, of course, reflects the individualist point of view. Rather than basing his theoretical framework on social relations, Marshall, true to the perspective of the utility theory of value, places the individual capitalist at the center of his argument. Thus, the change that does occur is capitalist change, and the capitalist is the starting and ending point of this change.

Coupled to this general theoretical framework is a necessary attack on socialism and militant trade unionism, both of which, in Marshall's view, tend to unsettle the 'normal' progression of capitalist society. In a letter to Lord Reay in 1909, Marshall writes:

> My own notion of Socialism is that it is a movement for taking the responsibility for a man's life and work, as far as possible, off his shoulders and putting it on to the State. In my opinion Germany is beneficially 'socialistic' in its regimentation of those who are incapable of caring for themselves: and we ought to copy Germany's methods in regard to our Residuum.
>
> But in relation to other classes, I regard the Socialistic movement as not merely a danger, but by far the greatest present danger to human well-being . . .
>
> I do not deny that semi-socialistic or Governmental methods are almost inevitable in ordinary railways etc . . . But the sting of socialism seems to lie in its desire to extend these rather than to check their expansion. I believe that they weaken character by limiting initiative and dulling aspiration; and that they lower character by diverting energy from creation to wire-pulling. I therefore regard

Protection as socialistic, in that, especially in a democratic country, it gives a first place to those business men who are 'expert' in hoodwinking officials, the legislature and the public as to the ability of their branch of industry to take care of itself. (Marshall in Pigou, [1925] 1956, p. 462)

And, from his 1907 essay, 'Social Possibilities of Economic Chivalry':

We are told sometimes that everyone who strenuously endeavours to promote the social amelioration of the people is a Socialist . . . In this sense nearly every economist of the present generation is a Socialist. In this sense I was a Socialist before I knew anything of economics . . . But I am convinced that, so soon as collectivist control had spread so far as to narrow considerably the field left for free enterprise, the pressure of bureaucratic methods would impair not only the springs of material wealth, but also many of those higher qualities of human nature, the strengthening of which should be the chief aim of social endeavour.

Let us, however, suppose, for the sake of argument, that some workable scheme (of collectivization) to this end could be devised. Even then we should need to face the difficulty already suggested that those improvements in method and in appliances, by which man's power over nature has been acquired in the past, are not likely to continue with even moderate vigour if free enterprise be stopped, before the human race has been brought up to a much higher general level of economic chivalry than has ever yet been attained. The world under free enterprise will fall short of the finest ideals until economic chivalry is developed. But until it is developed, every great step in the direction of collectivism is a grave menace to the maintenance even of our present moderate rate of progress. (Marshall in Pigou, [1925] 1956, pp. 334, 342)

Marshall's definition of socialism as government actions of a particular sort is erroneous; but the essential point is that he places the hope of progress squarely on the shoulders of the individual capitalist, i.e., the individualist view. To be sure, he would like this segment of society to be more genteel, kinder and more dutiful toward fulfilling their social responsibilities (to be more chivalrous), but such qualities are mere addenda to the essential characteristic of the businessman: aggressive, profit-maximizing behavior that brings with it the possibilities of economic progress (and which, of course, is antithetical to 'chivalry').

Marshall is favorably disposed toward government relief for the very poor (the Bismarckian model), but believes that to extend such relief to the remainder of the population is 'the greatest present danger to human well-being.' That is, relief payments to the 'residuum' take part of the sting out of the socialist movement. To the extent that they accomplish this end, such 'socialist' schemes are to the good. To socialize all of society, though, is a positive evil, because such a program eliminates the possibility of individual profit-gathering, which, according to Marshall and conventional wisdom, is the mainspring of economic progress. And, since progress is dependent on capitalist relations, it follows that whatever evolutionary (progressive) change does take place must do so within the context of capitalist society. Socialism may be tried, of course, but since it is not suitable to the rigors of the economic environment, it will not advance society, and thus must fail.

For Marshall, the fundamental issue within this evolutionary scene was that of controlling irresponsible competition and preventing socialism:

> Every year economic problems become more complex; every year the necessity of studying them from many different points of view and in many different connections becomes more urgent. Every year it is more manifest that we need to have more knowledge and to get it soon in order to escape, on the one hand, from the cruelty and the waste of irresponsible competition and the licentious use of wealth, and on the other from the tyranny and the spiritual death of an iron-bound socialism. (Marshall in Pigou, [1925] 1956, p. 291)

Marshall was quite aware of the charges directed against capitalism, in particular those connected with (supposedly) irresponsible, anti-social competition. His position was that of rescuing the competitive ethic by arguing that it could be made more responsive to the community's needs. In fact, if capitalism were to continue, it would, indeed, have to change if the socialist attack were to be defeated. But, responsible or not, the standard by which social organization was to be judged was that of (competitive) capitalism.

Marshall was decidedly pro-union as long as workers confined their demands to those that seemed amenable to continued accumulation of capital and pressed their demands within the constraints of capitalist authority. Two letters to Edward Caird, Master of Balliol College, regarding the strike of 1897, illustrate Marshall's position:

> I have followed this strike with an interest amounting to excitement. I am very much of an 8 hours man: I am wholly a trade-unionist of the old stamp. For the sake of trade unionism, and for that of labour as a whole, I hope that the employers will so far get the better of the leaders of the modern unionism, that the rank and file of the workers will get to see the futility as well as the selfishness of the policy which their new leaders are pressing. Everywhere the tried men, who had made modern unionism the greatest of England's glories, have been pushed aside – sometimes very cruelly . . .
>
> The 8 hours question is of course not the real issue *at all*. The real issue lies entirely in the question whether England is to be free to avail herself of the new resources of production.
>
> I have often said that T.U.'s are a greater glory to England than her wealth. But I thought then of T.U.'s in which the minority, who wanted to compel others to put as little work as possible into the hour, were overruled. Latterly they have, I fear, completely dominated the Engineers' Union. I want these people to be beaten at all costs: the complete destruction of Unionism would be as heavy a price as it is possible to conceive: but I think not too high a price. (Marshall in Pigou, [1925] 1956, pp. 398-9, 400)

In fact, given his individualist pe.spective, Marshall could not regard strikes or any significant union action as contributing to the commonweal. Any such activity would upset a natural (capitalist) social order that worked out its economic results independent of social action itself. Thus, unions, strikes, socialist agitation and the like were not and could not be the result of class conflict based on non-harmonious capitalist relations; they were merely the result of individual ineptitude or malfeasance, including that of 'bad' capitalist:

> Similarly a fair employer, when arranging for the pay of a carpenter, does not try to beat him down . . . offers at once whatever he knows to be the 'normal' rate of pay for that man's work . . . On the other hand he acts unfairly if he endeavours to make his profits, not so much by able and energetic management of his business, as by paying for labour at a lower rate than his competitors; if he takes advantage of the necessities of individual workmen, and perhaps of their ignorance of what is going on elsewhere; if he screws a little here and a little there; and perhaps in the course of doing this makes it more difficult for other employers in the same trade to go on paying straight-forwardly the full rates. It is this unfairness of bad masters which makes trades unions necessary and gives them their chief force: were there no bad masters, many of the ablest members of trades unions would be glad, not indeed entirely to forgo their organization, but to dispense with those parts of it which are most combative in spirit. (Marshall in Pigou, [1925] 1956, p. 214)

One does not have to question Marshall's sincerity regarding the amelioration of poverty or reform in general. Sincerity is not the point. Since his political perspective was capitalist at its very foundation, he necessarily arrived at a general theoretical framework that defended capitalist social relations. Certainly, he wished those relations to be more equitable and wished capitalists to behave in a more socially responsible manner. But any such improvements in the social order would have to develop within the constraints of capitalism. The 'perfect' world of Marshall was that of a smoothly functioning competitive capitalist society in which labor unions and socialism would be not only unnecessary, but unthinkable; that is, an idealized world that would conform to Marshall's own particular views.

Monopoly capital and the control of ideology

It has been demonstrated that Jevons, Menger and Walras shared a common ideological perspective, regardless of their national origins or diversities in the particulars of any aspect of this perspective. This same capitalist outlook was shared by Marshall, and can be demonstrated to have been held by all the major neoclassical authorities of the period. This point of view, based on the subjectivist utility theory of value, had been increasingly evident in the post-Smithian period (Say, Lauderdale *et al.*) and came to a position of dominance in the post-Ricardian world, the period when capitalism, in the still early period of its transition to imperialism, had begun to demonstrate its reactionary qualities. The 1870–1900 'revolution' was not that at all, but merely a period of systemization and consolidation. Thus, the Jevonian–Mengerian–Walrasian juggernaut was the capstone to a long gestation period in which the anti-scientific perspective had developed and had become increasingly vigorous.

In the final analysis, the position taken by Jevons *et al.* is not significant. Of course, such a development had to be forthcoming, and some intellectual(s) had to undertake the process of consolidating the argument. But it is society that determines the dissemination and, therefore, the authority of ideas. To the extent that ideas conform to the needs of society in any stage of development – or, more specifically, to the needs of the dominant class in class society – those ideas will be promoted. The social domination of the instruments of communication provides the basis for the domination of ideological structures. With the completion of the transition to monopoly capital, capitalists now allow a monopoly position to that ideological structure against which, in its progressive period, it had waged intellectual war.

The 1870–1900 period was one of intense class conflict: militant `·ade` unionism, the growth of the socialist movement, and, in countries that still contained a large petty producing class, the 'populist' challenge to the monopolization of the means of production. Capitalism had now reached its regressive stage of development, and it was necessary to confound these challenges to the continued rule of the oligarchy through a considered effort on the ideological front (in addition to massive use of force). However, given the enormity of the contradictions that could not be resolved amicably within the social context of a decadent economic system, this effort could only attempt to *conceal* those contradictions, thereby deceiving the underlying population into accepting an increasingly irrational and dangerous economic system. To accomplish such an end, economic theory had to be divorced from the actual economic life of society and concentrate on the elaboration of superficial aspects of capitalist relations:

> To the degree that economic analysis becomes more profound it not only describes contradictions, but is confronted by its own contradiction simultaneously with the development of the actual contradictions in the economic life of society. Accordingly, vulgar political economy deliberately becomes increasingly *apologetic* and makes strenuous attempts to talk out of existence the ideas which contain the contradictions. Because he finds the contradictions in Smith relatively undeveloped, *Say's* attitude still seems to be critical and impartial compared, for example, with that of *Bastiat*, the professional conciliator and apologist, who, however, found the contradictions existing in the economic life worked out in Ricardian economics and in the process of being worked out in socialism and in the struggles of the time. . .
>
> But Bastiat does not represent the last stage . . . The last form is the *academic form*, which proceeds 'historically' and, with wise moderation, collects the 'best' from all sources, and in doing this contradictions do not matter; on the contrary, what matters is comprehensiveness. All systems are thus made insipid, their edge is taken off and they are

peacefully gathered together in a miscellany. The heat of apologetics is moderated here by erudition, which looks down benignly on the exaggerations of economic thinkers, and merely allows them to float as oddities in its mediocre pap. Since such works only appear when political economy has reached the end of its scope as a science, they are at the same time the *graveyard* of this science. (Marx, [1905–10] 1971b, pp. 501–2)

With the monopolization of the economy as a whole came the monopolization of the means of communication. Ideas that were viewed as injurious to the maintenance of a decadent economic system had to be purged, or at least vulgarized to the point where they lost their revolutionary or even critical sting. In addition to the control established in the media (easily accomplished since these were generally owned by businessmen anyway: see Compaine, 1974; Schiller, 1973, 1976), it was crucial that the educational system be made to conform to the dictates of monopoly capitalism and that the ideas disseminated therein be uniform and supportive of the dominant class.

The school system that then existed was already supportive of minority ruling class interests. In Europe, institutionalized education had been established within a feudal context and modified to accommodate the changes required by capitalism. Now, however, it was necessary to enlarge the scope of *public* education in order to, as Jevons had argued, 'impress upon them the simple truths concerning their social position before the business of life has created insuperable prejudices' (Jevons, 1886, p. 4).

In countries like the United States, the school system had to be greatly enlarged and modernized. It was in this period that the basis was laid for the modern educational system (Bowles and Gintis, 1976, passim).

To some extent, to be sure, the growth and consolidation of the educational system – at all levels – was induced by purely technological requirements; skills had to be produced in sufficiently large quantities to satisfy the requirements of the economic organization. But more important than this, insofar as the maintenance of the existing social order was concerned, was the need to re-establish the domination of ruling-class ideology that had been undermined by the advances in both science and the working-class movement and by the increasingly obvious injurious social ramifications of monopoly capital. Summarizing the work of recent researches regarding the history of education in the United States (a position with which they do not fully agree), Bowles and Gintis write:

> The expansion of mass education and the evolution of its structural forms. . . was sparked by demographic changes associated with the industrialization and urbanization of economic and social activity. The main impetus for educational change was not, however, the occupational skills demanded by the increasingly complex and growing industrial sector, nor was it primarily the desire for the elimination of urban squalor. Rather, in their view, schools were promoted first and foremost as agents for the social control of an increasingly culturally heterogeneous and poverty-stricken urban population in an increasingly unstable and threatening economic and political system. (Bowles and Gintis, 1976, pp. 230-1)

The institution of education, along with other dominant institutions, is designed to maintain the hegemony of class relations. This is perfectly rational within the context of any given society. Any minority ruling class attempts to perpetuate itself. To accomplish such an end, it requires the establishment of authority to convince the rest of society to accept the continuation of that social order. If it can do this through the dissemination of scientific thought, it will; if it requires irrational (unscientific) thought, it will employ fraud. In any case, the instruments of communication, including institutionalized education, will be utilized to disseminate ideas conducive to the continuation of the social order.

To some extent (and, depending on the historical circumstances, sometimes to a large extent), this control of the educational system is exercised directly by the ruling class itself. In capitalist society, businessmen or their appointees sit on the governing boards of educational institutions, and thus control the decision-making processes that establish the contraints within which education occurs (Bowles and Gintis, 1976; Smith, 1974; Veblen, [1918] 1957). More generally, however, since the institution of education is one aspect of a larger social order, it must confine itself to the requirements of that order. Essentially, once established, a social order limits ideology – and limits those institutions responsible for the development and dissemination of that ideology to that which is amenable to society. What exists establishes the standards of 'normality'; all else is outside the pale. Questions concerning those standards are raised when the social order malfunctions, where social effects are of such enormous impact that conventional, 'normal' arguments simply are not tenable (as in the 1930s). But, in general, a social process is at work that induces acceptance of ideas conducive to the continuation of a given society and limits ideology to the conventional.

Because the educational system must conform to the dictates of society at large, it must necessarily train the individuals flowing through it to a perspective agreeable to that social order. Where contradictions exist between what is perceived as correct or just and the requirements of maintaining a social order, those contradictions must be resolved (or an attempt made) within the context of this training, either by providing a rationale for the problem at hand or by generating a view of society that eliminates the problem from consideration altogether.

As an example, one can cite the development of the modern engineering profession. Here, one observes the contradiction between the prime function of engineering – the production of use values that would enhance social welfare – and the requirement imposed by capitalist production relations – that output be produced to maximize profits. Since, under conditions of monopoly capital, profits are maximized by restricting the production of use values, a conflict exists that cannot be resolved within the framework of capitalism itself.

To deal with this problem, the training of engineers required a change in emphasis from the purely technical or physical aspects of construction, etc., to the profitability connected with these techniques. At the same time, an institutional shift occurred that placed schools of engineering outside the then-normal university program (liberal arts, in today's terms) to prevent engineers from being infected with ideas apparently opposed to the profit maximization motive (Noble, 1977).

The general problem faced by capitalists during the period was that of the disintegration of traditional authority, obeisance toward or acceptance of which is the necessary requirement for maintenance of a minority ruling-class society. Throughout the nineteenth century, traditional authority, particularly religion, was increasingly undermined by the growth of science and the growth and consolidation of the working-class movement (Haskel, 1977, passim). If capitalists were to hold on to power (maintain their form of social organization), new authority that seemed to be based on science had to be established. And it was in the 1870–1900 period that economics became firmly professionalized, separated itself from the 'ethics' curriculum, and instituted itself as a locus of authority. Obviously, the speed or extent of this professionalization varied from place to place, but, by the end of the nineteenth century, economics had firmly entrenched itself as a professionalized discipline throughout the capitalist world.

Professionalization requires standardization. The issue is: What standards, determined by whom? No one quarrels with the necessity of standards. The medical profession refuses to certify those who employ leeches as a curative mechanism; and this is commendable from a rational, objective standpoint. In economics, the standard applied in the professionalization process was neoclassical theory. This adoption altered the discipline from one in which non-neoclassical forces were still significant to one in which, for all practical purposes, the neoclassical perspective assumed a monopoly position. In a sense, the transition from an environment of competing ideologies to one of a monopolized perspective duplicated the transition from competition to monopoly capitalism itself.

This process of monopolization was accomplished not by sheer dint of demonstrated scholarly or scientific superiority, but rather through coercion. Non-orthodox economists were

225

simply expunged from their academic positions and others, threatened with removal, bowed to official pressure and modified their ideology (Furner, 1975, passim).

In her most interesting and informative examination of the formation of the American Economics Association, Furner has demonstrated that the initial contest was between the 'laissez-faire' neoclassicists and the 'interventionist' non-neoclassicals (who would be classified mainly as populist institutionalists). The latter, reformist group, as typified by Ely, was equated with the German 'socialist' economists, the same group attacked so vehemently by Menger (Furner, 1975, pp. 35–58). The adoption of the neoclassical utility-theory-of-value standard was thus part of a larger political struggle in which the dominant force was that which aligned itself with the ideological (though not practical) requirements of large businessmen in their attempt to establish new authority through which to subject (mislead) the underlying population. Essentially, the professionalization process drove economists into institutionalized structures (the university), which had been developed and modified to accommodate the needs of minority ruling class society. Thus, the discipline was sanitized.

Stigler, then, is perfectly correct in his argument equating the adoption of the utility theory of value as the discipline's standard with the professionalization of the discipline. From Stigler's perspective, this represented an advance allowed by the adoption of the superior idea in the so-called 'marketplace of ideas.' In reality, it was the result of coercion in the service of a reactionary class attempting to maintain the social organization that provided it with its privileges.

On the choice of the utility theory of value

The 1870–1900 neoclassical consolidation set forth a general point of view that had been in the process of redevelopment since the post-Smithian period and had carried over from the later feudal epoch. Like all general perspectives, this point of view rested on an underlying standard or theory of value – in this case, utility. But, why this particular standard? Why did the utility theory of value fulfill the requirements imposed upon economics by monopoly capitalist society?

The theory of value chosen for what would become orthodoxy was necessarily related to the problem at hand – the nature of capitalist society. Capitalism is a commodity-producing society, the highest form of such social organization. Here, the purpose of production is the generation of use values that are exchanged. As specified by Adam Smith (and those classical economists before him), a commodity has two basic characteristics of significance: use value and exchange value. In examining this commodity relationship, then, economists have essentially two choices as to the establishment of a standard upon which all other argumentation will be based: the *production* of use values, or the *exchange* of those values. The labor theorists obviously based their theory on the former point of view. Thus, since the neoclassical theory was developed and promoted to counter and eventually dominate this objective theory of value, the only possible standard that could have been adopted was that of utility – the very opposite of the labor theory of value, but a standard that, given the nature of a commodity, still appears reasonable.[16]

The adoption of the utility theory of value as the standard from which all subsequent theory would flow satisfied the general requirements that the dominant view of economics would have to fulfill. This standard allowed a point of view of capitalist society in general that not only concealed the essence of capitalist social relations (found in production), but also promoted a picture of capitalism that argued the system's permanence, naturalism and justice. That is, the utility theory of value satisfied the fundamental requirements of fraud.

Given the focal point of exchange, the essence of theory became the subjective relation of the individual to a commodity (or non-sentient *thing*). That is, value is determined by the subjective appraisal of the individual consumer. Given such a foundation, social relations – those existing among people or classes – disappear, or, at best, are reduced to a second order of importance and occupy a peripheral existence in the scheme of things. In fact, this individualist, non-social relationship is held to be essential for a proper understanding of economics altogether:

227

It is not because the life of a Crusoe is of much importance that it has been introduced into economic discussion: it is because the principles by which the economy of an isolated man are directed still guide the economy of a modern state. (Clark, 1899, p. 52)

I do not see how we can talk sense about economics without considering the economic behavior of an isolated individual. Only in that way can we expect to get rid by abstraction of all the social relationships . . . (Knight, 1960, p. 71)

But, the relation of the individual to the thing is not (in the main) influenced by historical or social differences or development. One can argue that the relation of a primitive, tribal person to a bean is essentially the same as that of a feudal peasant or a modern corporate lawyer to a bean. This standard of value generates a point of view in which economic laws are essentially above society, and thus have a natural and universal quality:

It is the purpose of this work to show that the distribution of the income of society is controlled by a natural law, and that this law, if it worked without friction, would give to every agent of production the amount of wealth which that agent creates. At the point in the economic system where titles to property originate – where labor and capital come into possession of the amounts that the state afterwards treats as their own – the social procedure is true to the principle on which the right of property rests. (Clark, 1899, p. v)

The generalisations of the theory of value are as applicable to the behaviour of isolated man or the executive authority of communist society, as to the behaviour of man in an exchange economy – even if they are not so illuminating in such contexts. (Robbins, 1952, p. 20)

This point of view is itself conditioned by the existence of a social organization *appearing* to contain no rational, ordered structure that can be rationally and orderly explained:

228

The characteristic feature of class society as opposed to primitive communism is the development of the production of exchange values, that is, of commodity production. The effect of commodity production was to break down the primitive relations, based on the production of use values and regulated by the palpable, personal ties of kinship, and to create a new nexus of relations based on the market, which brings men together simply as individuals, as owners of commodities; and, since the laws governing the market are beyond their understanding and control, the relation between them appears to them as a relation not between persons, but between things. (Thomson, 1977, p. 340)[17]

Now, if the general perspective is that of universal laws independent of and above society, resting on the subjectivist, individualist relation to a thing, then all economic orders, regardless of outward or superficial appearances, are essentially the same. And, since the model for the utility theory of value is a capitalist economy, then all social forms are capitalist at their foundations. Thus, since all society is and has been capitalist and, furthermore, must always be capitalist, there has been no real motion of society. True, quantitative change has taken place, but no qualitative (dialectical) changes have occurred. Not only does the origin and motion of capitalism not have to be explained, but one can ignore the study of a capitalist society altogether. Capitalism is an assumed constant. Economic laws are natural and universal, and what is the case now has always been and will always be the case:

Economics of the line represented at its best by Mr. Clark has never entered this field of cumulative change. . . but confines its interest to the definition and classification of a mechanically limited range of phenomena. Like other taxonomic sciences, hedonistic economics does not, and cannot, deal with phenomena of growth except so far as growth is taken in the quantitative sense of a variation in magnitude, bulk, mass, number, frequency. In its work of taxonomy this economics has consistently bound itself, as Mr. Clark does, by distinctions of a mechanical, statistical nature, and has drawn its categories of classification on those grounds.

Concretely, it is confined, in substance, to the determination of and refinements upon the concepts of land, labor, and capital, as handed down by the great economists of the classical era, and the correlate concepts of rent, wages, interest and profits . . . The facts of use and wont are not of the essence of this mechanical refinement. These several categories are mutually exclusive categories, mechanically speaking . . . They are hedonistically 'natural' categories of such taxonomic force that their elemental lines of cleavage run through the facts of any given economic situation, regardless of use and wont, even where the situation does not permit these lines of cleavage to be seen by men and recognised by use and wont; so that, e.g., a gang of Aleutian Islanders slushing about in the wrack and surf with rakes and magical incantations for the capture of shell-fish are held, in point of taxonomic reality, to be engaged on a feat of hedonistic equilibration in rent, wages, and interest. And that is all there is to it. Indeed, for economic theory of this kind, that is all there is to any economic situation. The hedonistic magnitudes vary from one situation to another, but, except for variations in the arithmetical details of the hedonistic balance, all situations are, in point of economic theory, substantially alike. (Veblen, [1908] 1961, pp. 192–3)

Now, if society in its essential features has been an historical constant, there must be an underlying harmony to existing relations. If this were not true, if there were fundamental (irreconcilable) social conflicts, then a social process would be set in motion to resolve those conflicts through changes in the social order itself. Certainly, neoclassical theory admits of *problems*, but such problems can be solved within the existing order *if* economic theory is properly understood by the population. If problems exist, they must be the result of ignorance or incorrect ideas:

We are drifting toward industrial war for lack of mental analysis. Classes in society are at variance over a ratio of division, and have no clear conception of the thing to be divided. (Clark, 1887, p. 35)

The underlying harmony-of-interests doctrine is, of course, the very opposite of the doctrine of class conflict. Moreover, in the Marxian scheme, the individual's perception was not the only, nor even the primary, motive force of history, whereas in the neoclassical argument it is everything (if one allows history at all).

And, if capitalism is characterized by an underlying harmony of interests, the system must then be just and, in some sense, equitable:

[There is a law that . . .] tends in the direction of a fair division of products between employer and employee, and if it could work entirely without hindrances, would actually give to every laborer substantially what he produces. In the midst of all prevalent abuses this basic law asserts itself like a law of gravitation, and so long as monopoly is excluded and competition is free . . . its action cannot be stopped, while that of the forces that disturb it can be so. In this is the most inspiriting fact for the social reformer. If there are 'inspirational points' on the mountain-tops of science . . . this is one of them, and it is reached whenever a man discovers that in a highly imperfect society the fundamental law makes for justice, that it is impossible to prevent it from working and that it is entirely possible to remove the hindrances it encounters . . . Nature is behind the reformer . . . To get a glimpse of what it can do and what man can help it do is to get a vision of the kingdoms of the earth, and the glory of them – a glory that may come from a moral redemption of the economic system. (Clark, 1914, pp. 34–6)

This just, equitable arrangement must necessarily be the case, for, if injustice prevailed, again, movement would occur to change the existing state of affairs. But, since that state of affairs is natural, universal and harmonious, there can be nothing in the established order to warrant such motion.

In essence, then, the utility theory of value presents a

picture of society as a well-ordered, natural structure, universal in its underlying foundations. And this is in keeping with the fundamental illusion put forward by a minority ruling class:

> It is characteristic of the ruling class in each epoch of class society to regard the established social order as a product, not of history, but of nature. This is what Marx and Engels called 'the illusion of the epoch'. . .
>
> Each epoch has introduced a new illusion, determined by the new class relations, the new relations of production. Thus the mode of exploitation characteristic of ancient society was slavery; and slavery was justified by Aristotle on the ground that the slave is naturally inferior to the freeman. The mode of exploitation characteristic of feudal society was serfdom; and serfdom was justified by John of Salisbury on the ground that 'according to the law of the universe all things are not reduced to order equally and immediately, but the lowest through the intermediate and the intermediate through the higher.' The mode of exploitation characteristic of capitalist society is wage labour, the labourer being 'free' to sell his labour power, just like any other commodity, on the open market; and this 'free competition' was justified by Rousseau's *contrat social*, 'which makes naturally independent individuals come in contact and have mutual intercourse.'
>
> These 'illusions' are inevitably reflected in the philosophical and scientific theories of the ruling class. The world of nature and of man is interpreted on the basis of certain assumptions which are accepted without question as absolute truths, although in fact they are historically determined by the position of the given class in the given epoch. (Thomson, 1977, p. 342)

By removing theory from its social and historical foundations (its practice), the neoclassicists succeeded in liquidating political economy altogether:

> By consistently avoiding the examination of social relations, the subjectivist trend avoids the consideration of

those great issues which were the concern of classical political economy and today form the subject of Marxist political economy. These are the problems of economic relations among men – relations of production and relations of distribution . . . The subjectivist trend, by devoting itself exclusively to the relation of man to things even in connection with the problem of exchange, turned its back on the proper subject matter of political economy . . .

The transformation of subjectivist economics into a branch of praxiology is the last step in its liquidation as political economy. When changed in this way subjectivist economics ceases to have anything to do with the examination of a definite field of social reality and concerned itself with a particular aspect of behaviour common to all rational human activities directed to the maximization of a given end. Understood as the science of the application of the economic principle, economics becomes a universal science covering the most varied fields of human activity. The economic principle can be applied . . . in many fields; in technology, military strategy and tactics, surgery and medicine, teaching, the art of swimming and horse-riding, chess, the art of painting, the methodology of scientific investigation etc. Every normal man employs the economic principle when he goes every morning to work taking the shortest route or the quickest tram . . .

All this would have to be counted as part of the subject matter of political economy if political economy is the study of behaviour according to the economic principle . . .

It would be difficult to put it more forcibly; the transformation of economic science into a branch of praxiology whether in hedonistic interpretation or in the form of the logic of rational choice implies its liquidation as political economy. (Lange, 1963, pp. 247-9)

But, in liquidating political economy, the neoclassicists accomplished more than this end. By duplicating in theory the world view of an exploiting class in decline, they turned the world upside down. To defend the interests of a regressive minority ruling class, the view of the world and society offered had to be directly counter to that which existed. The real world had to be hidden, concealed, and a rationalization of the existing state of affairs had to replace that world and ideology based squarely on an objective understanding of that world: class harmony rather than class struggle; universality rather than an historically ordered social system; competition rather than monopoly; individualism rather than class analysis. This is the very essence of fraud.

Lastly, it should be noted that the utility theory of value bears a strong resemblance to religion, that form of fraud that has the longest tenure and which was increasingly undermined by the growth of science in the nineteenth century, thus weakening its role as a principle agent of authority. Religion, like the utility theory of value, argues that universal laws exist independent of society and impose themselves on society. Failure to abide by those laws violates the basic principles that assure a smoothly functioning, harmonious social structure: chaos replaces order. Both contain an external agent (the Devil in religion; sunspots, for example, in Jevons) to 'explain' readily apparent deviations from the theoretically ideal society which the theory argues would obtain if society were modeled on the theory. And both are idealist in their very foundations. One could add that both religion and neoclassicism have their priestly castes, but that might be viewed as stretching the point. Thus, in a sense, neoclassicism serves as a lay religion, a substitute for a form of authority that at the time was losing its ability to maintain the underlying population in a servile state. The utility theory of value helped fill that apparently growing void.[18]

Notes: Chapter 6

1   Dissent, within the bounds of decency to be sure, has an impact under conditions of extreme social duress, when it becomes patently obvious that received doctrine is incapable of addressing fundamental problems. Hence Keynes's *General Theory* of the 1930s. With the return to normalcy, though, the 'vulgar' (neoclassical, equilibrium) version quickly rose to prominence: see Robinson, 1981, pp. 96–140.
2   Spiegel then goes on (1971, p. 514) to show how a subjective theory

of value was an 'alternative if not an antidote' to the ideas of Marx.

3   Though see his 1973 account, in which he does reference the socialist (and Georgian) threat as a reason for the adoption of the utility theory: Blaug, 1973, p. 13.

4   By 'completion' I do not wish to connote finality. As with any social system, change continues, and capitalism persists in undergoing modification. Competition does not end all at once (witness agriculture into the post-World War I period), and remnants of the older order continue into the present.

5   In orthodox Marxist literature, monopoly capitalism is synonymous with imperialism: see Lenin, [1916] 1939. A work that attempts to develop an understanding of this transition in its myriad effects is Hobsbawm, 1987, a study that one can turn to with great benefit.

6   We omit from this analysis various aspects of monopoly capital such as war and modern colonialism. While these are obviously of import, they are not directly pertinent to the argument at hand.

7   This generality should not be understood to mean that a full-fledged Marxist perspective seized all working-class organizations in one fell swoop. Rather, a socialist orientation, increasingly Marxist in its approach was becoming the dominant tendency within these organizations. Even in England, where, following the defeat of the Chartists, the ideological institutions had succeeded in promoting a generally pro-capitalist outlook, and where the union leadership was markedly conservative, we see such a development culminating in the formation of the Social Democratic Federation in 1881 and the Socialist League in 1884.

8   Given the ability of oligopoliostic business organizations to control output in order to maximize profits, it becomes necessary to regulate the flow of raw materials into the production process. Otherwise, new ventures may develop which undermine the existing cartel-like agreements. Thus, sources of raw materials are brought under the control of these organizations. As raw materials are found throughout the world, we observe that one basis for the modern colonization movement of this period is the monopolization of natural resources.

9   Austria, rather than the economic and political backwater depicted by some, was a veritable 'hotbed' of experimentation, with varied social movements, 'Political Crisis Providing the Heat': see Schorske, 1980, pp. xxvii, passim.

10 For a recent expression of this subjective idealist perspective from a leading physicist, see Born, 1968, pp. 160–89. In particular:

> We also have to be careful that scientific thinking in abstract terms does not extend to other domains where it is not applicable. Human and ethical values cannot be based on scientific thinking . . . It simply has to be accepted and believed in. However attractive and satisfactory abstract thinking is for the scientist, however valuable his results for the material aspect of our civilization, it is most dangerous

235

to apply these methods beyond the range of their validity, to religion, ethics, art, literature, and all humanities.

Thus my excursion into philosophy is intended to be not only an illustration of the foundation of science, but also an exhortation to restrict the scientific methods to that domain where they reasonably belong (p. 189).

I am aware that 'positivism' means different things to different people. As employed herein, the term is understood to mean 'an entire tendency in philosophy which, while maintaining that all knowledge is based on experience, says that knowledge cannot reflect objective reality existing independent of experience': see Cornforth, 1950, p. v.

11 It should be noted that what natural scientists *do* in their laboratories and what they *say* they do when they engage in philosophizing about their practice may be two quite different things. Obviously, when they practice science they must be materialists. But it is the philosophy or general perspective that is of moment here. To say that the material world does not exist or cannot be known, or is only a thing of one's ideas, is to generate a general ideology of obscurantism, pessimism and quiescence.

12 It is clear that the Nobel Laureate's philosophical discourse is directed specifically against Marxism, which Monod equates with the older 'animist' theories of Plato, Bergson *et al.*

13 The English Fabians did the same: see Shaw [1889] 1949, pp. 12–18, 38–9. Organized in 1884, the Fabian Society quickly rid itself of its left-wing, Marxist segment, led by William Morris, and eventually established itself as the reformist leadership of the British working class. The Fabians and the resultant Labour Party have been a principle reason why the British workers have not succumbed to the 'infection' of Marxism and, thus, why British economists could simply avoid discussing that issue. This political aspect of the Fabians and its relation to the utility theory of value was recognized quite early by Engels: see Marx, [1894] 1971a, p. 10. It should be noted that Shaw, along with some other Fabians, was not a consistent utility theorist. Rather, his general outlook was something of an eclectic hodgepodge that included some Marxist elements: see Dobb, [1924] 1955a.

For a general criticism of the abandonment of Marxist principles by ostensible socialists and the relationship of this to the embracing of orthodox economic (and other) general theory, see Engels, [1885] 1939.

14 For a concise statement of the contents of *Problems* from a sympathetic point of view, see Hutchinson, 1973.

15 Different neoclassical economists surely have different specific *tactical* programs in recommending policy to deal with particular issues. However, all such programs are contained within (and constrained by) an individualist, exchange economy rooted in privately controlled

means of production. Since Keynes, the amalgam sometimes called the 'neoclassical synthesis' has somewhat blurred this *general* outlook. Essentially, if all economists were both pure neoclassicists and consistent, they should reach the same end from a shared theoretical framework – just as, say, a body of chemists would.

16 As one illustration of how this choice of a standard influences how one approaches problems, consider Marshall's testimony before the Gold and Silver commission of 1887 in which, discussing the depression of the period, his only concerns were with, . . . depression of prices, a depression of interest and a depression of profits': see Marshall, 1926, p. 99. Of course, *the* issue of any depression is the reduction in output. Marshall, looking at the world through a utility standard, emphasizes aspects of exchange.

17 Actually, Thomson reverses the sequential order of things. The disintegration of primitive communism allowed the development of commodity production.

18 As something of a last word, consider the following: 'Until the econometricians have the answer for us, placing reliance upon neoclassical theory is a matter of faith' (Ferguson, 1975, p. xv). Recent research on the development of the economics tripos at Cambridge indicates that the search for an appropriate substitute for religion was of prime consideration for at least Marshall and Sedgwick in their arguments, which resulted in the establishment of this curricular adjustment to the (religious) institution. See, Groenewegen, 1988, esp. pp. 628, 634-5, 649.

CHAPTER SEVEN
Conclusion

All ideological structures are inextricably connected to the underlying society within which they are created. Ideas are the product of human activity, and humans must exist within a social environment in which they are physically and mentally nurtured. Society shapes not only ideas concerned with society itself (including social science) but also those ideas, seemingly devoid of social implications, dealing with nature. As Bernal (among others) has demonstrated, the physical sciences *are* affected by social formations, being either advanced or retarded by underlying social forces (Bernal, 1971).

The utility theory of value is no exception to this assertion. Initially a feudal theoretical postulate, it was resurrected within the confines of capitalist society to do ideological battle with the labor theory of value. Both theoretical structures, then, were 'bourgeois' theories.

With the progressive stage of capitalist development, the labor theory of value held a position of dominance. But this position began to deteriorate during the industrial revolution stage of development. Following Ricardo, it was increasingly reduced to a secondary position, eventually residing in the economic underworld of Marxism.

There should be no great surprise at this development. Any society organizes to protect itself, and, if a minority ruling-class society, to advance the interests of its dominant class. When the capitalists were consolidating their power after successfully waging war upon feudalism, the labor theory facilitated the growth of a progressive capitalist society. However, as capitalism became increasingly retrogressive, the labor theory became increasingly dangerous (and embarrassing), and the utility theory of value was resuscitated

238

to replace it as the ideological core of the new economic apparatus. Moreover, by Ricardo's period, the labor theory of value had demonstrated its growing allegiance to the working class. Hence, the ideological contests surrounding the respective theories of value were but reflections of the underlying class struggles contained within capitalism itself. And, since the dominant class controls the instruments of communication in any class society, any ideological structure conducive to that class's interests will be promoted while those not conducive will be squashed.

The above argument is obviously not congenial to those holding conventional ideas, ideas they have been trained to hold. Surely, so it is argued, prevalent ideas are those that come out of the wash of intellectual combat and are prevalent because they have been selected as the best or most correct ideas. It is, in fact, difficult for an individual to evaluate those ideas once they have seized on his or her mind, regardless of the objective evidence. However, the case may be more compelling if one steps outside existing society and ideology.

From the point of view of modern society, slavery is seen as unjust and irrational. Surely, none could defend this form of social organization from an objective position. Yet it is noted that slavery existed, was defended, and commanded a certain legitimacy among enough of the population to allow its maintenance. And the majority of intellectuals in such a society would have seen nothing fundamentally absurd in the prevailing ideology supportive of such a vile institution. Slavery and the ideology supporting that society were accepted because people were trained to accept them as a result of the slaveholders' control over the means of communication, including education.

Within this social context, the role of the individual ideologist, while important, is of a secondary significance. Did Jevons, Menger, Walras *et al.* consciously develop a fraudulent argument in order to defend the interests of an exploiting class?

These individuals were defending the *status quo* – that much they understood. They also understood that the labor theory was antithetical to the interests of established authority, and this demanded, then, an allegiance to the utility theory, the only reasonable alternative. Also, the neoclassical apparatus was already much in place by the time of the 'marginal revolution.' Jevons *et al.* based their ideas on those theoretical structures developed in the heat of battle by Say, Senior, etc., merely systematizing and elaborating an already extant doctrine that was in conformity with the continuation of a social organization to which these intellectuals owed their allegiance:

> The preservation of traditional ideology, vital to the protection of the existing order, is not wholly a fraudulent imposture, whatever deliberate fraud and imposture may be employed. To maintain the loyalty upon which the structure depends is the primary function of the process. (Briffault, 1935, p. 62)

Most ideologists are separated from the production process itself. The longer a social system is in place, the more entrenched it becomes, the more 'natural' it appears to be. It is doubtful that Jevons *et al.* saw capitalism as exploitative. Since this was the system to which they had been accustomed and in which they had been trained, given their relative degree of comfort, there was no reason to question its very foundations. There was reason, however, to defend it from its enemies – at both the practical and the theoretical levels. In other words, their ideas conformed to the interests of the ruling class, possibly without an understanding of the nature of that class. At the same time, it must be remembered that the great neoclassicists (Morgan *et al.*) rejected the developments in science that did demonstrate the falsity of neoclassical theory.

In the world of politics, one can readily find quite overt, conscious dishonesty geared to a particular situation or toward the development of a 'favorable' cast of mind. One need go no further than the dishonesty of government officials, media journalists, etc., surrounding wars of aggression. In the world of the intellectual (now, basically, academe), the case is not quite the same. The dishonesty here is directed more toward the development of general ideas that conform to the long-run interests of a ruling class and the continuation of a 'natural' state of affairs.

For example, we are aware that various predominant explanations for war have no basis in objective reality – e.g. innate aggression. The individual ideologist who develops or maintains such a general theory may well be opposed to a particular war. Yet the holding of the innate aggression theory serves to provide an ideological environment that permits the use of war as an instrument of coercion. In this sense, then, the innate aggression ideologist is culpable, though he may be unaware of the direct relationship between the general idea and the specific bases of the war itself. Sufficient information exists which, if pursued, demonstrates the falsity of innate aggression theories. At the same time, it must be observed that some theorists *do* overtly assist in the planning, selling, and execution of such wars.

As well, one may be dishonest merely by omitting mention of competing theories. And once the minority ruling class ideology is in place, and is the sole ideology to which one is trained, it is not surprising that such an omission occurs. Of course, this is an example of unconscious dishonesty, and merely continues the conscious fraud that was initially developed.

Even where vulgarization of heretical theories takes place, this is not necessarily a sign of conscious dishonesty. If one holds orthodox ideology by virtue of one's training, then examines heretical theory on the basis of that ideology, it is almost inevitable that bastard notions of that theory will develop. However, this position does not excuse conscious vulgarization that aims at dismembering a theory by overtly lying about some or all of its characteristics.

Basically, the degree to which individual ideologists are guilty of conscious fraud depends on what they *know*. One cannot consciously develop falsehood unless one knows truth at the same time. And the extent to which Jevons *et al.* (and Say and Senior *et al.*) were knowledgeable about the nature of capitalist society is arguable. What we do know and have proved is this: that all the major contributors to the neoclassical apparatus were sufficiently informed and sufficiently elitist (anti-democratic) to understand the necessity of developing an ideological structure that would serve to blunt or sidetrack majority class opposition to capitalism and allow the continuation of a society controlled by a minority class.

In the final analysis, though, the dominance of the utility theory of value did not depend on the economic ideologists. They did not control the means of communication and thus could not, by themselves, determine the eventual victory of this perspective. The utility theory of value was promoted because it was in the interests of capitalists to push it: the economists merely provided the agar.

Moreover, one must resist the continuing effort to lift these theoreticians out of their social environment; to force upon them the view that they were somehow equipped with different or better minds that allowed them to override their social foundations and develop their ideas apart from society and its constraints – the 'Great Man' theory. Such a view, in addition to obscuring the social base of all ideas, demeans the individual. Rather than being one who sees more clearly the social imperatives facing him, he becomes a freak, the idea itself an accident of history.

Jevons *et al.* were the culmination of a long tradition in which a hard-fought intellectual struggle had been waged. They cannot be understood apart from that struggle and from the social changes that lay beneath that struggle.

With the consolidation of monopoly capitalism and the consonant (and temporary) halting of the revolutionary movement, the old, relatively open, intellectual battles came to an end. Orthodoxy was firmly entrenched in all areas, disciplines were professionalized, and the ideas antagonistic to those dominant were pushed into the world of the heretics – Marx, Veblen, and the like – where they could be safely ignored (or vulgarized) to the point where they were no longer dangerous. Once this was accomplished, orthodox theory then had a life of its own, safe from critical evaluation until society itself generated an environment in which the prevailing theory was simply untenable – the 1930s for example. But, should society survive such a catastrophe and manage to patch itself up sufficiently to, once again, appear respectable, orthodoxy, with modifications certainly, continues in its dominant position.

However, a minority ruling-class ideology during the regressive epoch of that class's rule must increasingly divorce itself from reality – so the longer that irrational society exists, the more irrational, abstract, and irrelevant the theory supporting it must become. Witness the appeal of existentialism in the modern period. As argued above, to remove theory from its historical and social context is to allow the rationalization of any phenomenon on a purely idealistic basis, whether this is of the axiomatic or the religious approach. As society becomes increasingly irrational, the theory must increasingly divorce itself from its social foundation, analyze increasingly mythical and abstract notions, and, thus, prove increasingly incapable of assisting that society in attempting to solve the problems which it throws up. That is, the theory becomes hopelessly bankrupt though considerably more 'elegant.'

And so, economics has come full circle since its early, revolutionary period. Now it has returned, in its general philosophical position, to the old, idealist point of view of the Aristotelians – which was criticized by Bacon as being the bane of intellectual and societal advance. If one examines modern orthodox theory, particularly at the ethereal level of the 'frontier,' the same charge can be directed against it that Bacon levelled against the Oxford scholars who were the neoclassicists of their day:

> This kind of degenerate learning did chiefly reign amongst the schoolmen; who having sharp and strong wits, and abundance of leisure, and small variety of reading; but their wits being shut up in the cells of a few authors (chiefly Aristotle their dictator) as their persons were shut up in the cells of monasteries and colleges; and knowing little history, either of nature or time; did out of no great quantity of matter, and infinite agitation of wit, spin out unto us those laborious webs of learning which are extant in their books. For the wit and mind of man, if it works upon matter, which is the contemplation of the

creatures of God, worketh according to the stuff, and is limited thereby; but if it work upon itself, as the spider worketh his web, then it is endless, and brings forth indeed cobwebs of learning, admirable for the fineness of thread and work, but of no substance or profit. (Bacon; quoted in Farrington, 1949, pp. 285–6)

References

Albee, Ernest (1957 [1901]), *A history of English utilitarianism* (London: Allen & Unwin).

Anikin, A. V. (1979), *A science in its youth* (New York: International Publishers).

Appleby, Joyce (1978), *Economic theory and ideology in seventeenth-century England*. (Princeton: University Press).

Bacon, Francis (1859 [1605]), 'The Advancement of Learning'. In *The Works of Francis Bacon*, Vol. 3, ed. James Spedding, Robert Ellis and Douglas Heath (London: Longman).

Bailey, Samuel (1967 [1825]), *A critical dissertation on the nature, measure and causes of value*. (New York: Augustus M. Kelley).

Barbon, Nicholas (1903 [1690]), *A discourse of trade*, ed. J. Hollander (Baltimore: Johns Hopkins Press).

Bastiat, Frederic (1964a [1850]), *Economic harmonies* (Princeton, NJ: Van Nostrand).

Bastiat, Frederic (1964b [1848–50]), *Selected essays in political economy*. (Princeton, NJ: Van Nostrand).

Bentham, Jeremy (1954), *Jeremy Bentham: economics writing*, 3 vols, ed. W. Stark (London: Allen & Unwin).

Bentham, Jeremy (1969 [1780]), 'An Introduction to the Principles of Morals and Legislation'. In *A Benthamite reader*. ed. Mary Mack (New York: Pegasus), pp. 78–167.

Berg, Maxine (1980), *The machinery question and the making of political economy, 1815–1848* (Cambridge: University Press).

Berkeley, George (1929 [1710]) 'Treatise Concerning the Principles of Human Knowledge' In *Essays, principles, dialogues, with selections from other writings*, ed. M. W. Calkins (New York: Scribner's).

Bernal, J. D. (1967), *The social function of science* (Cambridge, Mass.: MIT Press).

Bernal, J. D. (1971), *Science in history*, 4 vols. (Cambridge, Mass.: MIT Press).

Bernstein, Eduard (1961 [1898]), *Evolutionary socialism* (New York: Schocken Books).

Bharadwaj, J. (1978), *Classical political economy and rise to dominance of supply and demand theory* (New Delhi: Orient Longman).

Blackett, P. M. S. (1935), 'The Frustration of Science'. In Sir Daniel Hall et al., *The frustration of science* (New York: W. W. Norton).

References

Blanqui, Jerome (1968 [1880]), *History of political economy in Europe* (New York: Augustus M. Kelley).

Blaug, Mark (1962), *Economic theory in retrospect* (Homewood, Ill.: Richard D. Irwin).

Blaug, Mark (1973), 'Was There A Marginal Revolution?' In R. D. C. Black *et al.*, *The marginal revolution in economics* (Durham, NC: Duke University Press).

Böhm-Bawerk, Eugene von (1959 [1884]), *Capital and interest* (South Holland, Ill: Libertarian Press).

Bonar, James (1968 [1893]), *Philosophy and political economy* (New York: Augustus M. Kelley).

Born, Max (1968), *My life and my views* (New York: Scribner's).

Bowles, Samuel, and Gintis, Herbert (1976), *Schooling in capitalist America* (New York: Basic Books).

Brady, Robert (1971. [1937]), *The spirit and structure of German fascism* (New York: Citadel Press).

Briffault, Robert (1927), *The mothers*, 3 vols (London: Allen & Unwin).

Briffault, Robert (1930), *Rational evolution*. (New York: Macmillan).

Briffault, Robert (1935), *Breakdown* (New York: Coward-McCann).

Caudwell, Christopher (1939) *The crisis in physics* (London: John Lane in Bodley Head).

Childe, V. Gordon (1964), *What happened in history* (Harmondsworth: Penquin).

Clark, John Bates (1887), 'Profits under modern conditions', *Political Science Quarterly*, 1 (4), 35–51.

Clark, John Bates (1899), *The distribution of wealth* (New York: Macmillan).

Clark, John Bates (1914), *Social justice without socialism* (Boston: Houghton Mifflin).

Compaine, Benjamin (ed.) (1974), *Who owns the media* (New York: Harmony Books).

Cornforth, Maurice (1947), *Science and idealism* (New York: International Publishers).

Cornforth, Maurice (1950), *In defense of philosophy* (New York: International Publishers).

Cournot, Augustin (1960 [1858]), *Researches into the mathematical principles of the theory of wealth* (New York: Augustus M. Kelley).

Cox, Oliver C. (1948), *Caste, class and race* (New York: Monthly Review Press).

Dmitriev, V. K. (1974 [1898–1902]), *Economic essays on value, competition and utility*, ed. D. M. Nuti (Cambridge: University Press).

Dobb, Maurice (1955a [1924]), 'Bernard Shaw and Economics', In *On economic theory and socialism* (London: Routledge & Kegan Paul).

Dobb, Maurice (1955b [1924]), 'The entrepreneur myth'. In *On economic theory and socialism* (London: Routledge & Kegan Paul).

Dobb, Maurice (1963), *Studies in the development of capitalism*, rev. edn

(New York: International Publishers).

Dobb, Maurice (1972), *Political economy and capitalism* (Westport, Conn.: Greenwood Press).

Dobb, Maurice (1973), *Theories of value and distribution since Adam Smith* (Cambridge: University Press).

Dunham, Barrows (1953), *Giant in chains* (Boston: Little, Brown).

Dunham, Barrows (1964), *Heroes and heretics* (New York: Alfred A. Knopf).

Dunn, John (1983), 'From Applied Theology to Social Analysis: The Break Between John Locke and the Scottish Enlightenment'. In I. Hont and M. Ignatieff (eds), *Wealth and virtue: the shaping of political economy in the Scottish enlightenment* (Cambridge: University Press).

Engels, Frederick (1939 [1885]), *Herr Duhring's revolution in science* (New York: International Publishers).

Engels, Frederick (1941 [1888]), *Ludwig Feuerbach and the outcome of classical German philosophy* (New York: International Publishers).

Engels, Frederick (1956 [1868–96]), *On Marx's Capital* (Moscow: Progress Publishers).

Engels, Frederick (1966 [1850]), *The peasant war in Germany* (New York: International Publishers).

Engels, Frederick (1968 [1880]), *Socialism: utopian and scientific* (New York: International Publishers).

Engels, Frederick (1972 [1925]), *Dialectics of nature* (Moscow: Progress Publishers).

Farrington, Benjamin (1949), *Francis Bacon* (New York: Henry Schuman).

Farrington, Benjamin (1953), *Greek science* (London: Penguin).

Farrington, Benjamin (1966), *Science and politics in the ancient world*, 2nd edn (New York: Barnes & Noble)

Ferguson, C. E. (1975), *The neoclassical theory of production and distribution* (London: Cambridge University Press).

Foster, William Z. (1956), *Outline history of the world trade union movement* (New York: International Publishers).

Franklin, Benjamin (1959 [1729]), 'A Modest Inquiry Into the Nature and Necessity of Paper-Currency'. In *The papers of Benjamin Franklin*. Vol. 1, L. W. Labaree (New Haven, Conn.: Yale University Press), pp. 141–57.

Furner, Mary (1975), *Advocacy and objectivity: a crisis in the professionalization of American social science, 1865–1905* (Lexington, Ky: University Press of Kentucky).

Furniss, Edgar (1965), *The position of the labourer in a system of nationalism* (New York: Augustus M. Kelley).

Gould, Stephen Jay (1979), *Ever since Darwin* (New York: W. W. Norton).

Gould, Stephen Jay (1982), *The panda's thumb* (New York: W. W. Norton).

Groenewegen, Peter D (1988), 'Alfred Marshall and the establishment of the Cambridge economic tripos', *History of political economy*, 20 (4), 627–67.

References

Halévy, Elie (1934), *The growth of philosophical radicalism* (London: Faber & Faber).

Hammond, J. L. and Hammond, Barbara (1967 [1930]), *The age of the Chartists* (New York: Augustus M. Kelley).

Hanke, Lewis (1959), *Aristotle and the American Indians* (Chicago: H. Regnery).

Haskell, Thomas (1977), *The emergence of professional social science: The American social science association and the nineteenth-century crisis of authority* (Urbana, Ill.: University of Illinois Press).

Hayek, Friedrich A. (1934), 'Carl Menger', *Economica*, 4, 393–420.

Hayek, Friedrich A. (1944), *The road to serfdom* (Chicago: University of Chicago Press).

Hayek, Friedrich A. (1955), *The counter-revolution of science* (London: Free Press of Glencoe).

Henry, John (1975), 'Productive labour, exploitation and oppression—a perspective', *Australian economic papers*, 14, 35–40.

Hessen, B. (1931), 'The Social and Economic Roots of Newton's *Principia*'. In *Science at the crossroads*. (London: Kniga).

Hicks, J. R. and Weber, W. (eds) (1973), *Carl Menger and the Austrian school of economics* (Oxford: Clarendon Press).

Hill, Christopher (1949), *The English revolution*, 2nd edn (London: Lawrence & Wishart).

Hill, Christopher (1964), *Puritanism and revolution* (New York: Schocken Books).

Hill, Christopher (1979), *Milton and the age of revolution* (Harmondsworth: Penguin).

Hill, Christopher (1980), *Some intellectual consequences of the English revolution* (Madison, Wis.: University of Wisconsin Press).

Hobbes, Thomas (1955 [1651]), *Leviathan* (Oxford: Basil Blackwell).

Hobsbawm, Eric (1987), *The age of empire, 1875–1914* (New York: Pantheon Books).

Hobsbawm, Eric, and Rudé, George (1975), *Captain swing* (New York: W. W. Norton).

Hollander, Samuel (1980), 'The post-Ricardian dissension: a case-study in economics and ideology', *Oxford economic papers* (n.s.), 32 (3), 370–410.

Horowitz, Irving (1954), *Claude Helvetius: philosopher of democracy and enlightenment* (New York: Paine-Whitman).

Howey, Richard S. (1960), *The rise of the marginal utility school 1870–1889* (Lawrence, Kans.: University of Kansas Press).

Howey, Richard S. (1973), 'The Origin of Marginalism'. In R. D. C. Black, *et al.*, *The marginal revolution in economics* (Durham, NC: Duke University Press).

Hull, David (1973), *Darwin and his critics* (Cambridge, Mass.: Harvard University Press).

Hume, David (1964 [1748]), 'An Enquiry Concerning Human Understanding. In *The philosophical works*, Vol. 4, ed. T. H. Green and T. H. Grose (Darmstadt: Scientia Verlag Aalen).

References

Hume, David (1967 [1739]), *A treatise of human nature* (Oxford: Clarendon Press).

Hunt, E. K. (1979), *History of economic thought: a critical perspective* (Belmont, Calif.: Wadsworth).

Hutchison, T. W. (1953), *A review of economic doctrines 1870–1929* (Oxford: Clarendon Press).

Hutchison, T. W. (1960 [1938]), *The significance and basic postulates of economic theory* (New York: Augustus M. Kelley).

Hutchinson, T. W. (1973), 'Some Themes From Investigation Into Method'. In J. R. Hicks and W. Weber (eds), *Carl Menger and the Austrian school of economics* (Oxford: Clarendon Press), pp. 15–37.

James, Patricia (1979), *Population Malthus* (London: Routledge & Kegan Paul).

Jennings, Richard (1969 [1855]), *Natural elements of political economy* (New York: Augustus M. Kelley).

Jevons, William Stanley (1883), *Methods of social reform and other papers* (London: Macmillan).

Jevons, William Stanley (1886), *Letters and journal* (London: Macmillan).

Jevons, William Stanley (1968 [1882]), *The state in relation to labour* (New York: Augustus M. Kelley).

Jevons, William Stanley (1970 [1871]), *The theory of political economy*, 2nd edn (Harmondsworth: Penguin).

Jevons, William Stanley (1972), *Papers and correspondence*, Vol. 1, ed. R. D. C. Black and Rosamond Konekamp (London: Macmillan).

Jevons, William Stanley (n.d. [1878]), *Political economy* (New York: American Book Co.).

Kauder, Emil (1965), *A history of marginal utility theory* (Princeton: Princeton University Press).

Keynes, John M. (1936), 'Herbert Somerton Foxwell, 1849–1936', *Economic journal*, 46, 589–611.

Knight, Frank (1960), *Intelligence and democratic action* (Cambridge, Mass.: Harvard University Press).

Kregel, J. A. (1973), *The reconstruction of political economy: an introduction to post-Keynesian economics* (London: Macmillan).

Kuczynski, Jurgen (1967), *The rise of the working class* (New York: McGraw-Hill).

Lange, Oscar (1963), *Political economy*, Vol. 1 (New York: Pergamon Press).

Law, John (1966 [1705]), *Money and trade considered* (New York: Augustus M. Kelley).

Lenin, V. I. (1939 [1916]), *Imperialism: the highest stage of capitalism* (New York: International Publishers).

Lenin, V. I. (1970 [1908]), *Materialism and empirio-criticism* (New York: International Publishers).

References

Lenin, V. I. (1977 [1917]), *The state and revolution* (New York: International Publishers).

Lilley, Samuel (1965), *Men, machines and history*, rev. edn (New York: International Publishers).

Lissagary, P. (1967 [1886]), *History of the commune of 1871* (New York: Monthly Review Press).

Lloyd, Wm. F. (1968 [1833]), 'On the notion of value'. In *Lectures on population, value, poor laws and rent* (New York: Augustus M. Kelley).

Locke, John (1912 [1690]), *Essay concerning human understanding* (Chicago: Open Court Publishing Co.).

Locke, John (1924 [1690]), *Two treatises of government* (London: Everyman's Library).

Longfield, Mountifort (1971 [1834]), 'Lectures on Political Economy'. In *The economic writings of Mountiford Longfield* (New York: Augustus M. Kelley).

McCulloch, John (1965 [1864]), *The principles of political economy*, 5th edn (New York: Augustus M. Kelley).

Mach, Ernst (1897), *Contributions to the analysis of sensations* (Chicago: Open Court Publishing Co.).

Maitland, James (1966 [1804]), *An inquiry into the nature and origin of public wealth* (New York: Augustus M. Kelley).

Malson, Lucien (1972), *Wolf children and the problem of human nature* (New York: Monthly Review Press).

Malthus, Thomas (1951 [1820]), *Principles of political economy ...*, 2nd edn (New York: Augustus M. Kelley).

Malthus, Thomas (1957 [1823]), *The measure of value stated and illustrated...* (New York: Kelley and Millman).

Malthus, Thomas (1969 [1815]), *An inquiry into the nature and progress of rent* (New York: Greenwood Press).

Malthus, Thomas (1976 [1798]), *An essay on the principle of population*, ed. P. Appleman (New York: W. W. Norton).

Manhattan, Avro (1972), *The Vatican billions* (London: Paravision Books).

Marshall, Alfred (1926), *Official papers* (London: Macmillan).

Marshall, Alfred (1964 [1890]), *Principles of economics*, 8th edn (London: Macmillan).

Marx, Karl (1906 [1869]), *Capital*, Vol. 1 (Chicago: Charles H. Kerr).

Marx, Karl (1968 [1905–10]) *Theories of surplus value, part II* (Moscow: Progress Publishers).

Marx, Karl (1969 [1905–10]), *Theories of surplus value, part I* (London: Lawrence & Wishart).

Marx, Karl (1970a [1859]), *A contribution to the critique of political economy* (Moscow: Progress Publishers).

Marx, Karl (1970b [1852]), 'The Eighteenth Brumaire of Louis Bonaparte'. In *Karl Marx and Frederick Engels: selected works* (New York: International Publishers).

References

Marx, Karl (1971a [1894]), *Capital, volume III* (Moscow: Progress Publishers).

Marx, Karl (1971b [1905–10]), *Theories of surplus value, part III* (Moscow: Progress Publishers).

Marx, Karl (1973 [1875]), *Critique of the Gotha program* (New York: International Publishers).

Marx, Karl and Engels, Frederick, (1964 [1848]), *The communist manifesto.* (New York: Monthly Review Press).

Marx, Karl and Engels, Frederick, (1971 [1870–84]), *On the Paris commune* (Moscow: Progress Publishers).

Marx, Karl and Engels, Frederick, (1975 [1844]), *The holy family, or critique of critical criticism* (Moscow: Progress Publishers).

Marx, Karl and Engels, Frederick, (1976 [1896]), *The German ideology* (Moscow: Progress Publishers).

Matyas, Antal (1980), *History of modern non-Marxian economics* (Budapest: Hungarian Academy of Sciences).

Meek, Ronald (ed.) (1953), *Marx and Engels on Malthus* (London: Lawrence & Wishart).

Meek, Ronald (1963), *The economics of physiocracy* (Cambridge, Mass.: Harvard University Press).

Meek, Ronald (1967), 'The Decline of Ricardian Economics in England'. In *Economics and ideology and other essays* (London: Chapman & Hall).

Meek, Ronald (1975), *Studies in the labour theory of values*, 2nd edn (New York: Monthly Review Press).

Menger, Carl (1963 [1883]), *Problems of economics and sociology* (Urbana, Ill.: University of Illinois Press).

Menger, Carl (1981 [1871]), *Principles of economics* (New York: University Press).

Mill, John Stuart (1969 [1861]), 'Utilitarianism'. In *Collected Works*, Vol. X ed. J. M. Robson (Toronto: University Press).

Monod, Jacques (1971), *Chance and necessity* (New York: Alfred A. Knopf).

Morgan, Lewis Henry (1877), *Ancient society* (New York: Henry Holt).

Morton, A. L. (1975), *Freedom In arms: a selection of leveller writings* (New York: International Publishers).

Morton, A. L. (1978), *The life and ideas of Robert Owen* (New York: International Publishers).

Myrdal, Gunnar (1969), *The political element in the development of economic theory* (New York: Simon & Schuster).

Noble, David (1977), *America by design* (New York: Oxford University Press).

O'Brien, D. P. (1970), *J. R. McCulloch: A study in classical economics* (London: Allen & Unwin).

References

Opie, R. (1929), 'A neglected English economist: George Poulett Scrope', *Quarterly journal of economics*, 44, 101–37.

Ornstein, Martha (1963 [1913]), *The role of scientific societies in the seventeenth century* (London: Archmon Books).

Paglin, Morton (1973 [1961]), *Malthus and Lauderdale: the anti-Ricardian tradition* (Clifton, NJ: Augustus M. Kelley).

Pareto, Vilfredo (1935 [1916]), *The mind and society (treatise on general society)*, Vol. IV: *The general form of society* (New York: Harcourt, Brace).

Petty, William (1962 [1662]), 'A Treatise of Taxes and Contributions'. In the *Economic writings of Sir William Petty* Vol. 1 (New York: Augustus M. Kelley), pp. 1–95.

Pigou, A. C. (ed.) (1956 [1925]), *Memories of Alfred Marshall* (New York: Kelley and Millman).

Plamenatz, John (1958), *The English utilitarian* (Oxford: Basil Blackwell).

Plato (1963 [*c.* 370]), 'The Republic. In *The collected dialogues of Plato*, ed. H. Cairnes and E. Hamilton (New York: Pantheon Books).

Plekhanov, Georgi (1976a [1896]), 'Essays on the Theory of Materialism'. In *Selected philosophical works*, Vol. 2 (Moscow: Progress Publishers), pp. 31–162.

Plekhanov, Georgi (1976b [1898]), 'On the Question of the Individual's Role in History'. In *Selected philosophical works*, Vol. 2 (Moscow: Progress Publishers), pp. 282–315.

Read, Samuel (1976 [1829]), *Political economy: an inquiry into the natural grounds of right to vendible property or wealth* (Fairfield, Conn.: Augustus M. Kelley).

Ricardo, David (1952a), 'Letters, 1819–June 1821'. In *The works and correspondence of David Ricardo*, Vol. III, ed. Piero Sraffa (Cambridge: University Press).

Ricardo, David (1952b), 'Letters, July 1821–1823'. In *The works and correspondence of David Ricardo*, Vol. IX, ed. Piero Sraffa (Cambridge: University Press).

Ricardo, David (1957), 'Notes on Malthus's Principles of Political Economy'. In *The works and correspondence of David Ricardo*, Vol. II, ed. Piero Sraffa (Cambridge: University Press).

Ricardo, David (1970 [1821]), 'On the Principles of Political Economy and Taxation', 3rd edn. In *The works and correspondence of David Ricardo*, Vol. I, ed. Piero Sraffa, (Cambridge: University Press).

Robbins, Lionel (1952), *An essay on the nature and significance of economic science*, 2nd edn (London: Macmillan).

Robertson, Archibald (1962), *The origins of christianity*, rev. edn (New York: International Publishers).

Robinson, Joan (1981), *What are the questions?* (Armonk, NY: M. E. Sharpe).

Rogin, Leo (1956), *The meaning and validity of economic theory* (New York: Harper and Brothers).

References

Roll, Eric (1956), *A history of economic thought*, rev. edn (London: Faber & Faber).

Routh, Guy (1977), *The origin of economic ideas* (New York: Vintage Books).

Rubin, Isaac (1979 [1929]), *A history of economic thought*, 2nd edn (London: Ink Links).

Say, Jean Baptiste (1827 [1803]), *A treatise on political economy*, 3rd US edn (Philadelphia: John Grigg).

Say, Jean Baptiste (1936 [1821]), *Letters to Thomas Robert Malthus on political economy* (London: George Harding's Bookshop).

Schiller, Herbert (1973), *The mind managers* (Boston: Beacon Press).

Schiller, Herbert (1976), *Communication and cultural domination* (White Plains, NY: M. E. Sharpe).

Schorske, Carl (1980), *Fin-de-siécle Vienna* (New York: Alfred A. Knopf).

Schumpeter, Joseph A. (1954), *History of economic analysis* (New York: Oxford University Press).

Scrope, George (1969 [1833]), *Principles of political economy: deduced from the natural laws of social welfare and applied to the present state of Britain* (New York: Augustus M. Kelley).

Seligman, E. R. A. (1903), 'On some neglected British economists', *Economic journal*, 13, 335–63; 511–35.

Senior, Nassau (1871), *Journals kept in France and Italy*, 2 vols, 2nd edn, (London: Henry S. King).

Senior, Nassau (1965 [1836]), *An outline of the science of political economy* (New York: Augustus M. Kelley).

Senior, Nassau (1966 [1831]), *Three lectures on the rate of wages*, 2nd edn (New York: Augustus M. Kelley).

Shaw, George Bernard (1949 [1889]), *Essays on Fabian socialism*. (London: Constable).

Sismonde, J. C. L. Simonde de (1966 [1815]), *Political economy* (New York: Augustus M. Kelley).

Smith, Adam (1937 [1776]), *An inquiry into the nature and causes of the wealth of nations* (New York: Modern Library).

Smith, David (1974), *Who rules the universities?* (New York: Monthly Review).

Smith, F. B. (1966), *Making of the second reform bill* (Cambridge: University Press).

Spiegel, Henry W. (1971), *The growth of economic thought* (Englewood Cliffs. NJ: Prentice-Hall).

Stephen, Leslie (1950 [1900]), *The English utilitarians*, 3 vols (London: London School of Economics and Political Science).

Stigler, George (1941), *Production and distribution theories* (New York: Macmillan).

Stigler, George (1973), 'The Adoption of Marginal Utility Theory'. In R. D. C. Black *et al.*, *The marginal revolution in economics* (Durham, NC: Duke University Press).

Thompson, E. P. (1968), *The making of the English working class* (Harmondsworth: Penguin).

Thompson, Noel (1984), *The people's science* (Cambridge: University Press).

Thomson, George (1965), *Studies in ancient Greek society: the prehistoric Aegean* (New York: Citadel Press).

Thomson, George (1974), *The human essence* (London: China Policy Study Group).

Thomson, George (1977), *The first philosophers*, 2nd edn (London: Lawrence & Wishart).

Thunen, Johann von (1966 [1826–63]), *The isolated state*, ed. Peter Hall (Oxford: Pergaman Press).

Veblen, Thorstein (1904), *The theory of business enterprise* (New York: Charles Scribner's Sons).

Veblen, Thorstein (1957 [1918]), *The higher learning in America* (New York: Hill & Wang).

Veblen, Thorstein (1961 [1908]), 'Professor Clark's economic's. In *The place of science in modern civilization* (New York: Russell & Russell), pp. 180–230.

Veblen, Thorstein (1967 [1923]), *Absentee ownership* (Boston: Beacon Press).

Walras, Leon (1954 [1874]), *Elements of pure economics* (Homewood, Ill: Richard D. Irwin).

Webb, R. K. (1955), *The British working class reader* (London: Allen & Unwin).

Wells, Harry (1954), *Pragmatism* (New York: International Publishers).

Wells, Harry (1956), *Ivan P. Pavlov* (New York: International Publishers).

Wells, Harry (1960), *Sigmund Freud: a Pavlovian critique* (New York: International Publishers).

Whately, Richard (1966 [1832]), *Introductory lectures on political economy* (New York: Augustus M. Kelley).

Whitaker, J. K. (ed.) (1975), *The early economic writings of Alfred Marshall, 1867–1890*, 2 vols (New York: Free Press).

White, Leslie (1959), *The evolution of culture* (New York: McGraw-Hill).

Wicksell, Knut (1934), *Lectures on political economy* (London: Routledge & Kegan Paul.

Index